BECOMING ANDY WARHOL

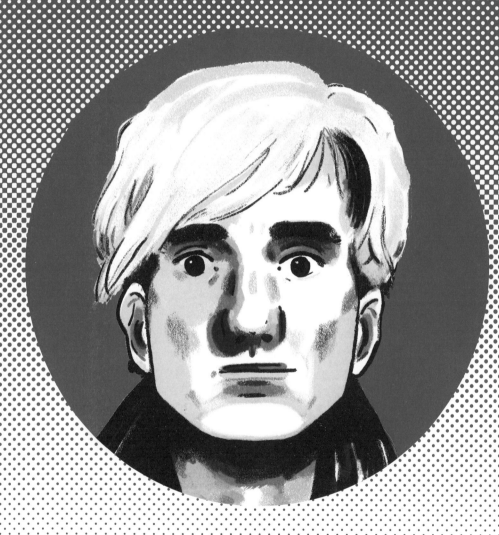

by **NICK BERTOZZI**

illustrated by **PIERCE HARGAN**

ABRAMS COMICARTS ● NEW YORK

At the dawn of the 1960s, commercial illustrator Andy Warhol wanted desperately to become a famous painter. He worked tirelessly to break into the flourishing New York City gallery scene, but he couldn't quite seem to rise above his misfit status . . . until he began to push the limits of everyone's imaginations, including his own.

After numerous gallery failures, Warhol finally scored a commission for the 1964 World's Fair—his only work of public art. His controversial mural of the *Thirteen Most Wanted Men* provoked a powerful response from urban planner Robert Moses, architect Philip Johnson, and New York Governor Nelson Rockefeller—igniting a firestorm that ultimately forced Warhol to make a choice that would either make or break his career.

By stubborn force of personality and sheer burgeoning talent, Warhol went up against the creative establishment and emerged to become one of the most significant and influential artists of the 20th century. This is the story of Warhol's path to that turning point, vividly reconstructed by *New York Times*-bestselling author Nick Bertozzi and breakout artist Pierce Hargan.

The World's Fair was out in Flushing Meadow . . . with my mural of the *Thirteen Most Wanted Men* on the outside of the building that Philip Johnson designed. Philip gave me the assignment, but because of some political thing I never understood, the officials had it whitewashed out. A bunch of us went to Flushing Meadow to have a look at it, but by the time we got there you could only see the images faintly coming through the paint they'd just put over them.

In one way I was glad the mural was gone: now I wouldn't have to feel responsible if one of the criminals ever got turned in to the FBI because someone had recognized him from my pictures.

—ANDY WARHOL
from his memoir, *Popism: The Warhol '60s*

PREFACE

I would have been the perfect young person for Andy Warhol to use: slightly broken, deeply gullible, and desperate to please. He would have chewed me up and spit me out, just as he did so many others over the course of his career. That Warhol—the one who was shot point-blank by a hanger-on, the artist who immortalized everyday objects with his depictions of Campbell's soup cans, who signed printed portraits of the wealthy and the famous that were created in his Factory—sits immovable at the foundation of glossy twenty-first-century pop culture. If that isn't obvious to you, turn on the television, Andy's favorite pastime, and witness the celebrity culture Warhol personified. But this book is not about the world-famous Andy Warhol; it's about the moment just before his fame, when he longed to get out of the illustration racket and be treated like a heavyweight. This book is his origin story, you might say.

Becoming Andy Warhol was originally titled *America's Thirteen Most Wanted Men*. A twenty-foot-by-twenty-foot mural titled *Thirteen Most Wanted Men* was commissioned by the architect Philip Johnson, to be hung on the side of the Johnson-designed New York State Pavilion at the 1964 World's Fair. When the installation caused a political uproar, Warhol was forced to make a choice. It was a choice deeply influenced by the young, non-mainstream crowd he met through his assistants Gerard Malanga and Billy Name; by his decision to leave the small Stable Gallery for the prestigious Castelli Gallery; and in defiance of the attitudes of his mother, who lived with him. It was the turning point of his transformation from the child of working-class immigrants into an artist with an American vision.

Becoming Andy Warhol is not meant to be read as a scholarly work. In writing this graphic novel, I followed the historical record as best I could, but I compressed some events and added or subtracted people from scenes to create a story that would serve as an engaging and thoughtful guide to the experiences that became his art. This is my interpretation of Warhol, pulled from biographies, documentaries, and interviews as well as his work. The sources are listed in the back of the book.

Now, allow me to tell you about my collaborator, Pierce Hargan. He's young, he's smart, he's from California, and he has a cartooning voice that is unique in the best manner possible. Look at the cover again (front and back). Look at the backgrounds of the interior art—and marvel, as I do, at the pitch-perfect depiction of 1960s New York City. But also look at his people—that's important. Pierce gets the poses, the facial nuances, and the hands exactly right. As a cartoonist myself, I found it difficult to let someone else draw my script, but I'm very glad it was Pierce. It's obvious that he's just beginning an amazing career.

My college art history classes consisted of surveys of painters and sculptors: their works, the dates they created them, and the movements they fell within. In this mode of presentation, artists become mythical legends, gracing mortals with their Olympian visions. But I wanted to know them as people, to know where they lived, to understand the experiences of their lives that pushed them to make their work, and to find out why it mattered where their work was displayed. That was also my objective for the book you hold in your hands—to make this creative and defining period of Warhol's life stand on its own, and serve as a very different kind of introduction to the career of this remarkable artist. One that has extended far beyond "fifteen minutes."

NICK BERT❂ZZI
Ridgewood, New York

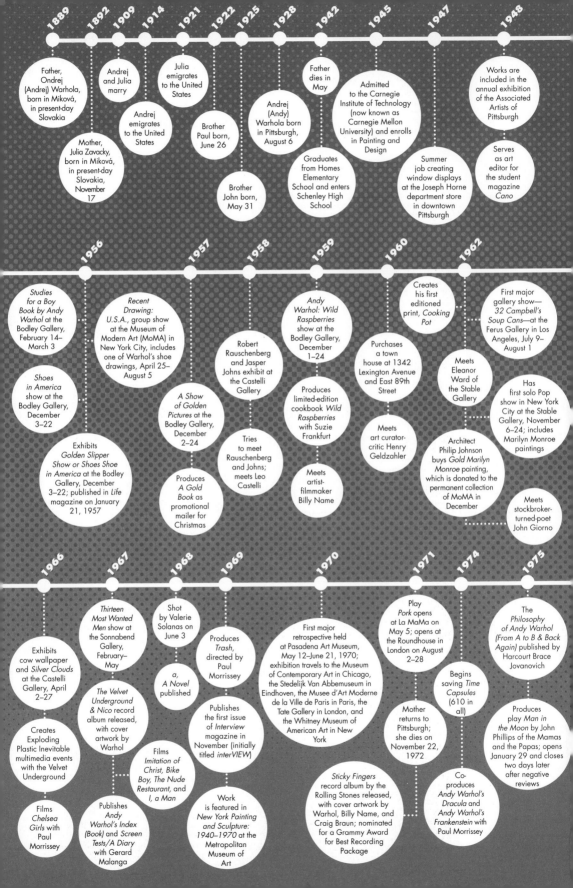

1889
Father, Ondrej (Andrej) Warhola, born in Miková, in present-day Slovakia

Mother, Julia Zavacky, born in Miková, in present-day Slovakia, November 17

1892
Andrej and Julia marry

1909
Andrej emigrates to the United States

1914
Julia emigrates to the United States

1921
Brother Paul born, June 26

Brother John born, May 31

1922

1925
Andrej (Andy) Warhola born in Pittsburgh, August 6

1928
Graduates from Homes Elementary School and enters Schenley High School

1942
Father dies in May

1945
Admitted to the Carnegie Institute of Technology (now known as Carnegie Mellon University) and enrolls in Painting and Design

1947
Summer job creating window displays at the Joseph Horne department store in downtown Pittsburgh

1948
Works are included in the annual exhibition of the Associated Artists of Pittsburgh

Serves as art editor for the student magazine *Cano*

1956
Studies for a Boy Book by Andy Warhol at the Bodley Gallery, February 14–March 3

Shoes in America show at the Bodley Gallery, December 3–22

Exhibits *Golden Slipper Show or Shoes Shoe in America* at the Bodley Gallery, December 3–22; published in *Life* magazine on January 21, 1957

1957
Recent Drawing: U.S.A., group show at the Museum of Modern Art (MoMA) in New York City, includes one of Warhol's shoe drawings, April 25–August 5

A Show of Golden Pictures at the Bodley Gallery, December 2–24

Produces *A Gold Book* as promotional mailer for Christmas

1958
Robert Rauschenberg and Jasper Johns exhibit at the Castelli Gallery

Tries to meet Rauschenberg and Johns; meets Leo Castelli

1959
Andy Warhol: Wild Raspberries show at the Bodley Gallery, December 1–24

Produces limited-edition cookbook *Wild Raspberries* with Suzie Frankfurt

Meets artist-filmmaker Billy Name

1960
Purchases a town house at 1342 Lexington Avenue and East 89th Street

Meets art curator-critic Henry Geldzahler

Creates his first editioned print, *Cooking Pot*

1962
First major gallery show—*32 Campbell's Soup Cans*—at the Ferus Gallery in Los Angeles, July 9–August 1

Meets Eleanor Ward of the Stable Gallery

Architect Philip Johnson buys *Gold Marilyn Monroe* painting, which is donated to the permanent collection of MoMA in December

Has first solo Pop show in New York City at the Stable Gallery, November 6–24; includes Marilyn Monroe paintings

Meets stockbroker-turned-poet John Giorno

1966
Exhibits cow wallpaper and *Silver Clouds* at the Castelli Gallery, April 2–27

Creates Exploding Plastic Inevitable multimedia events with the Velvet Underground

Films *Chelsea Girls* with Paul Morrissey

1967
Thirteen Most Wanted Men show at the Sonnabend Gallery, February–May

The Velvet Underground & Nico record album released, with cover artwork by Warhol

Films *Imitation of Christ, Bike Boy, The Nude Restaurant*, and *I, a Man*

Publishes *Andy Warhol's Index (Book)* and *Screen Tests/A Diary* with Gerard Malanga

1968
Shot by Valerie Solanas on June 3

a, A Novel published

1969
Produces *Trash*, directed by Paul Morrissey

Publishes the first issue of *Interview* magazine in November (initially titled *interVIEW*)

Work is featured in *New York Painting and Sculpture: 1940–1970* at the Metropolitan Museum of Art

1970
First major retrospective held at Pasadena Art Museum, May 12–June 21, 1970; exhibition travels to the Museum of Contemporary Art in Chicago, the Stedelijk Van Abbemuseum in Eindhoven, the Musee d'Art Moderne de la Ville de Paris in Paris, the Tate Gallery in London, and the Whitney Museum of American Art in New York

Sticky Fingers record album by the Rolling Stones released, with cover artwork by Warhol, Billy Name, and Craig Braun; nominated for a Grammy Award for Best Recording Package

1971
Play *Pork* opens at La MaMa on May 5; opens at the Roundhouse in London on August 2–28

Mother returns to Pittsburgh; she dies on November 22, 1972

1974
Begins saving *Time Capsules* (610 in all)

Co-produces *Andy Warhol's Dracula* and *Andy Warhol's Frankenstein* with Paul Morrissey

1975
The *Philosophy of Andy Warhol (From A to B & Back Again)* published by Harcourt Brace Jovanovich

Produces play *Man in the Moon* by John Phillips of the Mamas and the Papas; opens January 29 and closes two days later after negative reviews

TIMELINE

1949
- Graduates from the Carnegie Institute of Technology with a bachelor of fine arts in pictorial design
- Illustrates "Success Is a Job in New York" for the September issue of *Glamour* magazine

1950
- Produces *Holy Cats by Andy Warhol's Mother*, a series of lithographs by Julia Warhol
- Moves to New York City and begins work as a commercial artist
- His mother moves in with him
- Changes last name from Warhola to Warhol

1952
- Wins Art Directors Club Medal for illustrations related to CBS radio program *The Nation's Nightmare*
- First solo exhibition, *Fifteen Drawings Based on the Writings of Truman Capote*, at the Hugo Gallery, June 16–July 3

1953
- Illustrates *A Is an Alphabet* and *Love Is a Pink Cake* by Ralph Thomas (Corkie) Ward

1954
- Group and solo shows at the Loft Gallery with future studio assistant, Nathan Gluck, April–October
- Illustrates limited edition of *25 Cats Name Sam and One Blue Pussy*

1955
- Meets film production designer Charles Lisanby at a party
- Nephew James Warhola, born March 16
- *À La Recherche du Shoe Perdu* portfolio published
- Selected by I. Miller to illustrate weekly newspaper advertisements for their line of women's shoes; runs for almost three years

1963
- Moves into firehouse studio at 159 East 87th Street
- *Pop Art Américain*, group exhibition at the Ileana Sonnabend Gallery, May–June
- Screening of *Andy Warhol Films Jack Smith Filming Normal Love* at the New Bowery Theatre on March 2; film is confiscated in a raid by the NYPD the next night
- Meets artist Gerard Malanga; hires him as studio assistant
- Purchases a 16mm movie camera; films *Sleep* with John Giorno
- Travels cross-country for the Elvis Presley show at the Ferus Gallery in September

1964
- Begins *Four Jackies*, portraits of Mrs. Jacqueline Kennedy
- Establishes the Factory, located at 231 East 47th Street
- Creates shipping-box-sculptures, including Brillo, Del Monte, and Campbell's brands
- *Flowers*, first show at the Castelli Gallery, November 21–December 17
- Purchases his first tape recorder
- On April 15, installs *Thirteen Most Wanted Men* mural on New York State Pavilion; it's painted over in silver on April 17
- Films *Empire, Eat, Blow Job,* and *Couch*; begins *Screen Test* series
- Films *Batman Dracula* starring Jack Smith
- Shows his *Death and Disaster* paintings at the Sonnabend Gallery, January–February
- *The Personality of the Artist*, a sculpture show (including box facsimiles), at the Stable Gallery, April 21–May 9

1965
- Designs the cover for January 29 issue of *Time* magazine
- Makes the films *Drink, Vinyl, Horse, My Hustler,* and *Paul Swan*
- Meets Edie Sedgwick
- Meets Paul Morrissey
- Meets Lou Reed and the Velvet Underground

1977
- Regular at Studio 54 (until 1981)

1979
- Produces *Fashion*, a ten-episode video program
- Publishes *Andy Warhol's Exposures* by Bob Colacello with Grosset and Dunlap
- *Andy Warhol: Portraits of the 70s* at the Whitney Museum, November 20, 1979–January 27, 1980; companion book published by Random House

1980
- Meets Pope John Paul II at the Vatican on April 2, accompanied by manager, Fred Hughes
- *Popism: The Warhol '60s* by Warhol and Pat Hackett published by Harcourt Brace Jovanovich

1981
- Produces and stars in three episodes of *Andy Warhol's T.V.* for *Saturday Night Live*
- Creates official poster for Brooklyn Bridge Centennial in May

1983
- Collaborates with Jean-Michel Basquiat, Keith Haring, and Francesco Clemente

1984
- Directs music video for "Hello Again" by the Cars

1985
- Creates TV shows, including *Andy Warhol's Fifteen Minutes* for MTV (premieres October 20 and runs for five episodes through 1987)
- Creates paintings for Absolut Vodka ad campaign
- Guest-stars on *The Love Boat* (October 12) and in a TV commercial for Diet Coke

1987
- Dies of a heart attack on February 22, following routine gallbladder surgery

1989
- *The Andy Warhol Diaries* published by Warner Books, vedited by Pat Hackett

1994
- Andy Warhol Museum opens in Pittsburgh on May 15

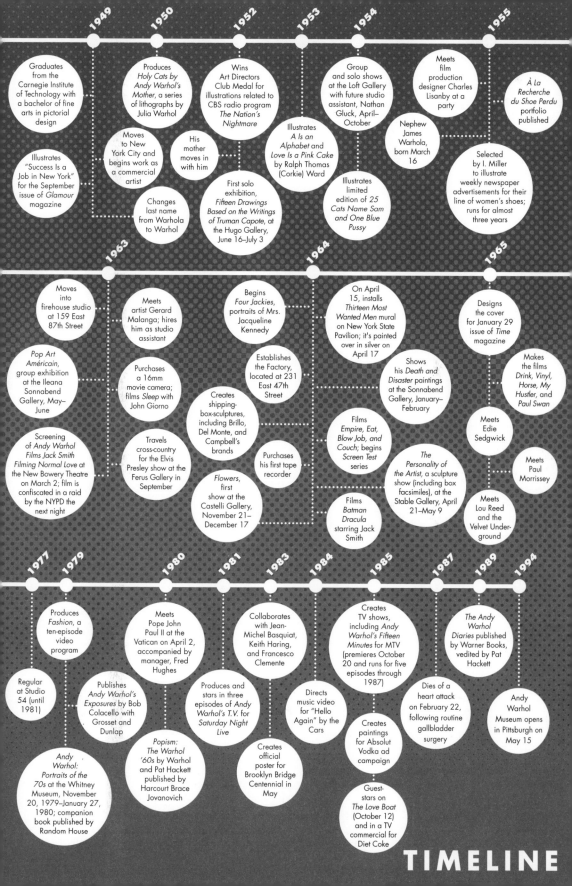

FEATURING

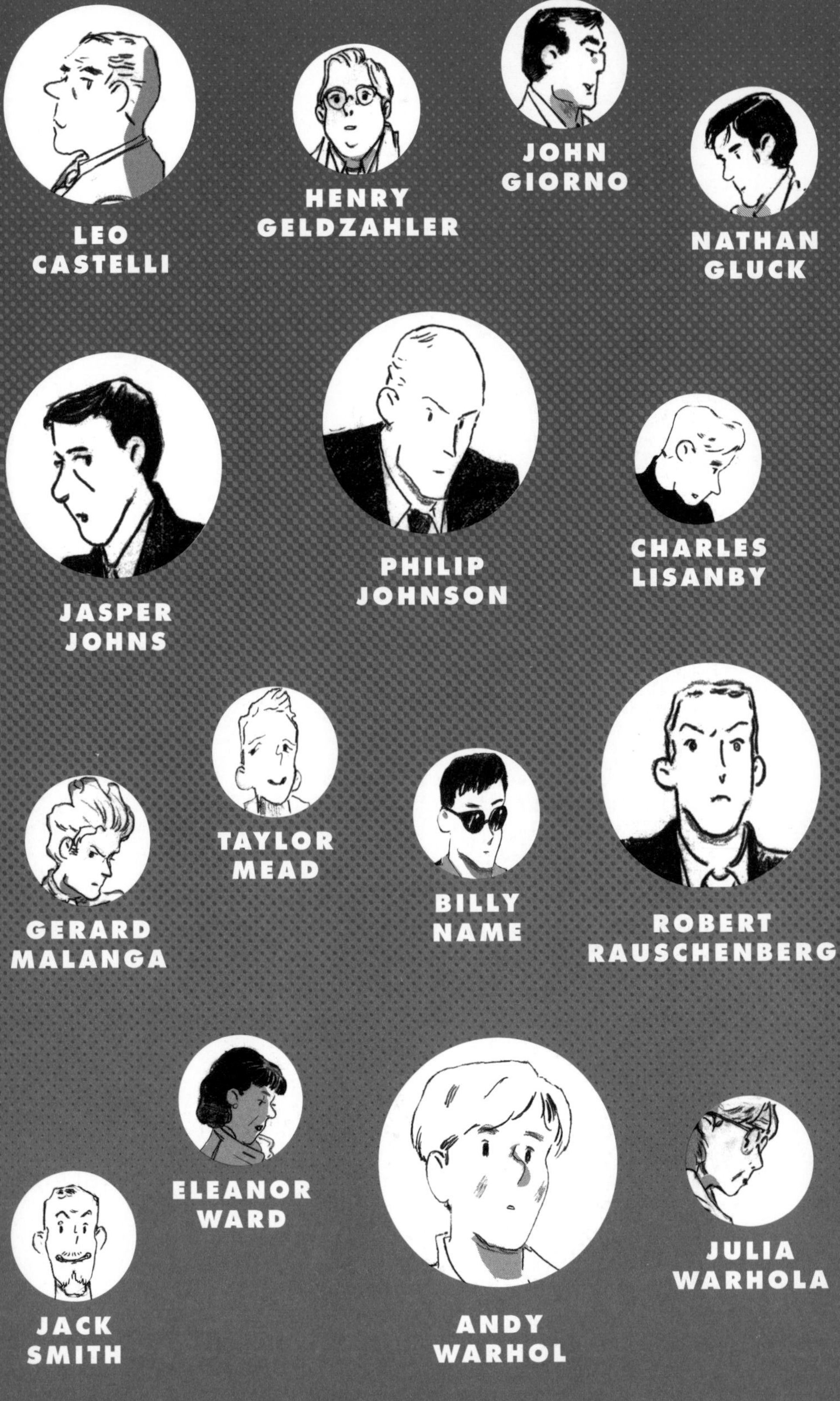
LEO CASTELLI
HENRY GELDZAHLER
JOHN GIORNO
NATHAN GLUCK
JASPER JOHNS
PHILIP JOHNSON
CHARLES LISANBY
GERARD MALANGA
TAYLOR MEAD
BILLY NAME
ROBERT RAUSCHENBERG
JACK SMITH
ELEANOR WARD
ANDY WARHOL
JULIA WARHOLA

CHAPTER ONE

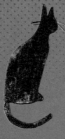

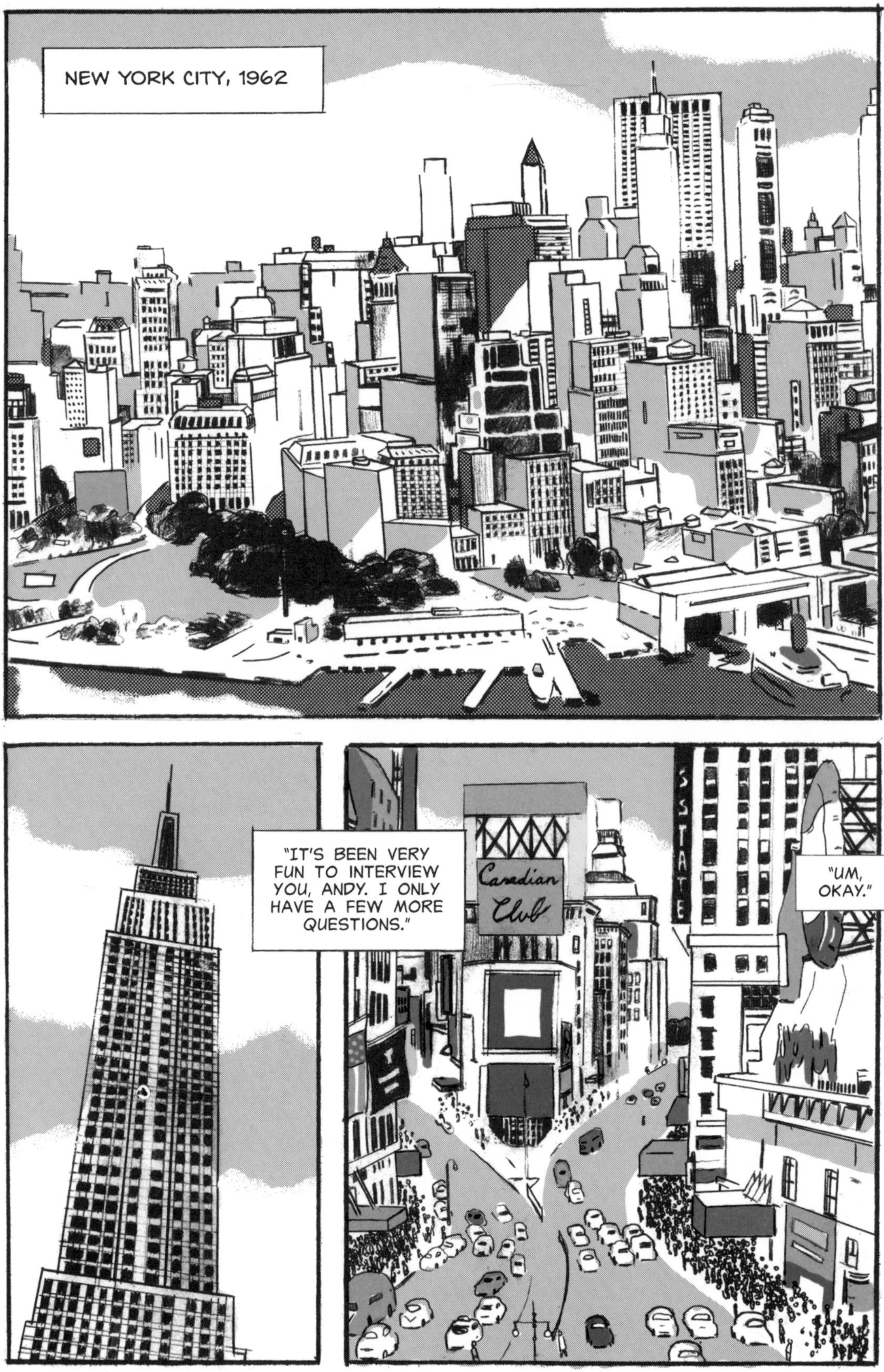
NEW YORK CITY, 1962
"IT'S BEEN VERY FUN TO INTERVIEW YOU, ANDY. I ONLY HAVE A FEW MORE QUESTIONS."
Canadian Club
"UM, OKAY."

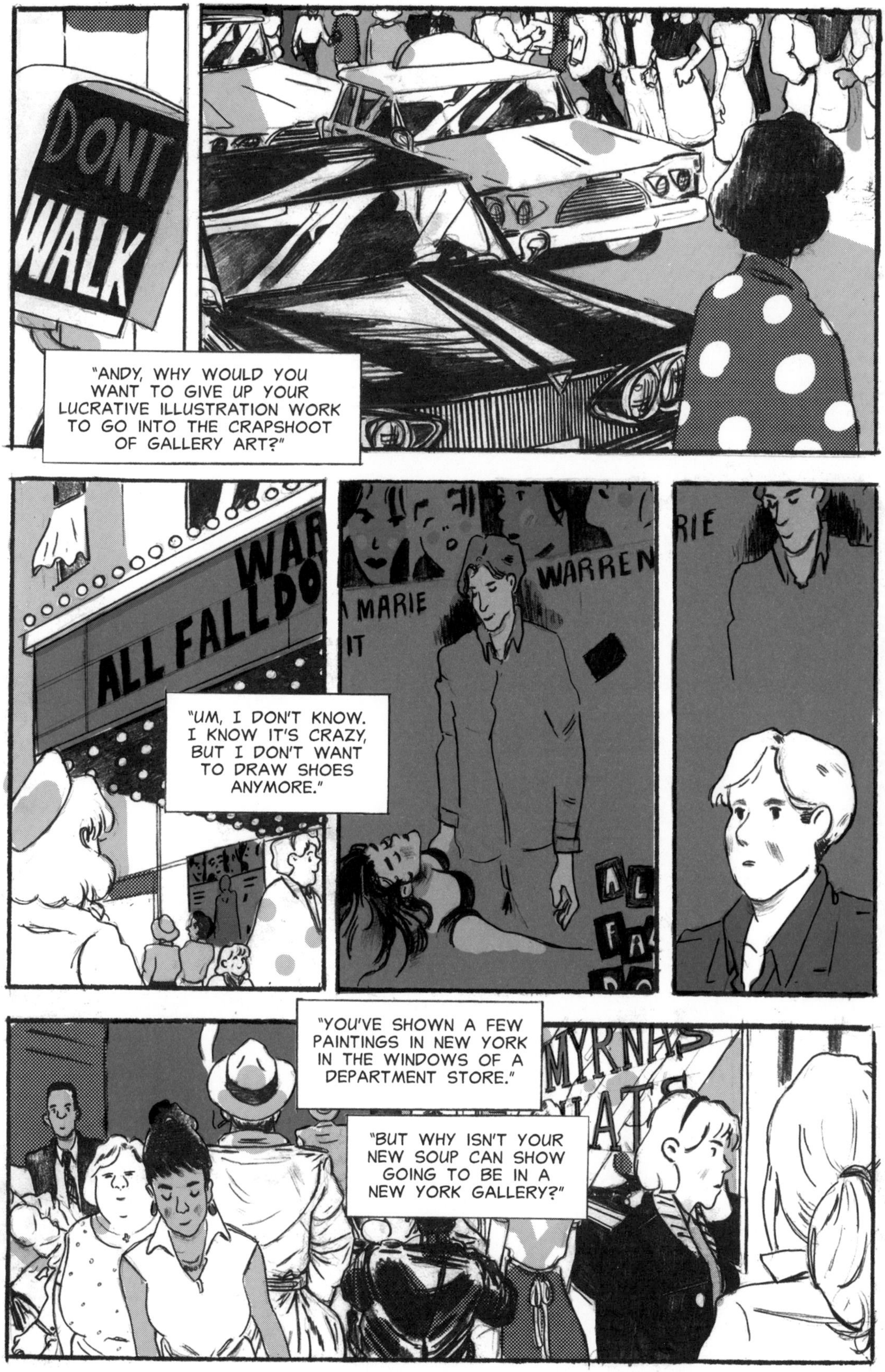
DONT WALK
"ANDY, WHY WOULD YOU WANT TO GIVE UP YOUR LUCRATIVE ILLUSTRATION WORK TO GO INTO THE CRAPSHOOT OF GALLERY ART?"
ALL FALL DO
WAR
"UM, I DON'T KNOW. I KNOW IT'S CRAZY, BUT I DON'T WANT TO DRAW SHOES ANYMORE."
WARREN
MARIE
RIE
"YOU'VE SHOWN A FEW PAINTINGS IN NEW YORK IN THE WINDOWS OF A DEPARTMENT STORE."
MYRNA'S
"BUT WHY ISN'T YOUR NEW SOUP CAN SHOW GOING TO BE IN A NEW YORK GALLERY?"

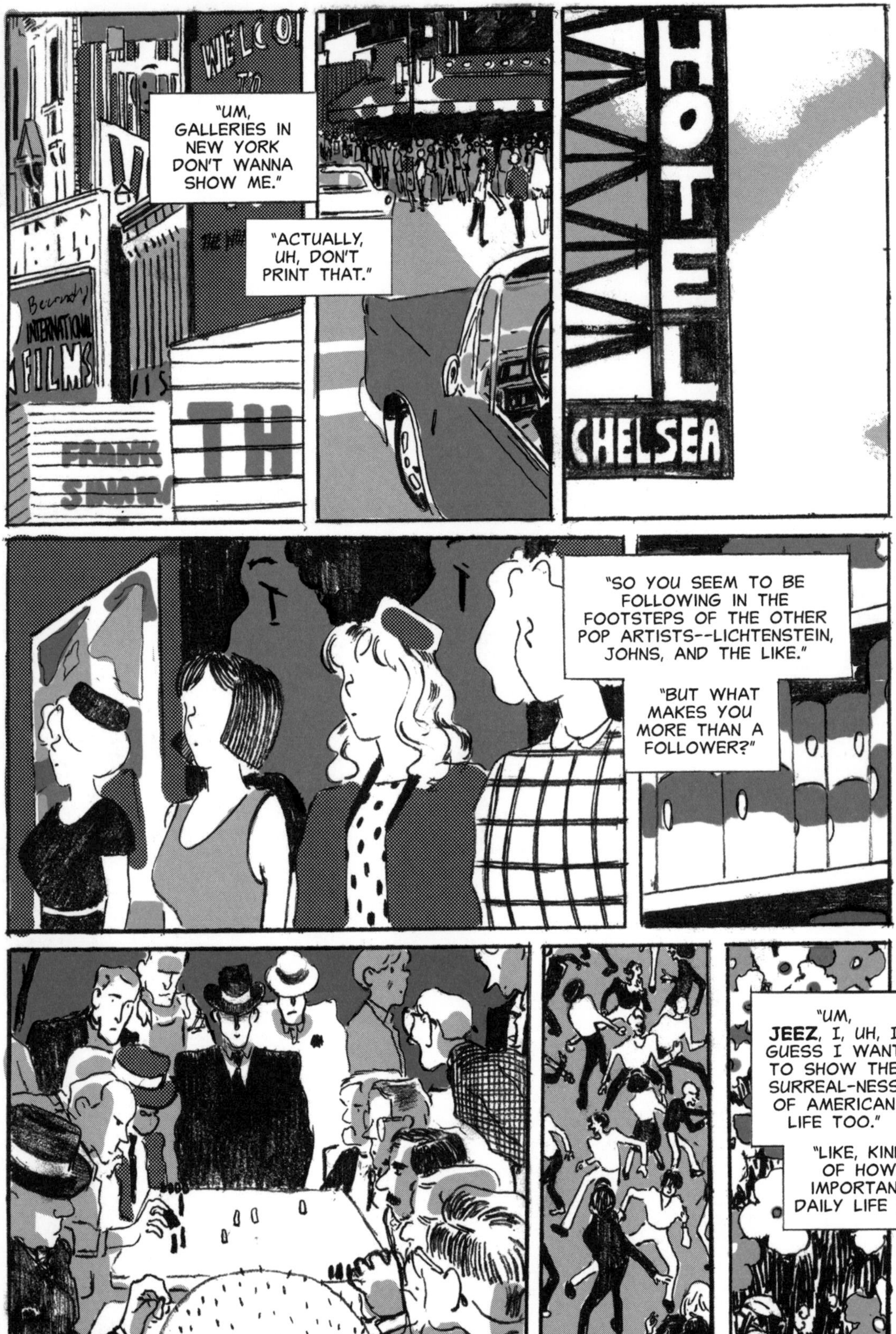
WELCO
TO
Beverly
INTERNATIONAL
FILMS
FRANK
TH
"UM, GALLERIES IN NEW YORK DON'T WANNA SHOW ME."
"ACTUALLY, UH, DON'T PRINT THAT."
HOTEL
CHELSEA
"SO YOU SEEM TO BE FOLLOWING IN THE FOOTSTEPS OF THE OTHER POP ARTISTS--LICHTENSTEIN, JOHNS, AND THE LIKE."
"BUT WHAT MAKES YOU MORE THAN A FOLLOWER?"
"UM, **JEEZ**, I, UH, I GUESS I WANT TO SHOW THE SURREAL-NESS OF AMERICAN LIFE TOO."
"LIKE, KIND OF HOW IMPORTANT DAILY LIFE IS."

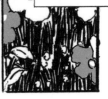

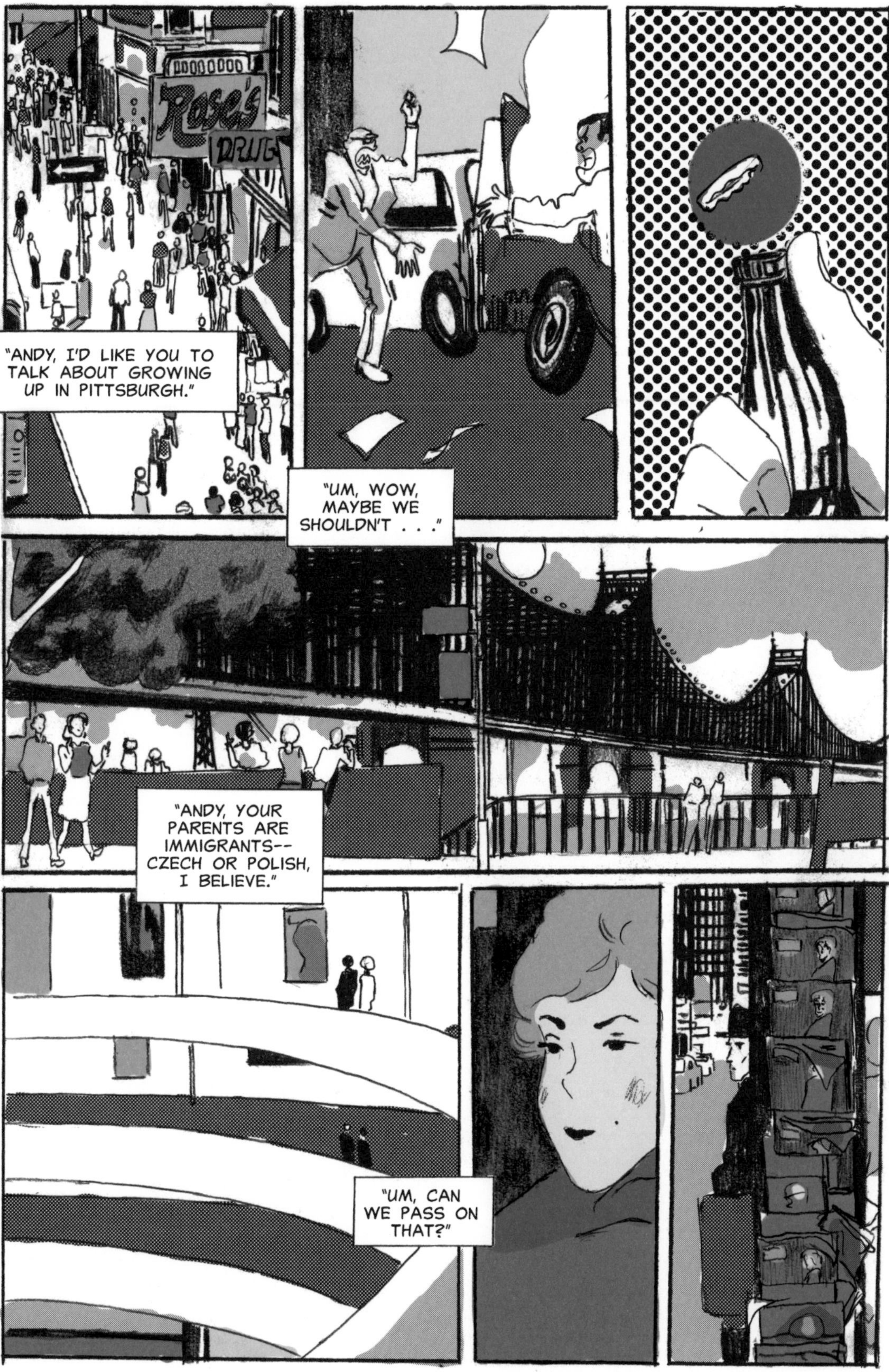
ROSE'S
DRUG
"ANDY, I'D LIKE YOU TO TALK ABOUT GROWING UP IN PITTSBURGH."
"UM, WOW, MAYBE WE SHOULDN'T . . ."
"ANDY, YOUR PARENTS ARE IMMIGRANTS-- CZECH OR POLISH, I BELIEVE."
"UM, CAN WE PASS ON THAT?"

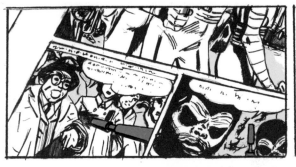

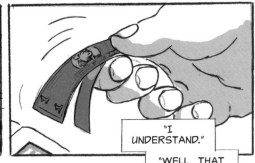

"I UNDERSTAND."

"WELL, THAT WAS MY LAST QUESTION."

"THANK YOU FOR YOUR TIME, ANDY."

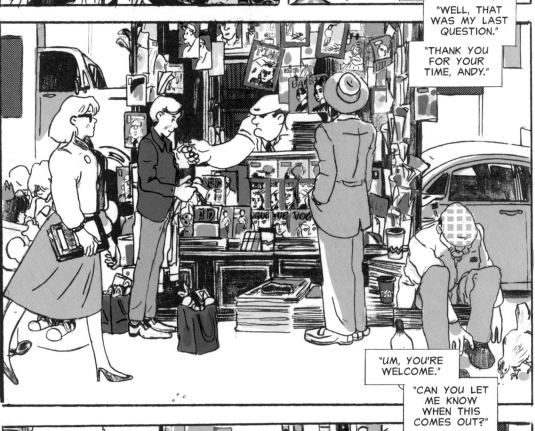

"UM, YOU'RE WELCOME."

"CAN YOU LET ME KNOW WHEN THIS COMES OUT?"

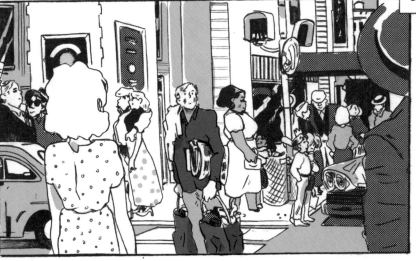

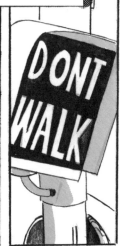

DONT WALK

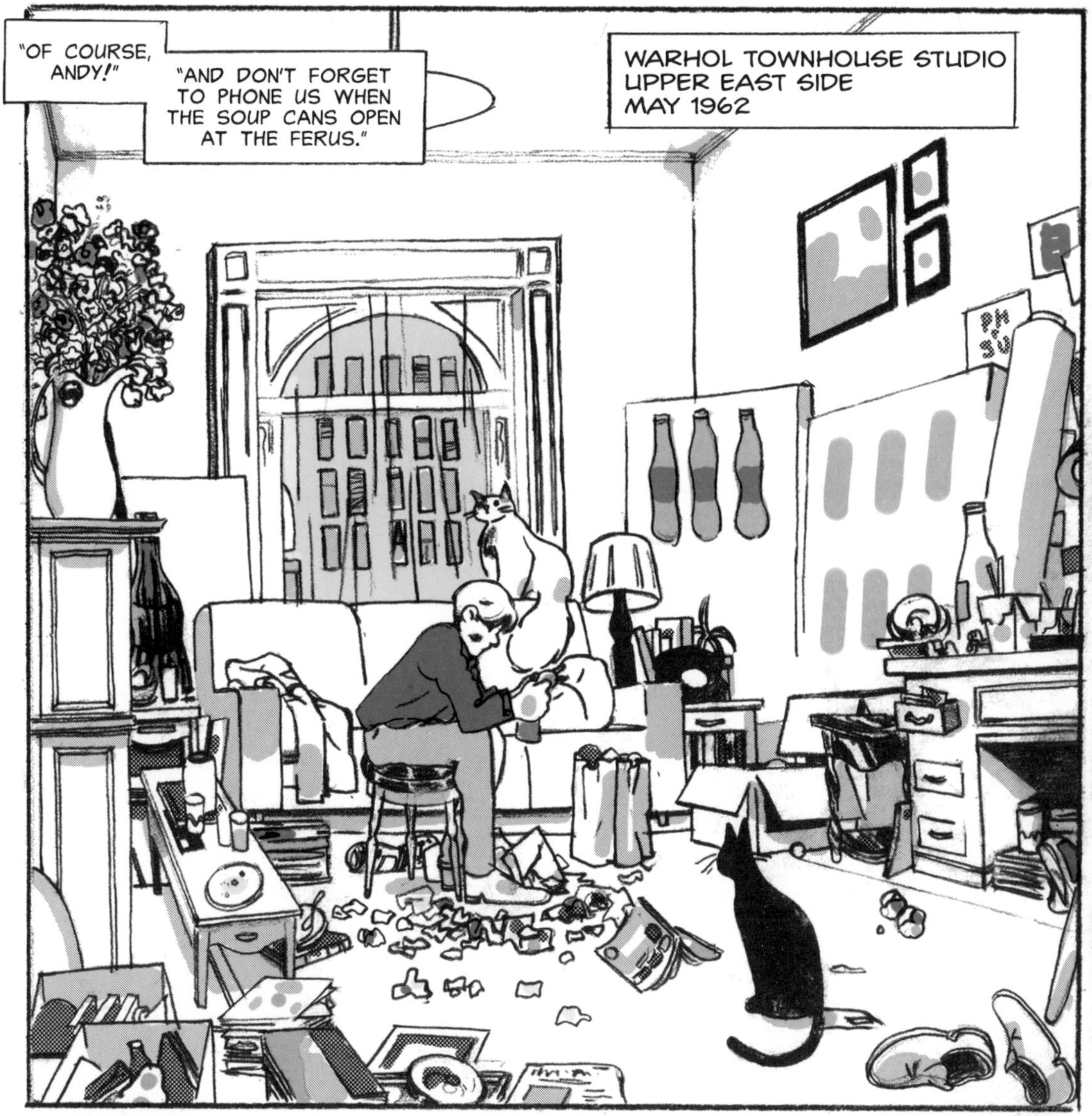
"OF COURSE, ANDY!"
"AND DON'T FORGET TO PHONE US WHEN THE SOUP CANS OPEN AT THE FERUS."
WARHOL TOWNHOUSE STUDIO
UPPER EAST SIDE
MAY 1962

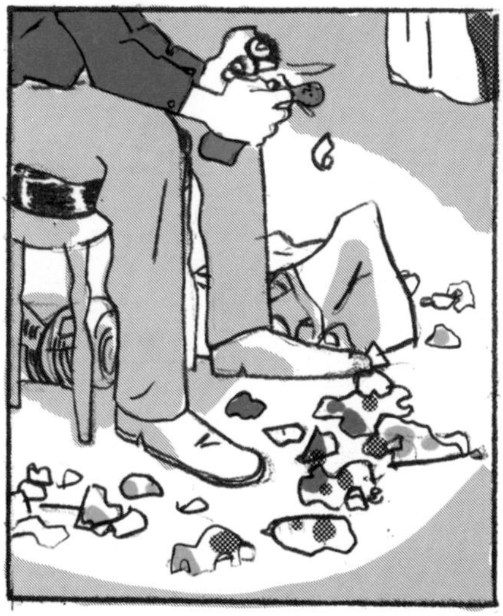

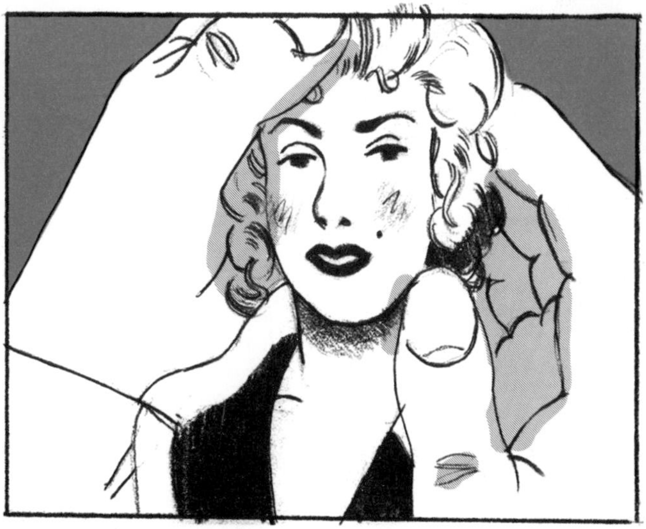

CHAPTER TWO

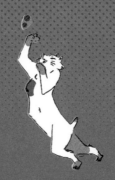

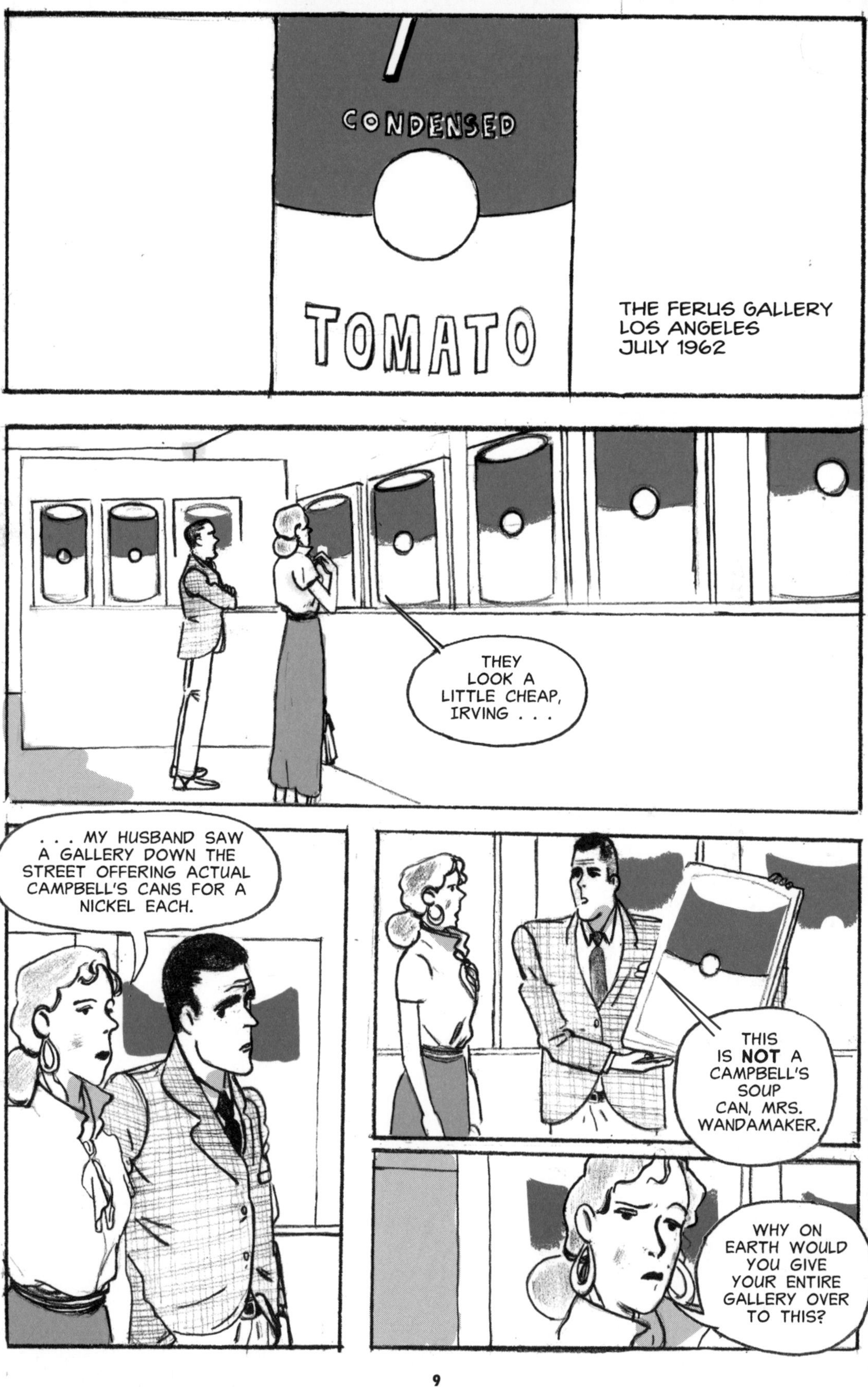
CONDENSED
TOMATO
THE FERUS GALLERY
LOS ANGELES
JULY 1962
THEY LOOK A LITTLE CHEAP, IRVING . . .
. . . MY HUSBAND SAW A GALLERY DOWN THE STREET OFFERING ACTUAL CAMPBELL'S CANS FOR A NICKEL EACH.
THIS IS **NOT** A CAMPBELL'S SOUP CAN, MRS. WANDAMAKER.
WHY ON EARTH WOULD YOU GIVE YOUR ENTIRE GALLERY OVER TO THIS?

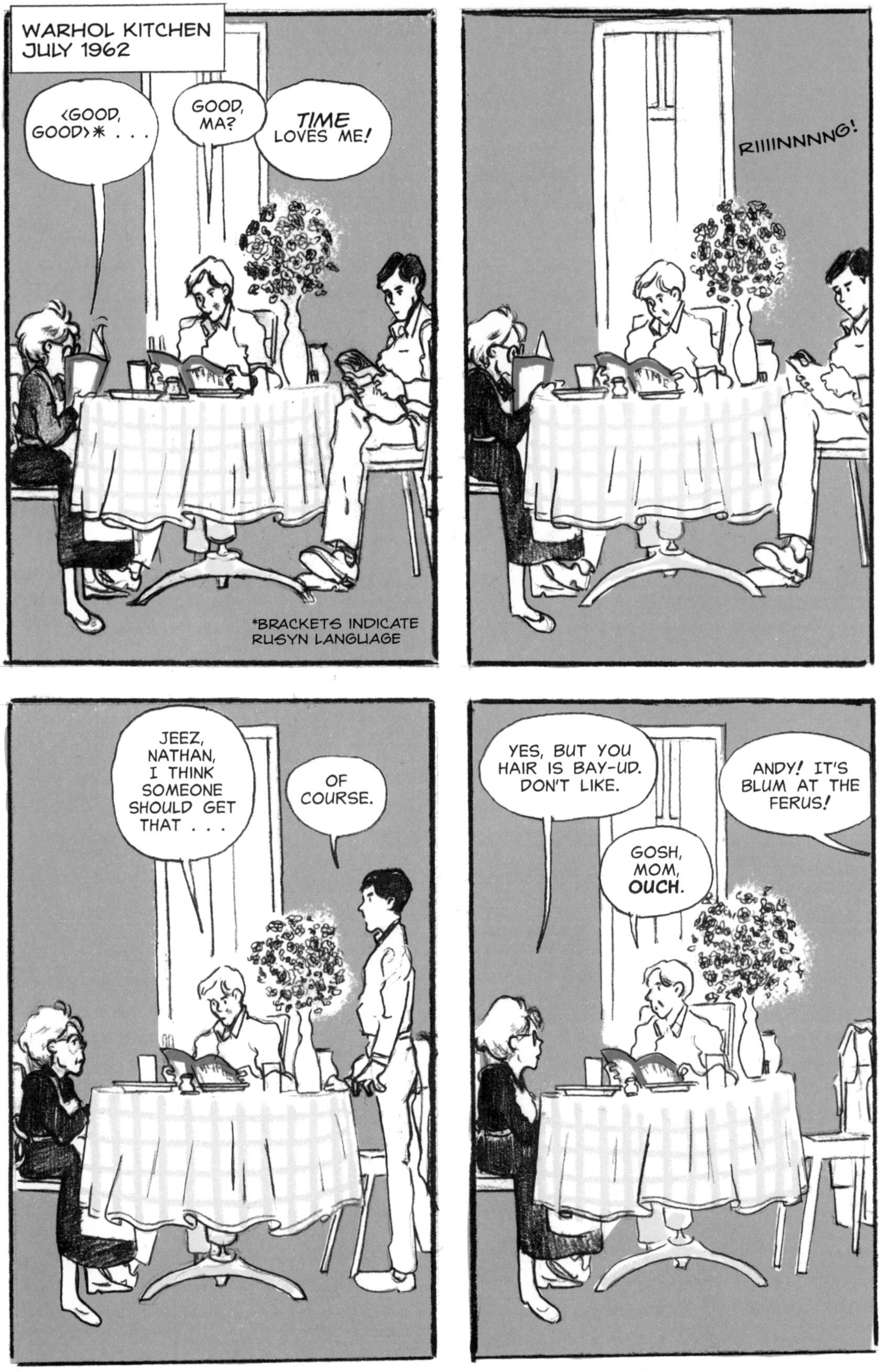
WARHOL KITCHEN
JULY 1962
‹GOOD, GOOD›* . . .
GOOD, MA?
TIME LOVES ME!
*BRACKETS INDICATE RUSYN LANGUAGE
RIIIINNNNG!
JEEZ, NATHAN, I THINK SOMEONE SHOULD GET THAT . . .
OF COURSE.
YES, BUT YOU HAIR IS BAY-UD. DON'T LIKE.
GOSH, MOM, OUCH.
ANDY! IT'S BLUM AT THE FERUS!

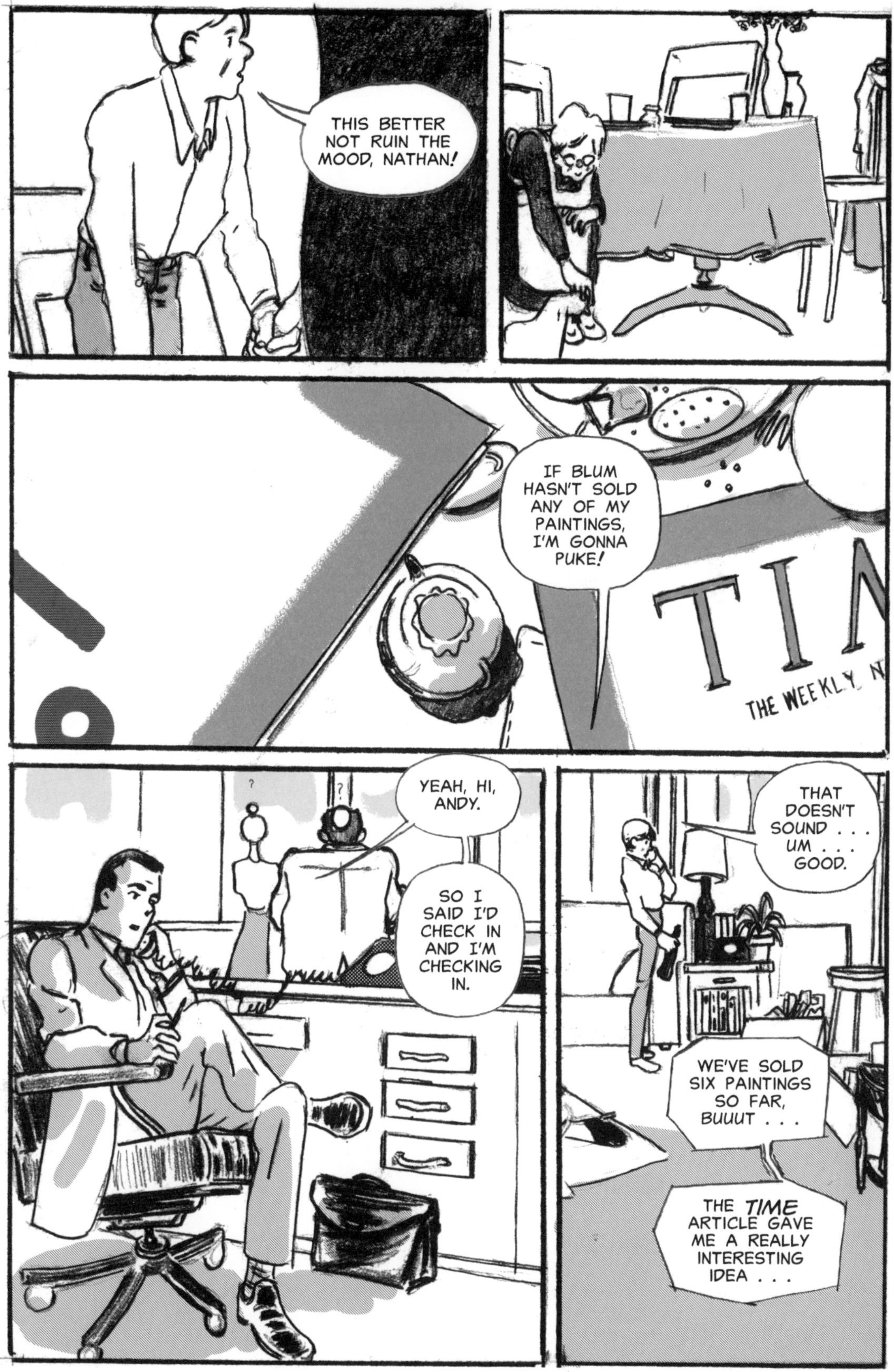
THIS BETTER NOT RUIN THE MOOD, NATHAN!
IF BLUM HASN'T SOLD ANY OF MY PAINTINGS, I'M GONNA PUKE!
TIM
THE WEEKLY N
YEAH, HI, ANDY.
SO I SAID I'D CHECK IN AND I'M CHECKING IN.
THAT DOESN'T SOUND . . . UM . . . GOOD.
WE'VE SOLD SIX PAINTINGS SO FAR, BUUUT . . .
THE *TIME* ARTICLE GAVE ME A REALLY INTERESTING IDEA . . .

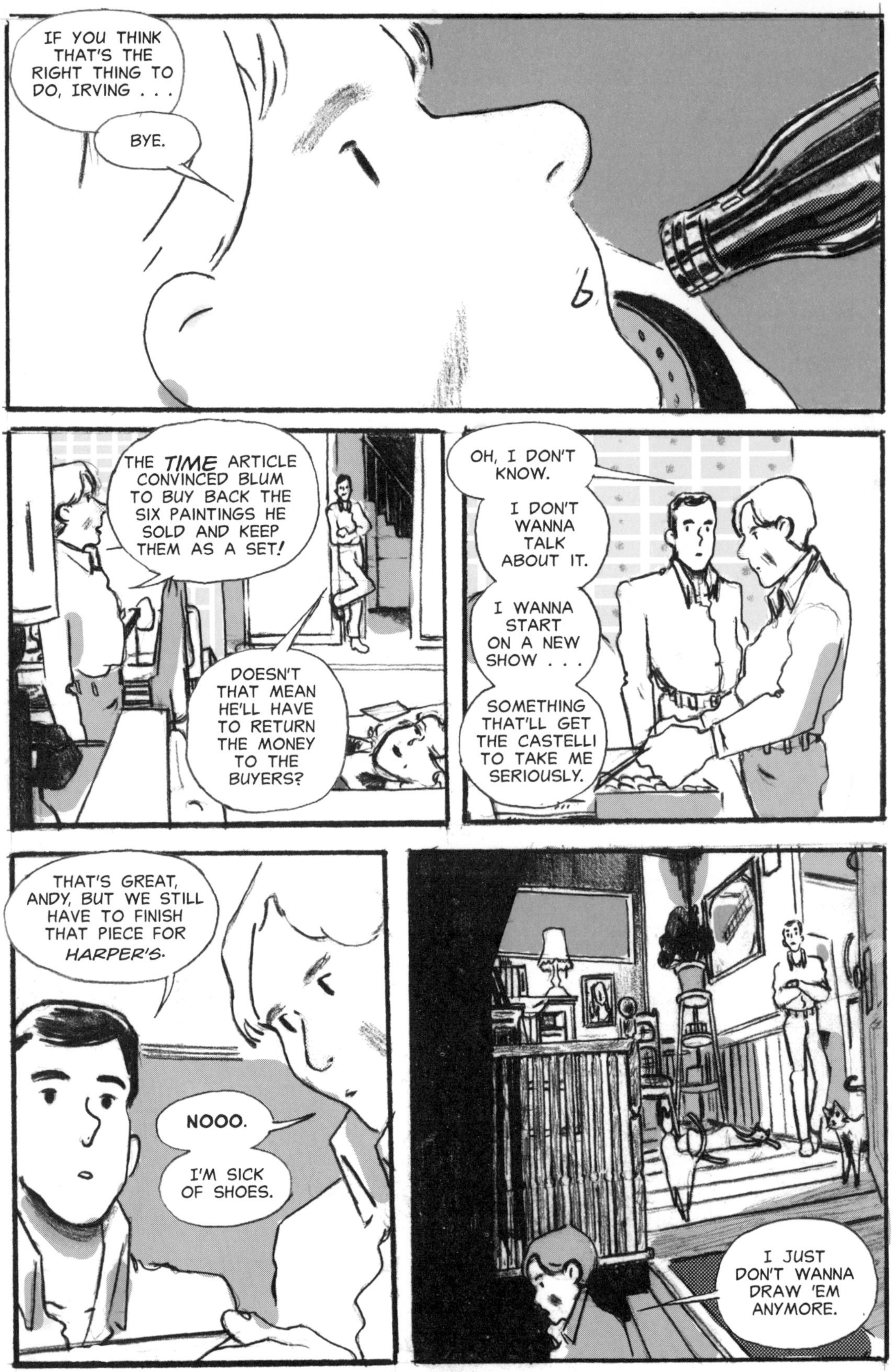
IF YOU THINK THAT'S THE RIGHT THING TO DO, IRVING . . .
BYE.
THE TIME ARTICLE CONVINCED BLUM TO BUY BACK THE SIX PAINTINGS HE SOLD AND KEEP THEM AS A SET!
DOESN'T THAT MEAN HE'LL HAVE TO RETURN THE MONEY TO THE BUYERS?
OH, I DON'T KNOW.
I DON'T WANNA TALK ABOUT IT.
I WANNA START ON A NEW SHOW . . .
SOMETHING THAT'LL GET THE CASTELLI TO TAKE ME SERIOUSLY.
THAT'S GREAT, ANDY, BUT WE STILL HAVE TO FINISH THAT PIECE FOR HARPER'S.
NOOO.
I'M SICK OF SHOES.
I JUST DON'T WANNA DRAW 'EM ANYMORE.

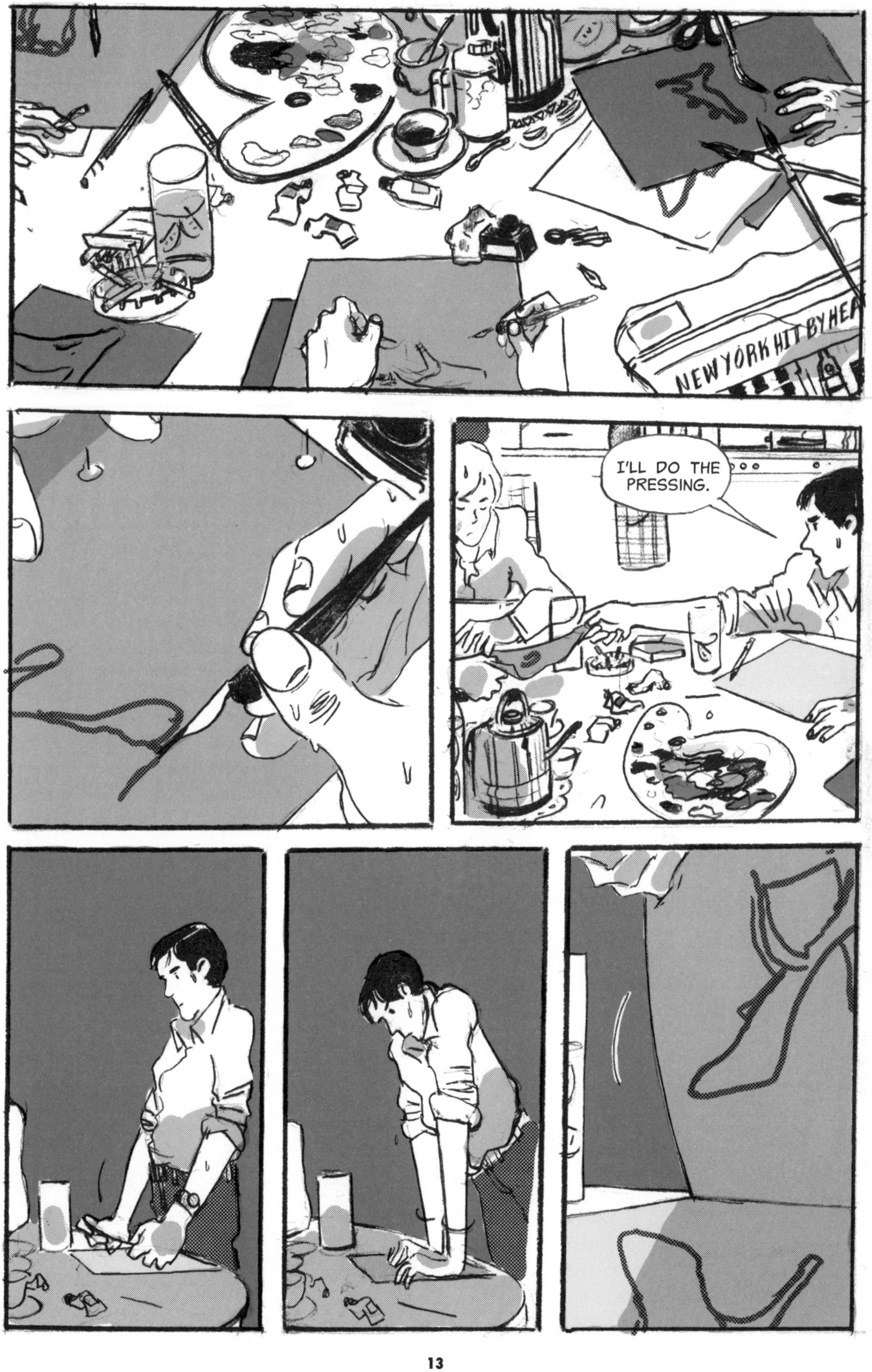
NEW YORK HIT BY HE
I'LL DO THE PRESSING.

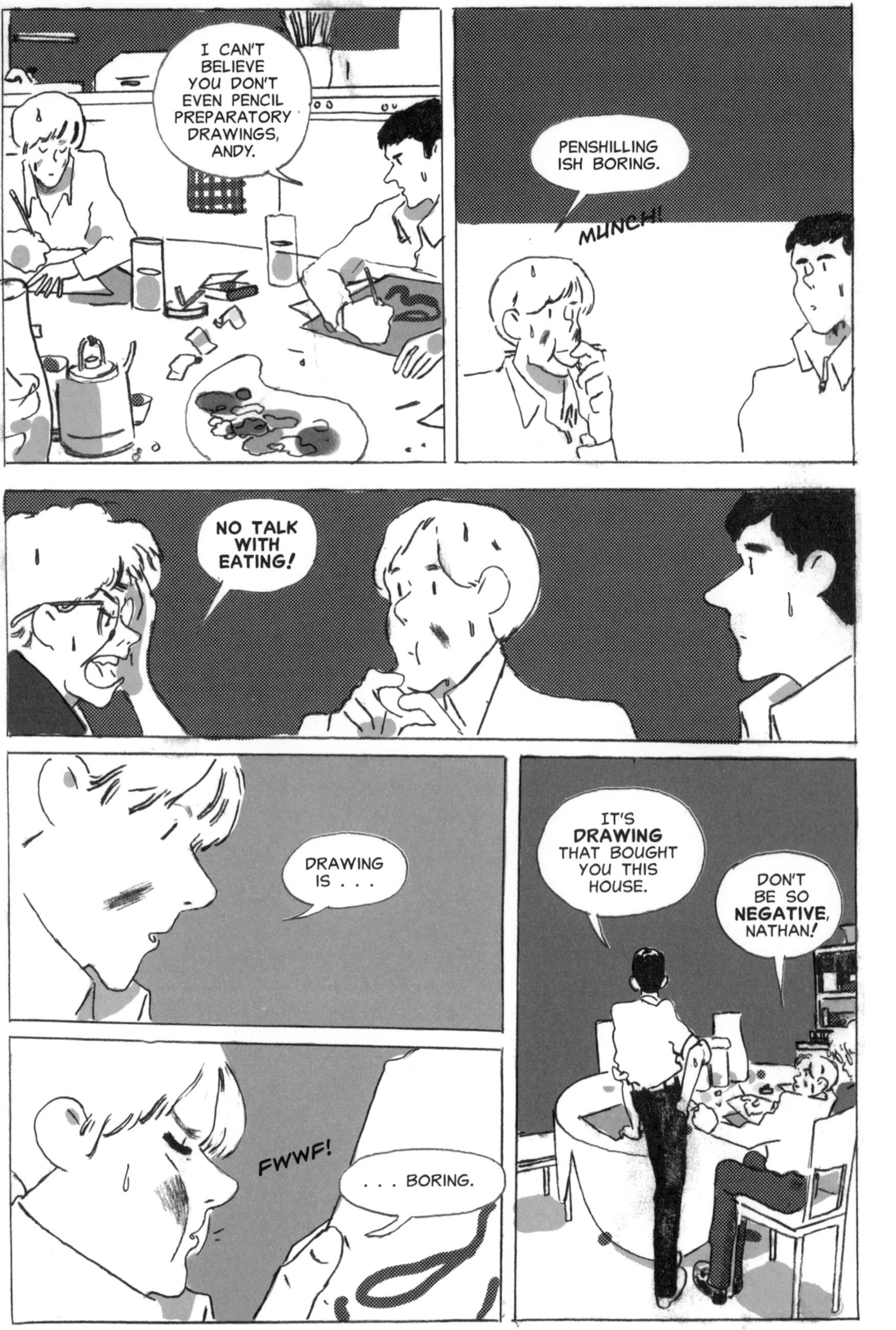
I CAN'T BELIEVE YOU DON'T EVEN PENCIL PREPARATORY DRAWINGS, ANDY.
PENSHILLING ISH BORING.
MUNCH!
NO TALK WITH EATING!
DRAWING IS . . .
FWWF!
. . . BORING.
IT'S DRAWING THAT BOUGHT YOU THIS HOUSE.
DON'T BE SO NEGATIVE, NATHAN!

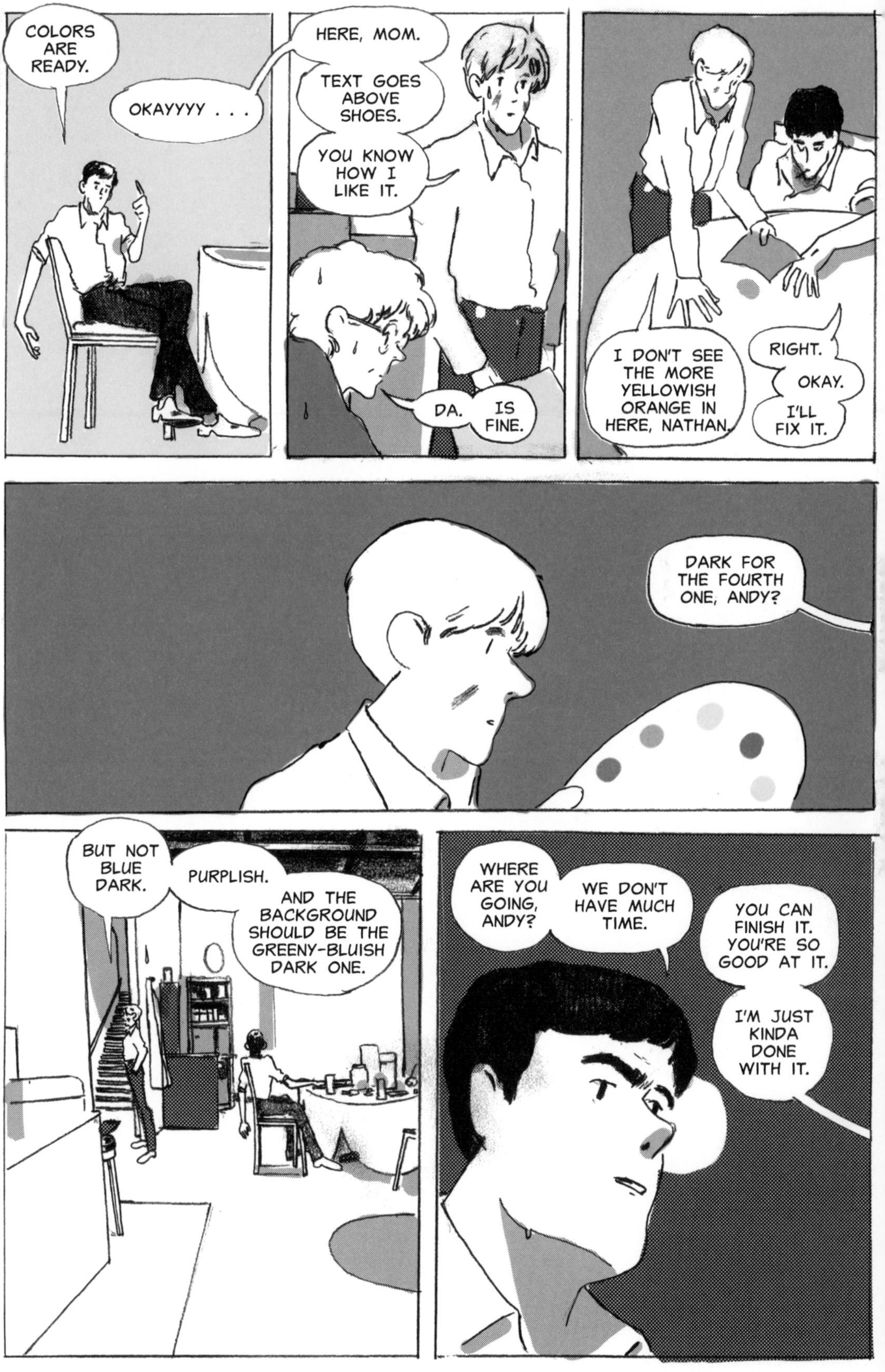
COLORS ARE READY.
OKAYYYY . . .
HERE, MOM.
TEXT GOES ABOVE SHOES.
YOU KNOW HOW I LIKE IT.
DA.
IS FINE.
I DON'T SEE THE MORE YELLOWISH ORANGE IN HERE, NATHAN.
RIGHT.
OKAY.
I'LL FIX IT.
DARK FOR THE FOURTH ONE, ANDY?
BUT NOT BLUE DARK.
PURPLISH.
AND THE BACKGROUND SHOULD BE THE GREENY-BLUISH DARK ONE.
WHERE ARE YOU GOING, ANDY?
WE DON'T HAVE MUCH TIME.
YOU CAN FINISH IT. YOU'RE SO GOOD AT IT.
I'M JUST KINDA DONE WITH IT.

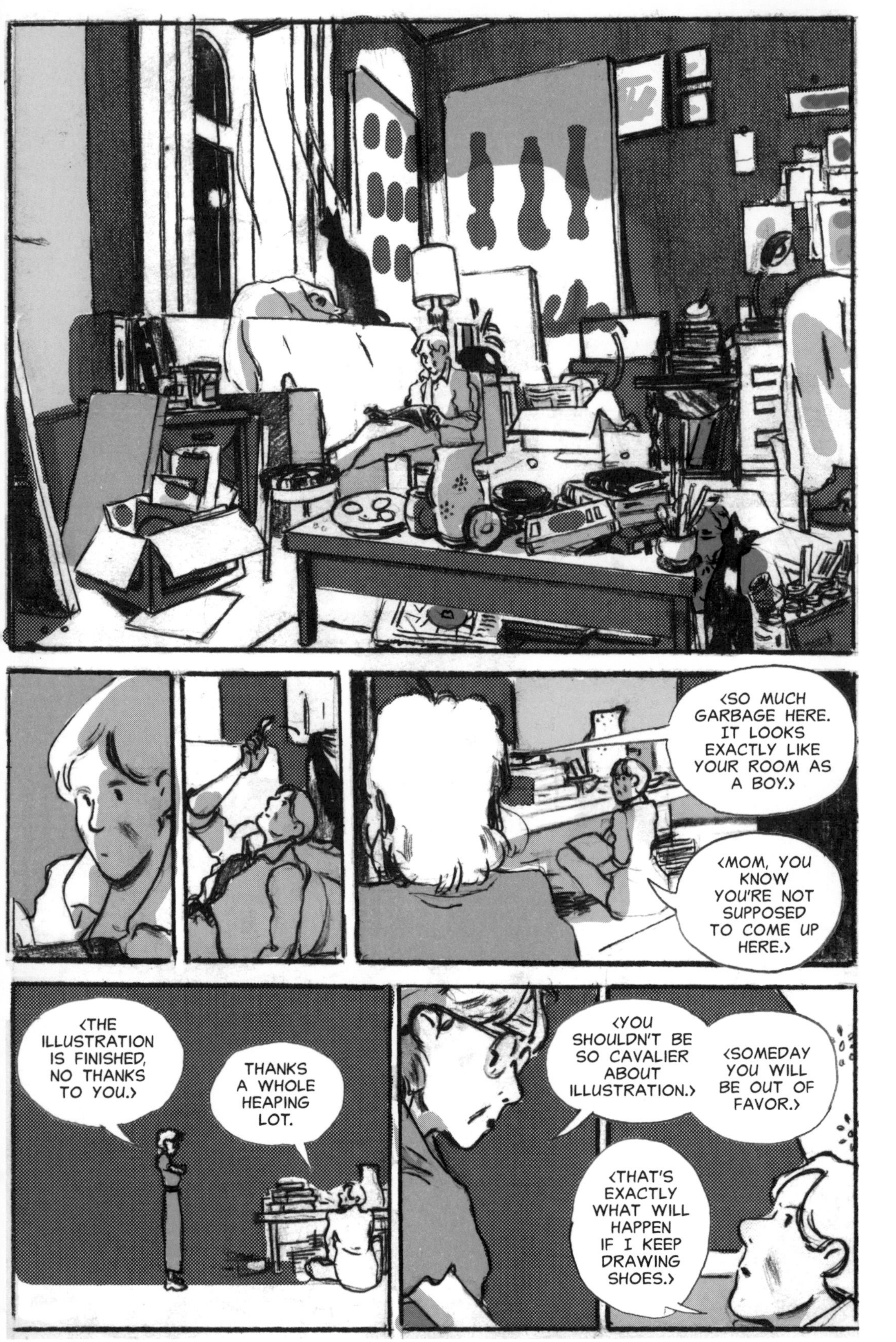
<SO MUCH GARBAGE HERE. IT LOOKS EXACTLY LIKE YOUR ROOM AS A BOY.>
<MOM, YOU KNOW YOU'RE NOT SUPPOSED TO COME UP HERE.>
<THE ILLUSTRATION IS FINISHED, NO THANKS TO YOU.>
THANKS A WHOLE HEAPING LOT.
<YOU SHOULDN'T BE SO CAVALIER ABOUT ILLUSTRATION.>
<SOMEDAY YOU WILL BE OUT OF FAVOR.>
<THAT'S EXACTLY WHAT WILL HAPPEN IF I KEEP DRAWING SHOES.>

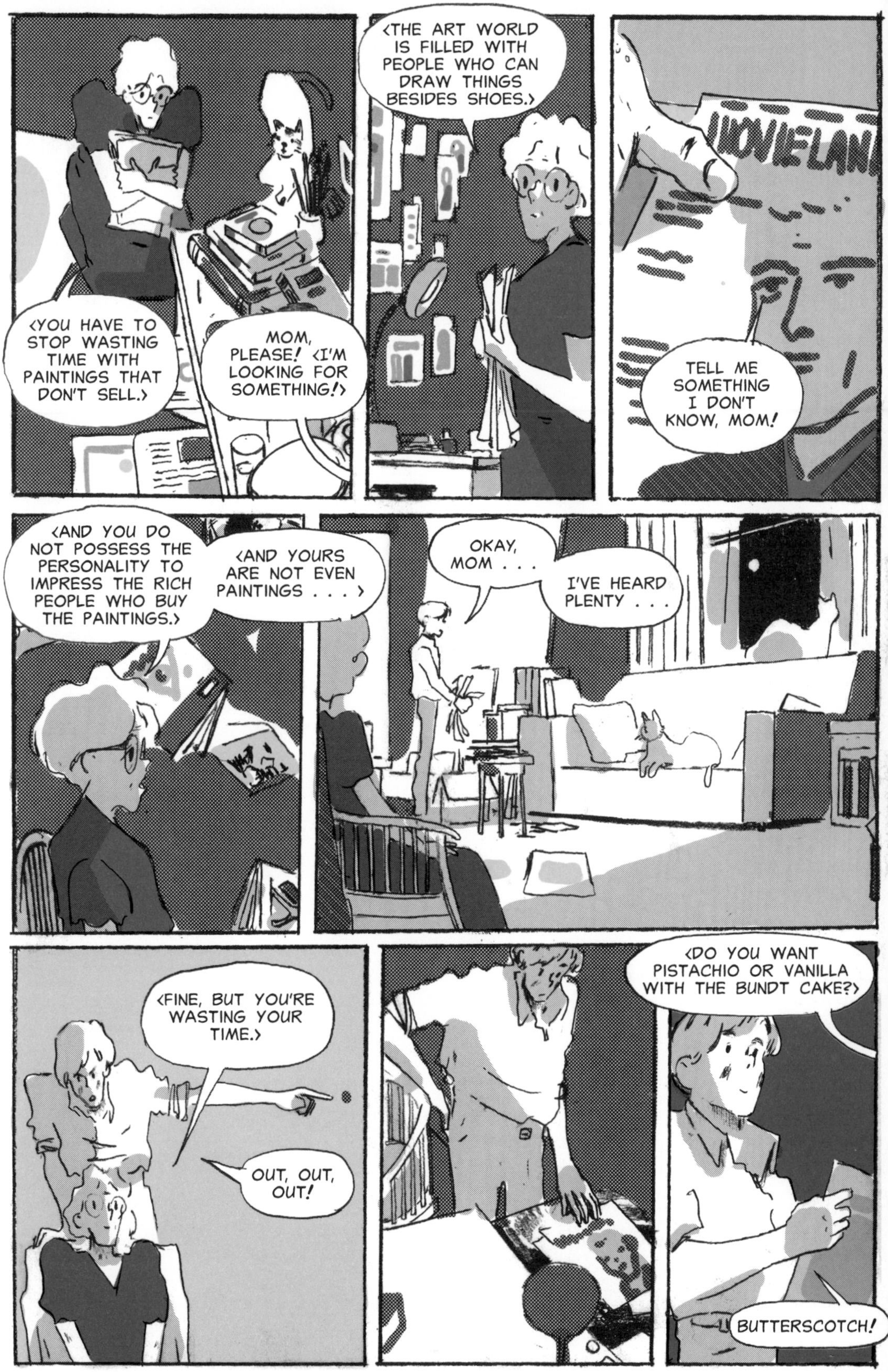
<YOU HAVE TO STOP WASTING TIME WITH PAINTINGS THAT DON'T SELL.>
MOM, PLEASE! <I'M LOOKING FOR SOMETHING!>
<THE ART WORLD IS FILLED WITH PEOPLE WHO CAN DRAW THINGS BESIDES SHOES.>
TELL ME SOMETHING I DON'T KNOW, MOM!
<AND YOU DO NOT POSSESS THE PERSONALITY TO IMPRESS THE RICH PEOPLE WHO BUY THE PAINTINGS.>
<AND YOURS ARE NOT EVEN PAINTINGS . . . >
OKAY, MOM . . .
I'VE HEARD PLENTY . . .
<FINE, BUT YOU'RE WASTING YOUR TIME.>
OUT, OUT, OUT!
<DO YOU WANT PISTACHIO OR VANILLA WITH THE BUNDT CAKE?>
BUTTERSCOTCH!

CHAPTER THREE

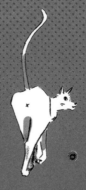

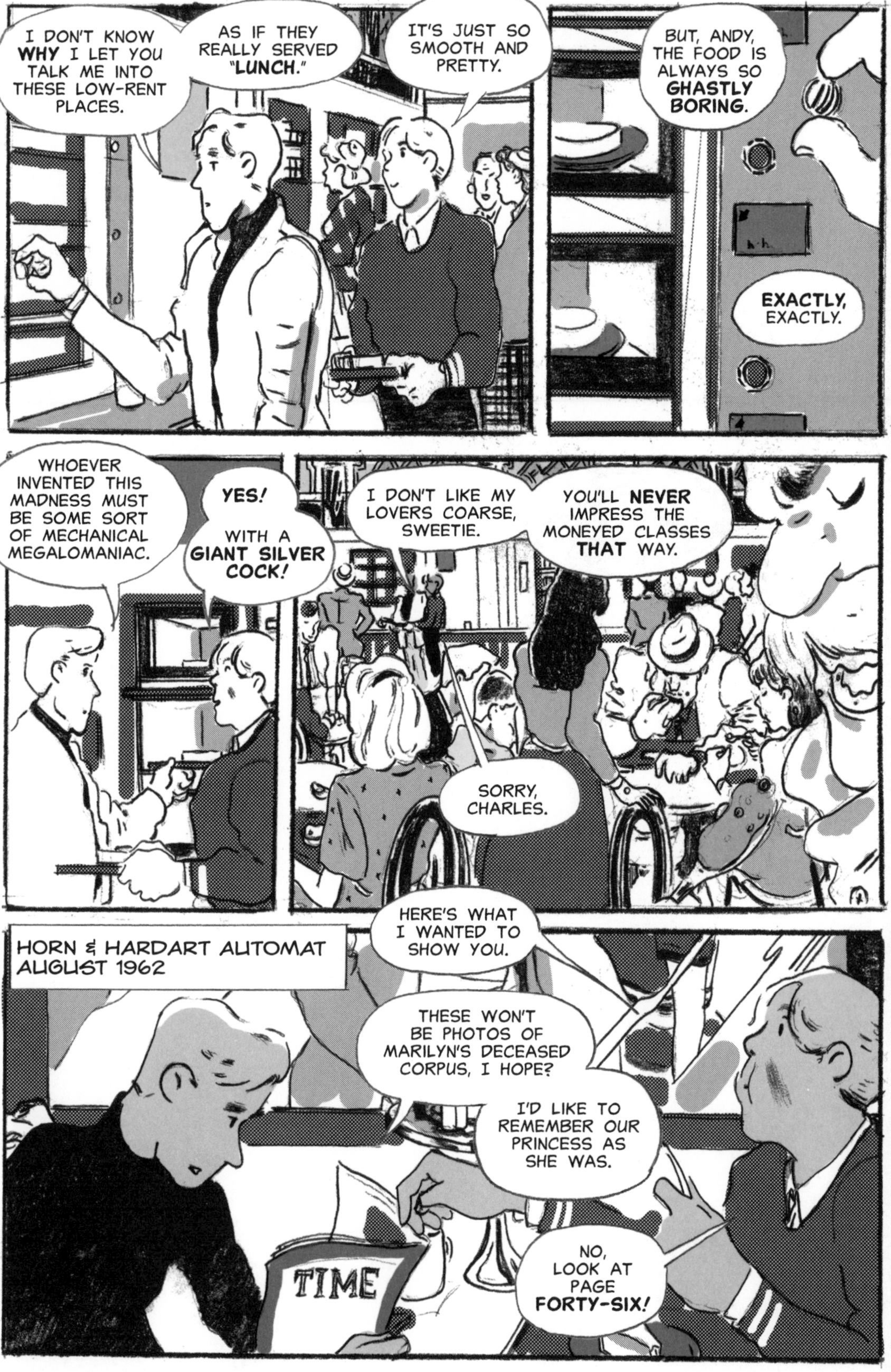
I DON'T KNOW WHY I LET YOU TALK ME INTO THESE LOW-RENT PLACES.
AS IF THEY REALLY SERVED "LUNCH."
IT'S JUST SO SMOOTH AND PRETTY.
BUT, ANDY, THE FOOD IS ALWAYS SO GHASTLY BORING.
EXACTLY, EXACTLY.
WHOEVER INVENTED THIS MADNESS MUST BE SOME SORT OF MECHANICAL MEGALOMANIAC.
YES!
WITH A GIANT SILVER COCK!
I DON'T LIKE MY LOVERS COARSE, SWEETIE.
YOU'LL NEVER IMPRESS THE MONEYED CLASSES THAT WAY.
SORRY, CHARLES.
HORN & HARDART AUTOMAT AUGUST 1962
HERE'S WHAT I WANTED TO SHOW YOU.
THESE WON'T BE PHOTOS OF MARILYN'S DECEASED CORPUS, I HOPE?
I'D LIKE TO REMEMBER OUR PRINCESS AS SHE WAS.
NO, LOOK AT PAGE FORTY-SIX!
TIME

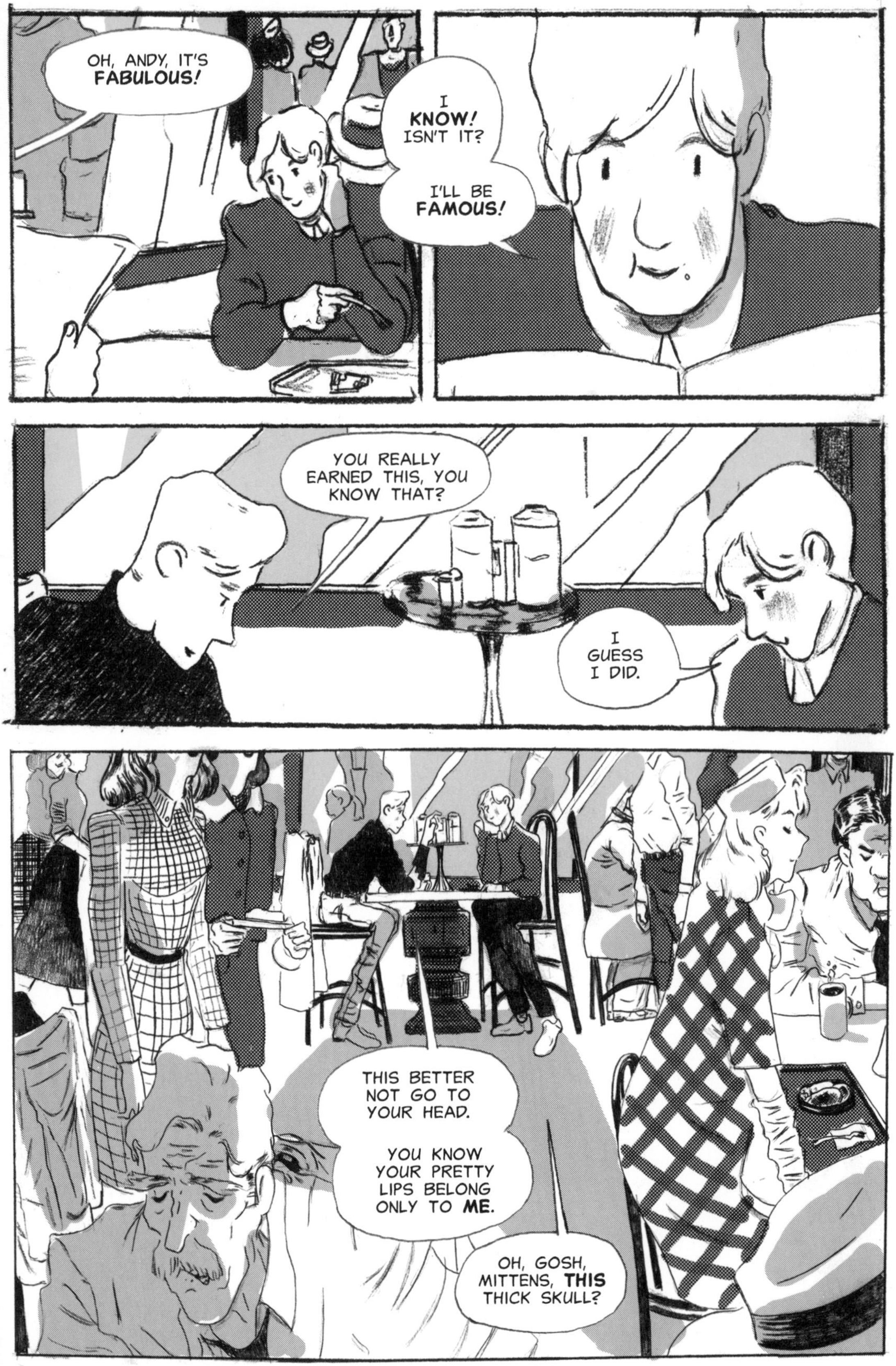
OH, ANDY, IT'S **FABULOUS!**
I **KNOW!** ISN'T IT?
I'LL BE **FAMOUS!**
YOU REALLY EARNED THIS, YOU KNOW THAT?
I GUESS I DID.
THIS BETTER NOT GO TO YOUR HEAD.
YOU KNOW YOUR PRETTY LIPS BELONG ONLY TO **ME**.
OH, GOSH, MITTENS, **THIS** THICK SKULL?

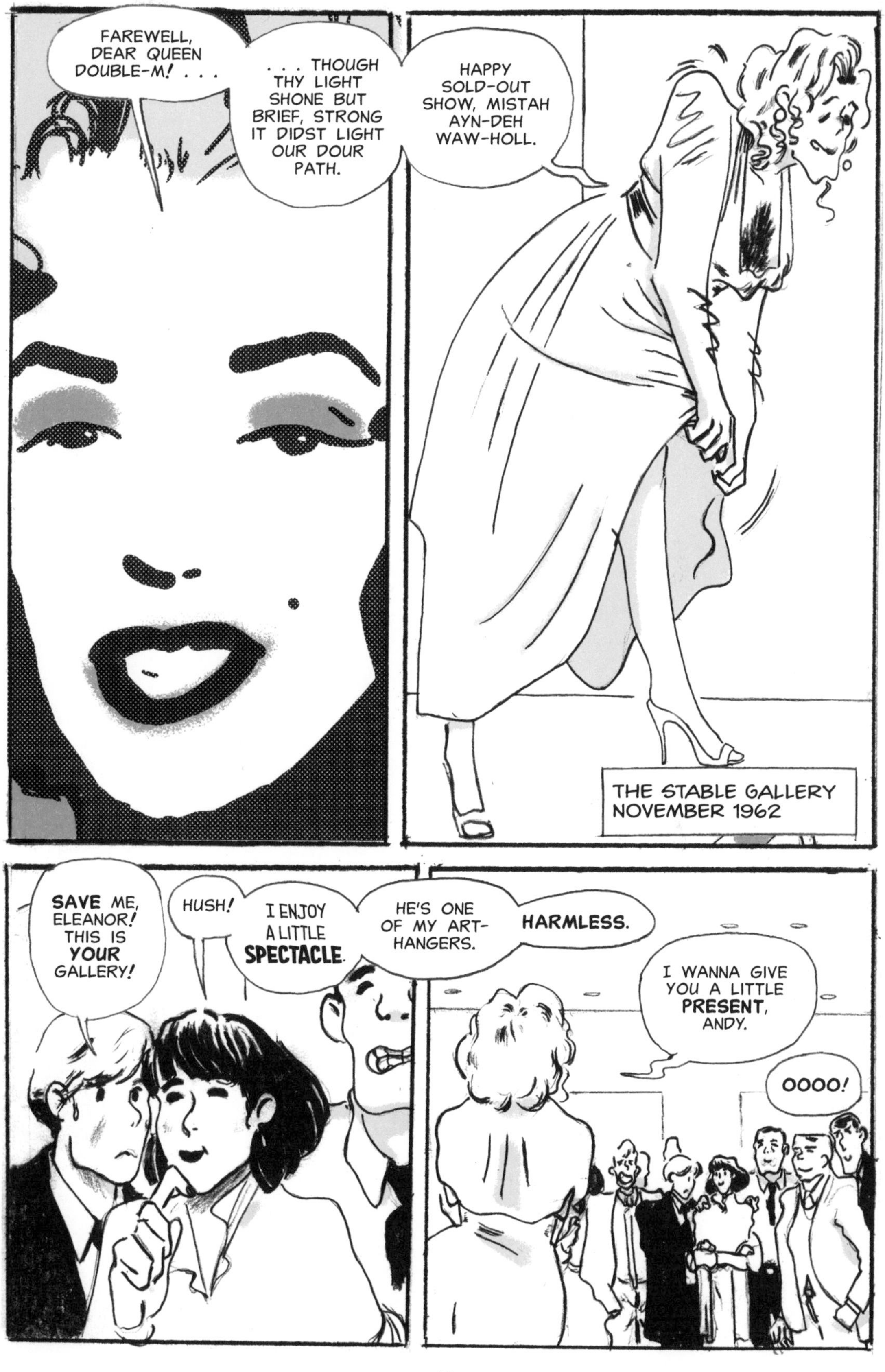
FAREWELL, DEAR QUEEN DOUBLE-M! . . .
. . . THOUGH THY LIGHT SHONE BUT BRIEF, STRONG IT DIDST LIGHT OUR DOUR PATH.
HAPPY SOLD-OUT SHOW, MISTAH AYN-DEH WAW-HOLL.
THE STABLE GALLERY NOVEMBER 1962
SAVE ME, ELEANOR! THIS IS YOUR GALLERY!
HUSH!
I ENJOY A LITTLE SPECTACLE.
HE'S ONE OF MY ART-HANGERS.
HARMLESS.
I WANNA GIVE YOU A LITTLE PRESENT, ANDY.
OOOO!

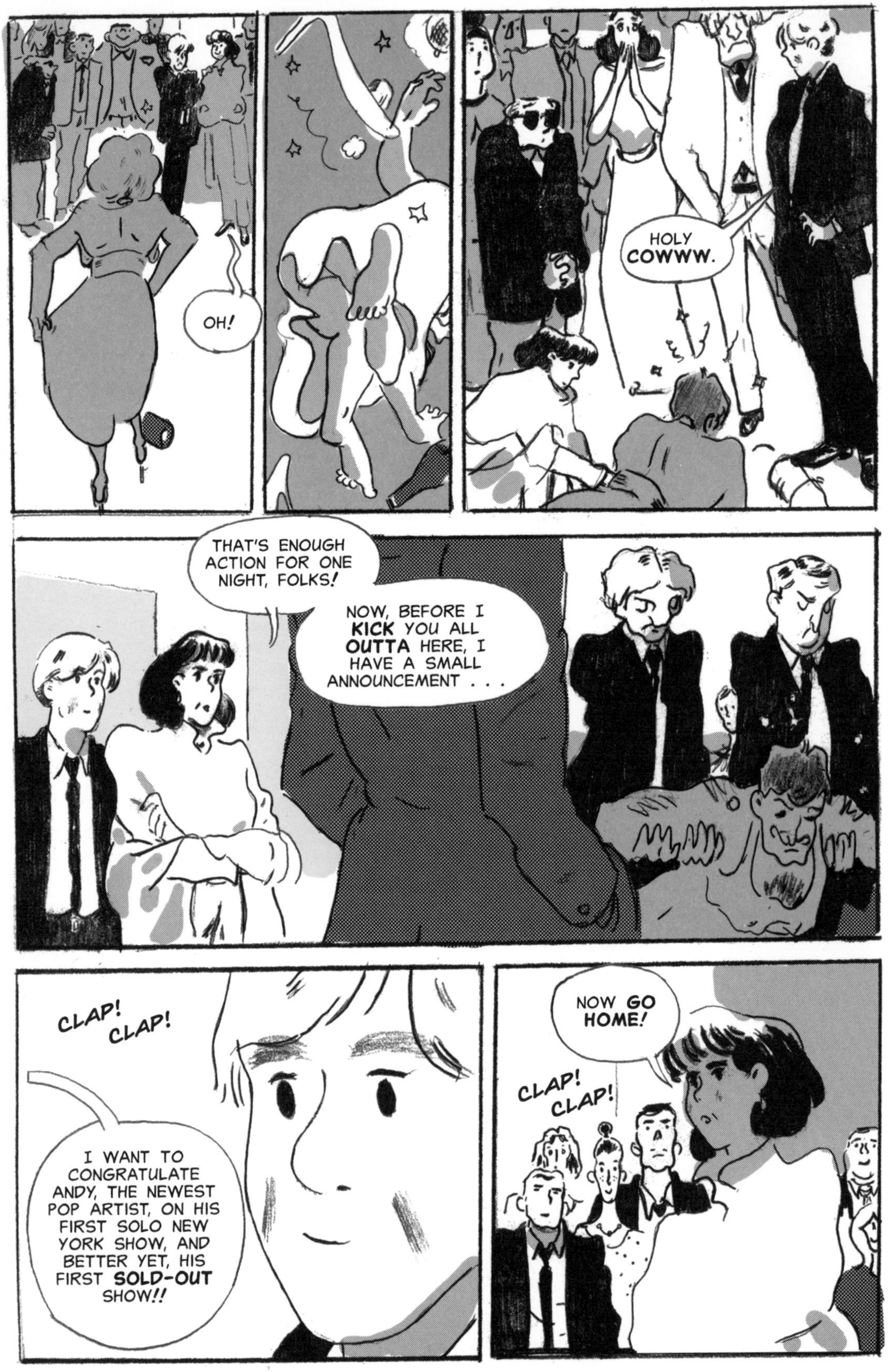
OH!
HOLY COWWW.
THAT'S ENOUGH ACTION FOR ONE NIGHT, FOLKS!
NOW, BEFORE I KICK YOU ALL OUTTA HERE, I HAVE A SMALL ANNOUNCEMENT . . .
CLAP! CLAP!
I WANT TO CONGRATULATE ANDY, THE NEWEST POP ARTIST, ON HIS FIRST SOLO NEW YORK SHOW, AND BETTER YET, HIS FIRST SOLD-OUT SHOW!!
NOW GO HOME!
CLAP! CLAP!

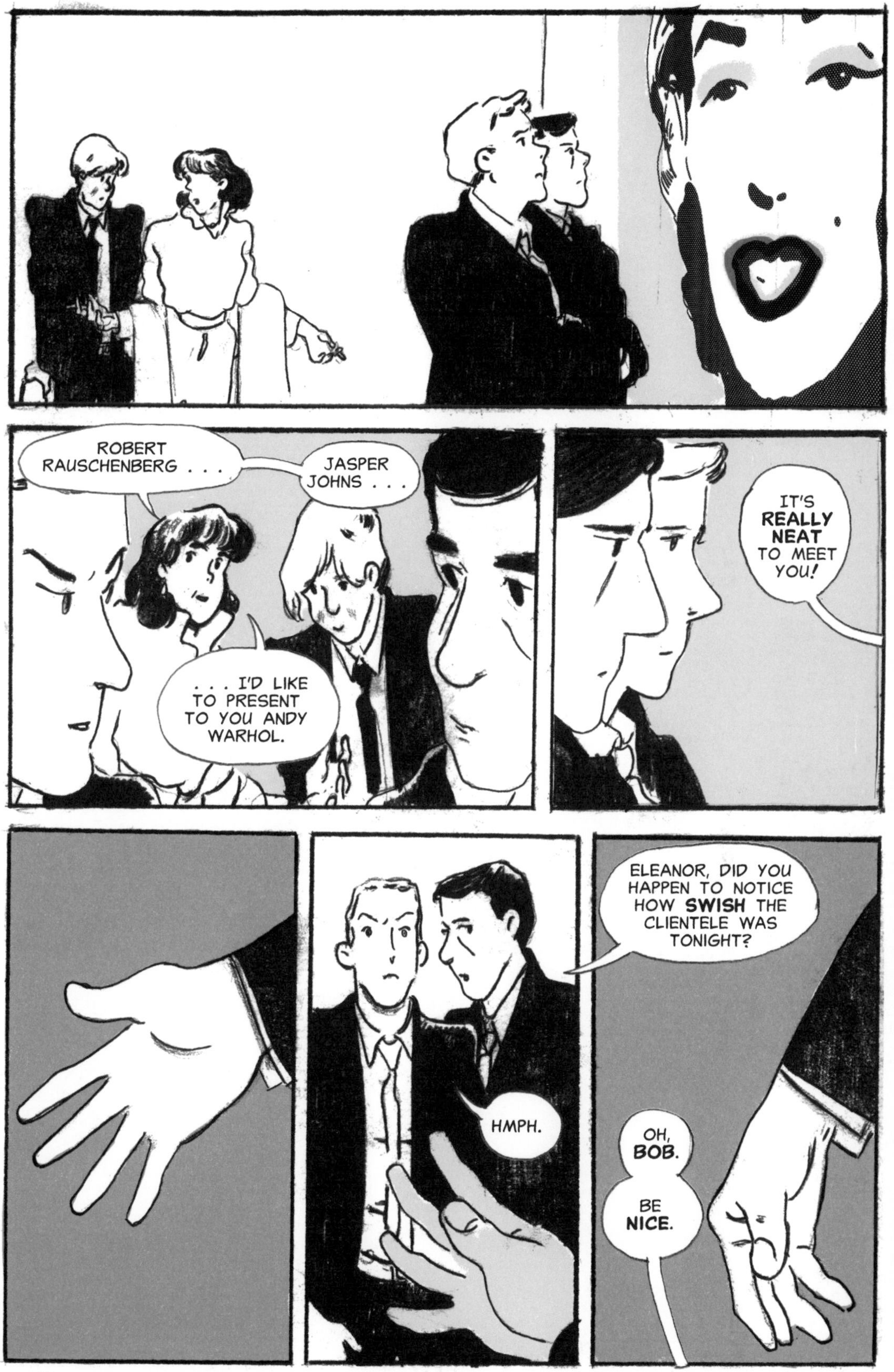
ROBERT RAUSCHENBERG . . .
JASPER JOHNS . . .
. . . I'D LIKE TO PRESENT TO YOU ANDY WARHOL.
IT'S REALLY NEAT TO MEET YOU!
ELEANOR, DID YOU HAPPEN TO NOTICE HOW SWISH THE CLIENTELE WAS TONIGHT?
HMPH.
OH, BOB.
BE NICE.

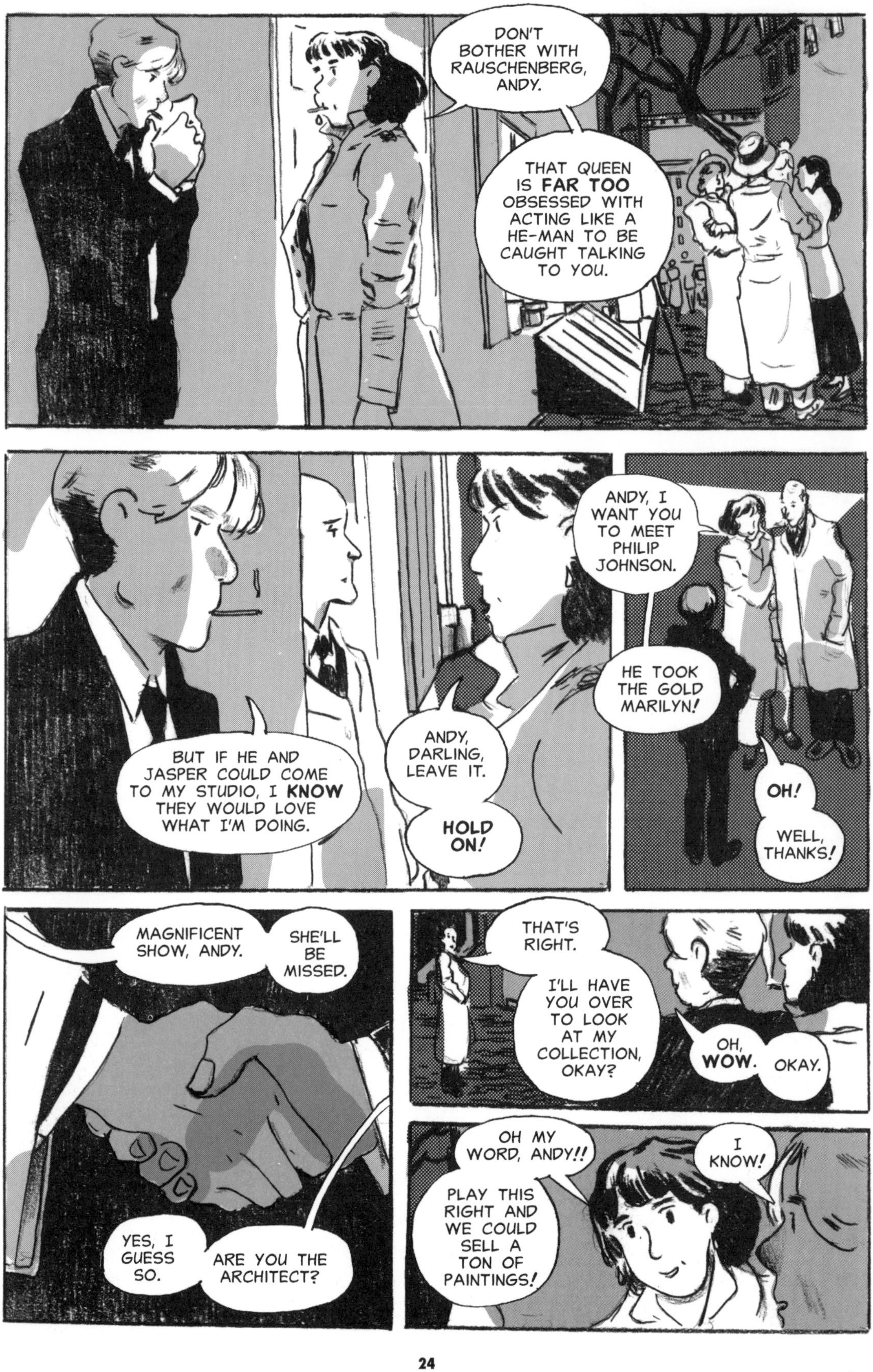
DON'T BOTHER WITH RAUSCHENBERG, ANDY.
THAT QUEEN IS **FAR TOO** OBSESSED WITH ACTING LIKE A HE-MAN TO BE CAUGHT TALKING TO YOU.
BUT IF HE AND JASPER COULD COME TO MY STUDIO, I **KNOW** THEY WOULD LOVE WHAT I'M DOING.
ANDY, DARLING, LEAVE IT.
HOLD ON!
ANDY, I WANT YOU TO MEET PHILIP JOHNSON.
HE TOOK THE GOLD MARILYN!
OH!
WELL, THANKS!
MAGNIFICENT SHOW, ANDY.
SHE'LL BE MISSED.
YES, I GUESS SO.
ARE YOU THE ARCHITECT?
THAT'S RIGHT.
I'LL HAVE YOU OVER TO LOOK AT MY COLLECTION, OKAY?
OH, **WOW.**
OKAY.
OH MY WORD, ANDY!!
PLAY THIS RIGHT AND WE COULD SELL A TON OF PAINTINGS!
I KNOW!

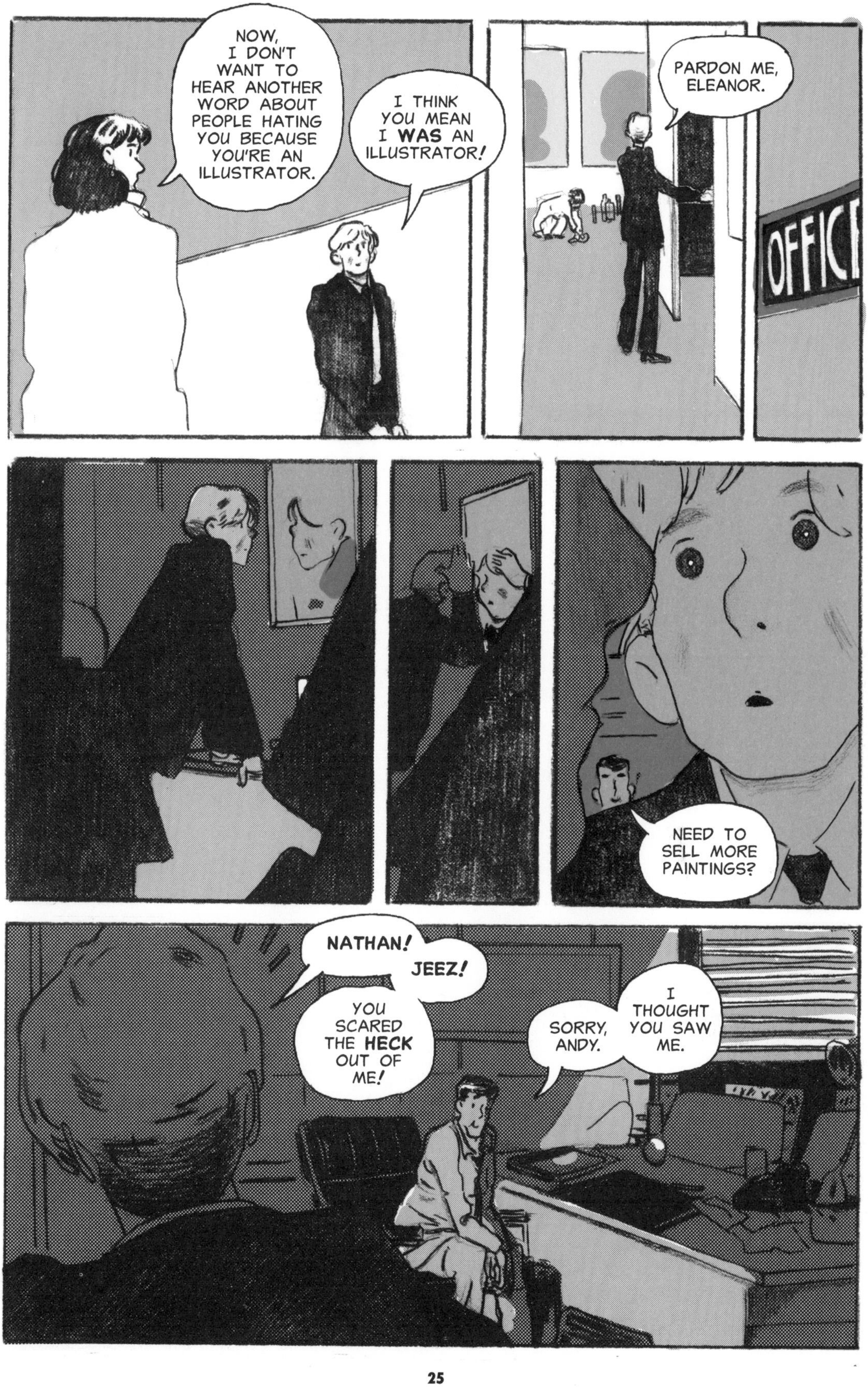
NOW, I DON'T WANT TO HEAR ANOTHER WORD ABOUT PEOPLE HATING YOU BECAUSE YOU'RE AN ILLUSTRATOR.
I THINK YOU MEAN I **WAS** AN ILLUSTRATOR!
PARDON ME, ELEANOR.
OFFICE
NEED TO SELL MORE PAINTINGS?
NATHAN!
JEEZ!
YOU SCARED THE **HECK** OUT OF ME!
SORRY, ANDY.
I THOUGHT YOU SAW ME.

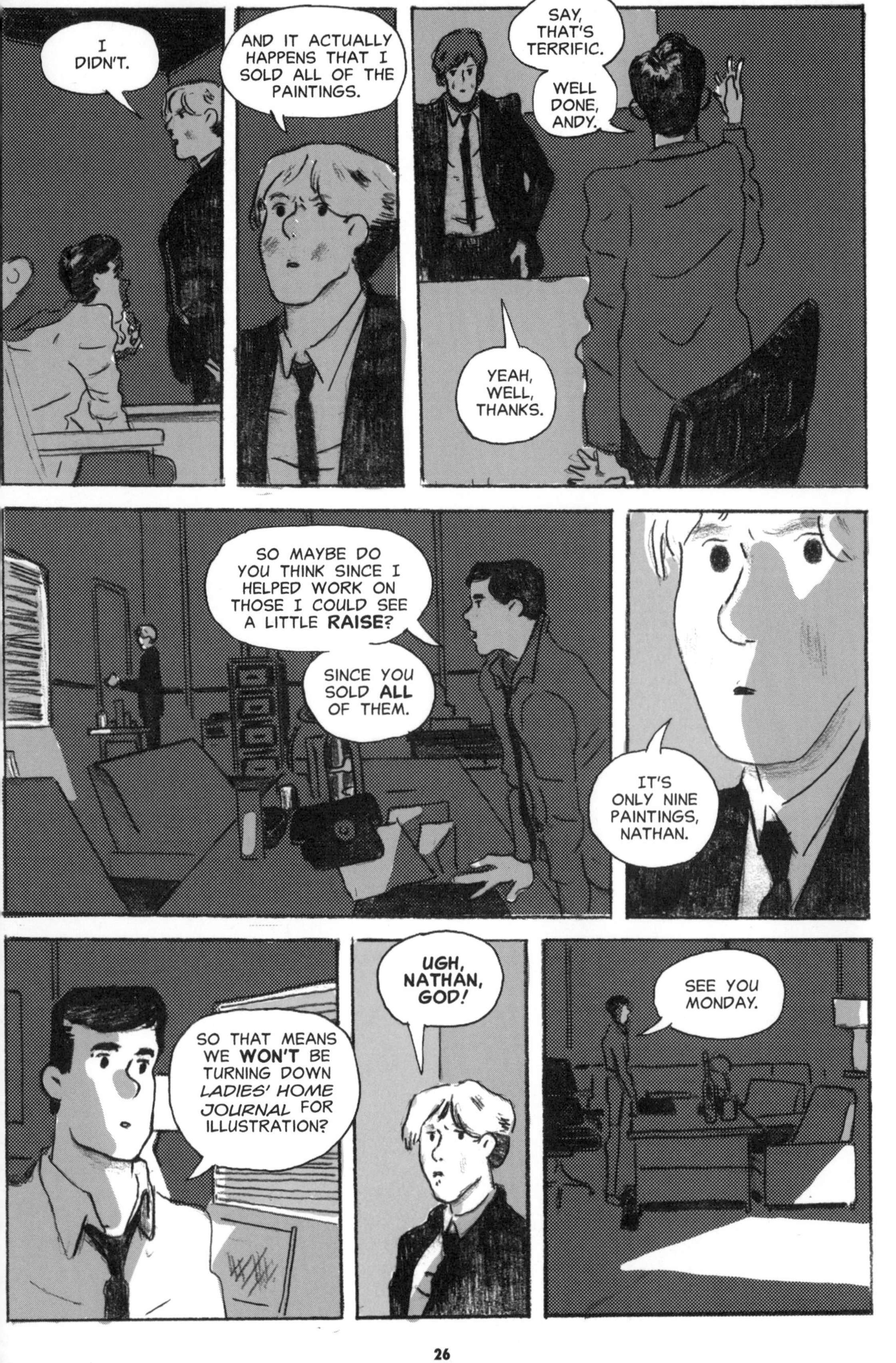
I DIDN'T.
AND IT ACTUALLY HAPPENS THAT I SOLD ALL OF THE PAINTINGS.
SAY, THAT'S TERRIFIC.
WELL DONE, ANDY.
YEAH, WELL, THANKS.
SO MAYBE DO YOU THINK SINCE I HELPED WORK ON THOSE I COULD SEE A LITTLE RAISE?
SINCE YOU SOLD ALL OF THEM.
IT'S ONLY NINE PAINTINGS, NATHAN.
SO THAT MEANS WE WON'T BE TURNING DOWN LADIES' HOME JOURNAL FOR ILLUSTRATION?
UGH, NATHAN, GOD!
SEE YOU MONDAY.

CHAPTER FOUR

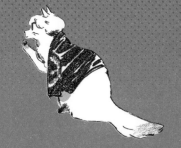

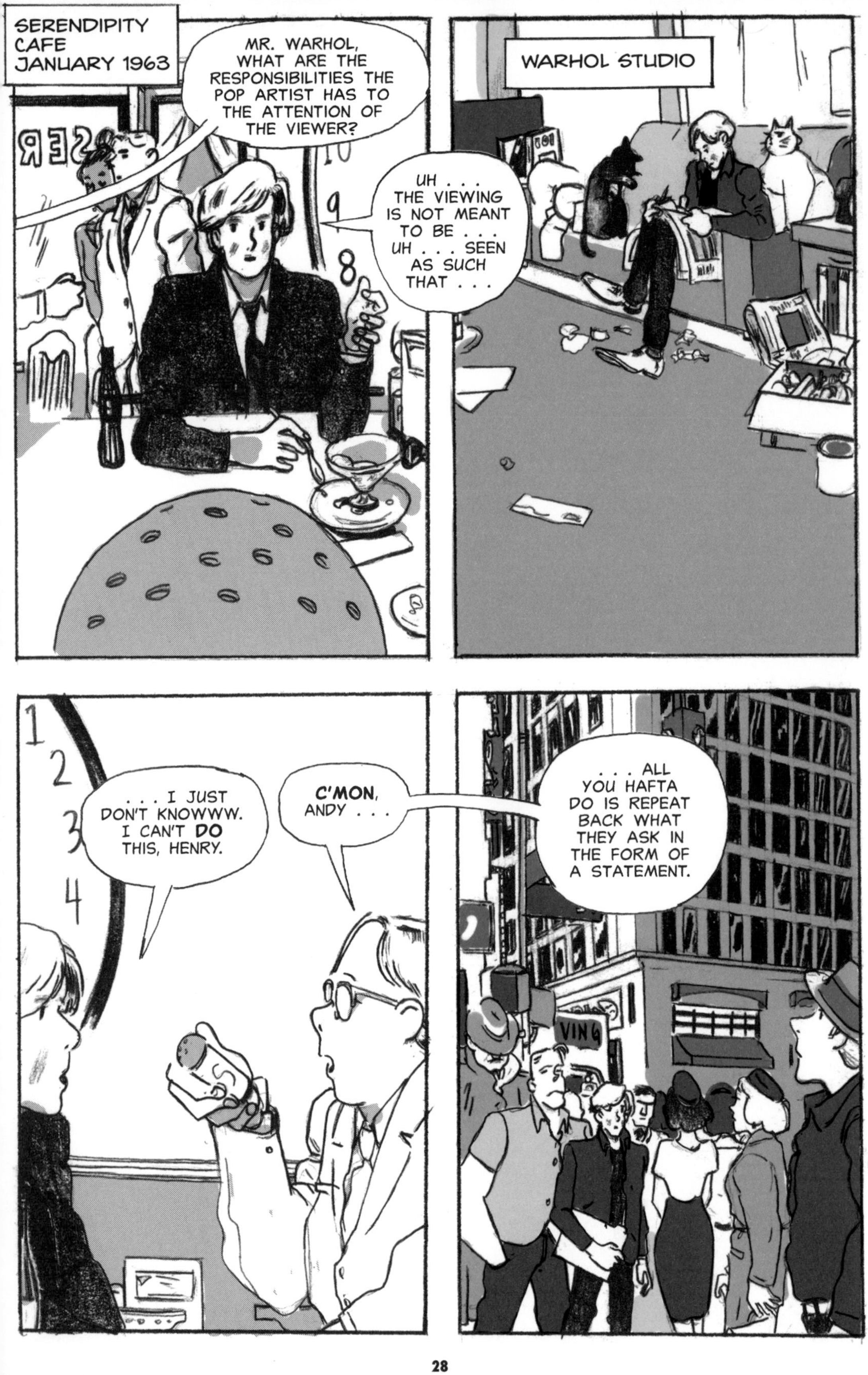
SERENDIPITY CAFE JANUARY 1963
MR. WARHOL, WHAT ARE THE RESPONSIBILITIES THE POP ARTIST HAS TO THE ATTENTION OF THE VIEWER?
UH . . . THE VIEWING IS NOT MEANT TO BE . . . UH . . . SEEN AS SUCH THAT . . .
WARHOL STUDIO
. . . I JUST DON'T KNOWWW. I CAN'T **DO** THIS, HENRY.
C'MON, ANDY . . .
. . . ALL YOU HAFTA DO IS REPEAT BACK WHAT THEY ASK IN THE FORM OF A STATEMENT.
VING

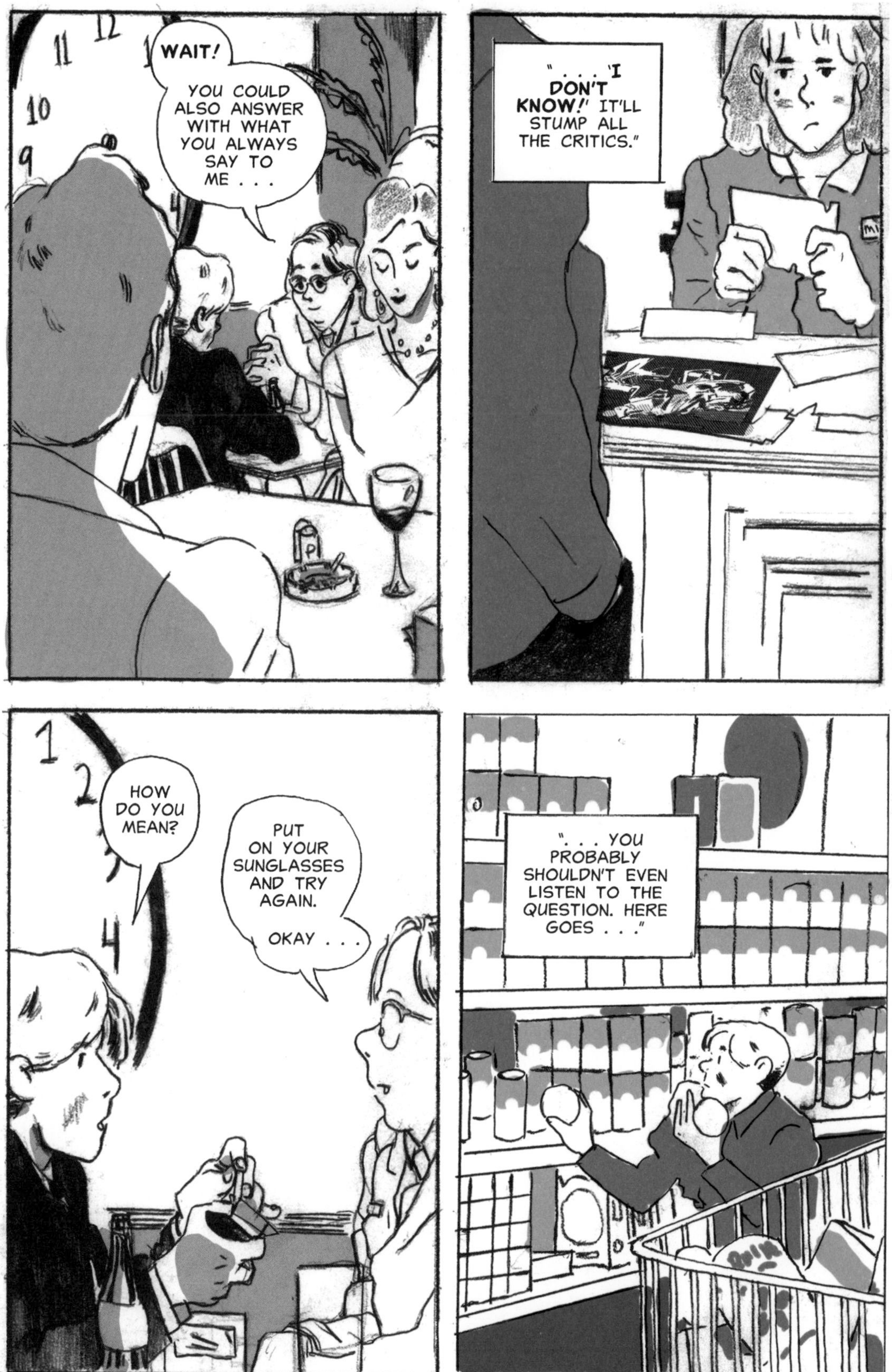
WAIT!
YOU COULD ALSO ANSWER WITH WHAT YOU ALWAYS SAY TO ME . . .
". . . 'I DON'T KNOW!' IT'LL STUMP ALL THE CRITICS."
HOW DO YOU MEAN?
PUT ON YOUR SUNGLASSES AND TRY AGAIN.
OKAY . . .
". . . YOU PROBABLY SHOULDN'T EVEN LISTEN TO THE QUESTION. HERE GOES . . ."

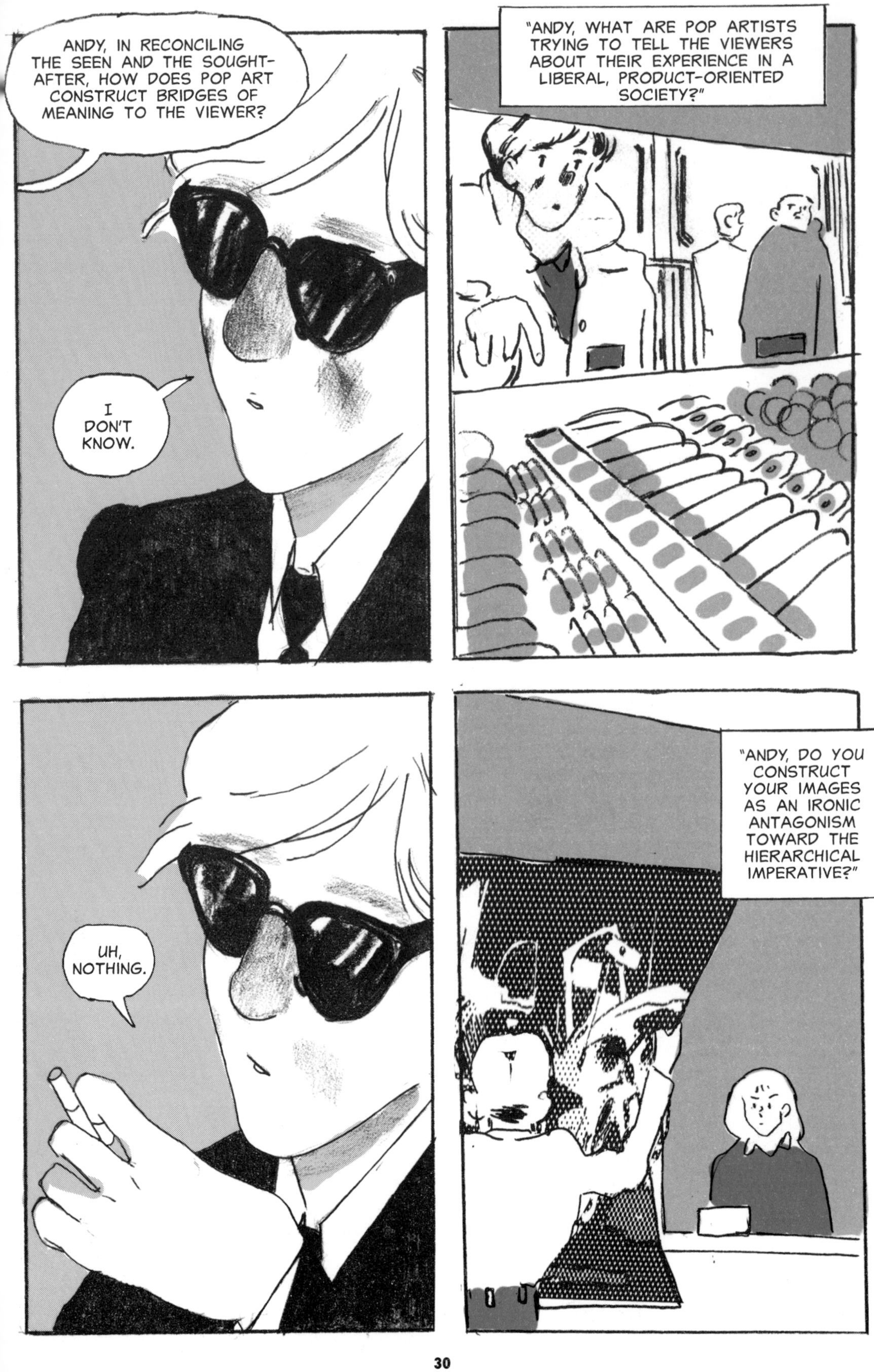
ANDY, IN RECONCILING THE SEEN AND THE SOUGHT-AFTER, HOW DOES POP ART CONSTRUCT BRIDGES OF MEANING TO THE VIEWER?
I DON'T KNOW.
"ANDY, WHAT ARE POP ARTISTS TRYING TO TELL THE VIEWERS ABOUT THEIR EXPERIENCE IN A LIBERAL, PRODUCT-ORIENTED SOCIETY?"
UH, NOTHING.
"ANDY, DO YOU CONSTRUCT YOUR IMAGES AS AN IRONIC ANTAGONISM TOWARD THE HIERARCHICAL IMPERATIVE?"

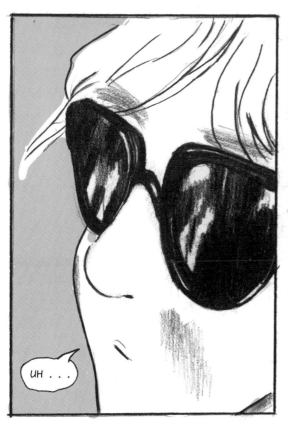

UH . . .

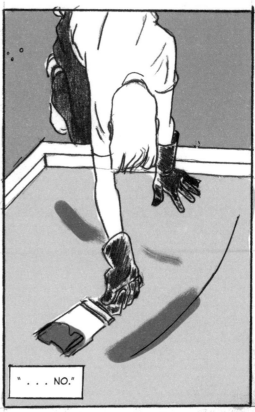

" . . . NO."

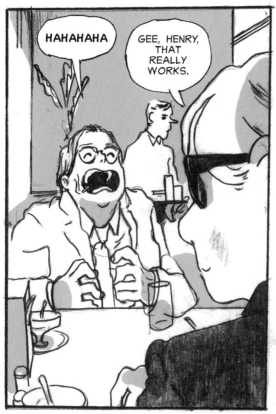

HAHAHAHA

GEE, HENRY, THAT REALLY WORKS.

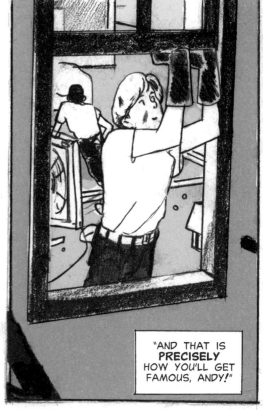

"AND THAT IS **PRECISELY** HOW YOU'LL GET FAMOUS, ANDY!"

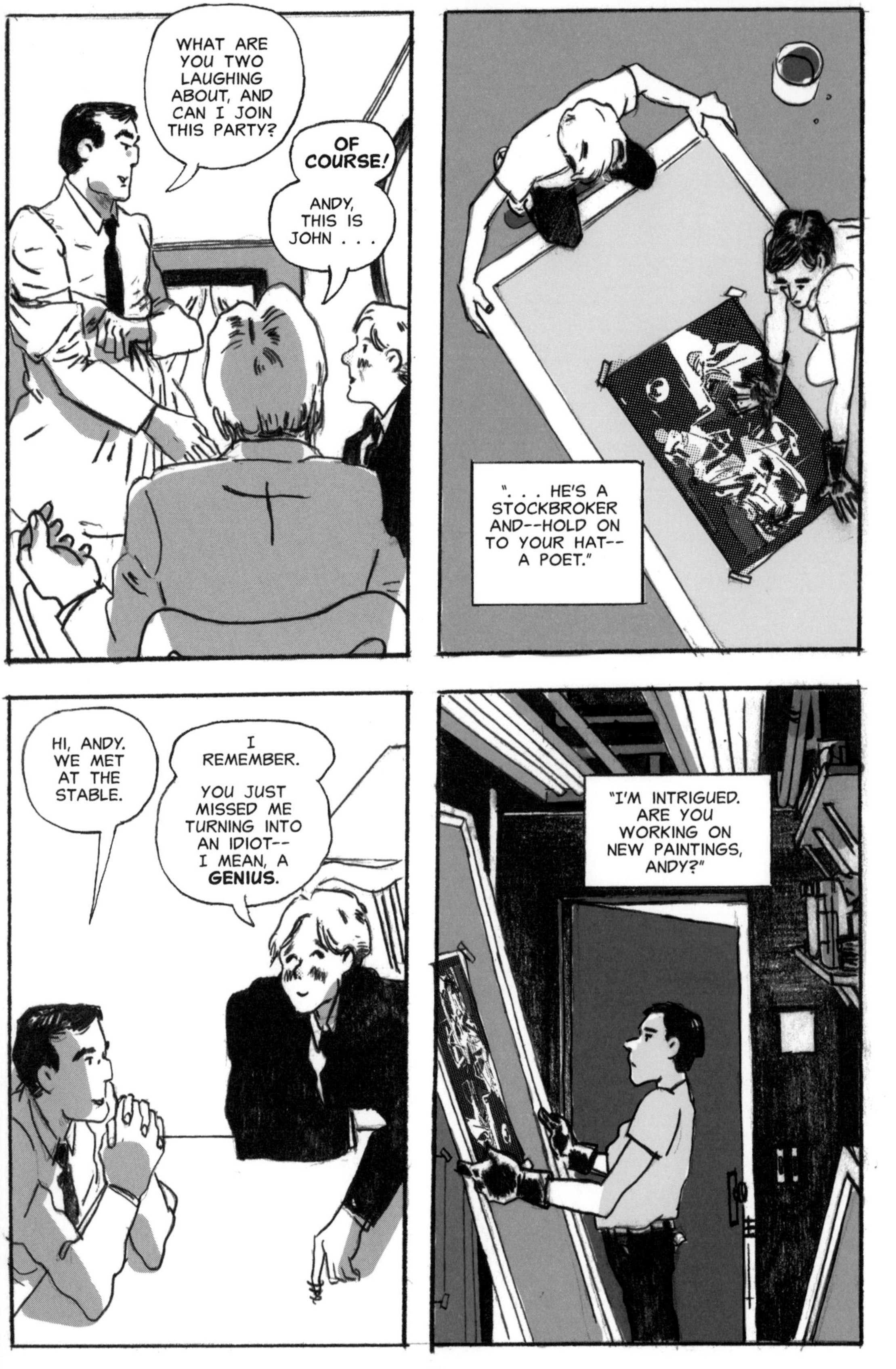
WHAT ARE YOU TWO LAUGHING ABOUT, AND CAN I JOIN THIS PARTY?
OF COURSE!
ANDY, THIS IS JOHN . . .
". . . HE'S A STOCKBROKER AND--HOLD ON TO YOUR HAT-- A POET."
HI, ANDY. WE MET AT THE STABLE.
I REMEMBER.
YOU JUST MISSED ME TURNING INTO AN IDIOT-- I MEAN, A GENIUS.
"I'M INTRIGUED. ARE YOU WORKING ON NEW PAINTINGS, ANDY?"

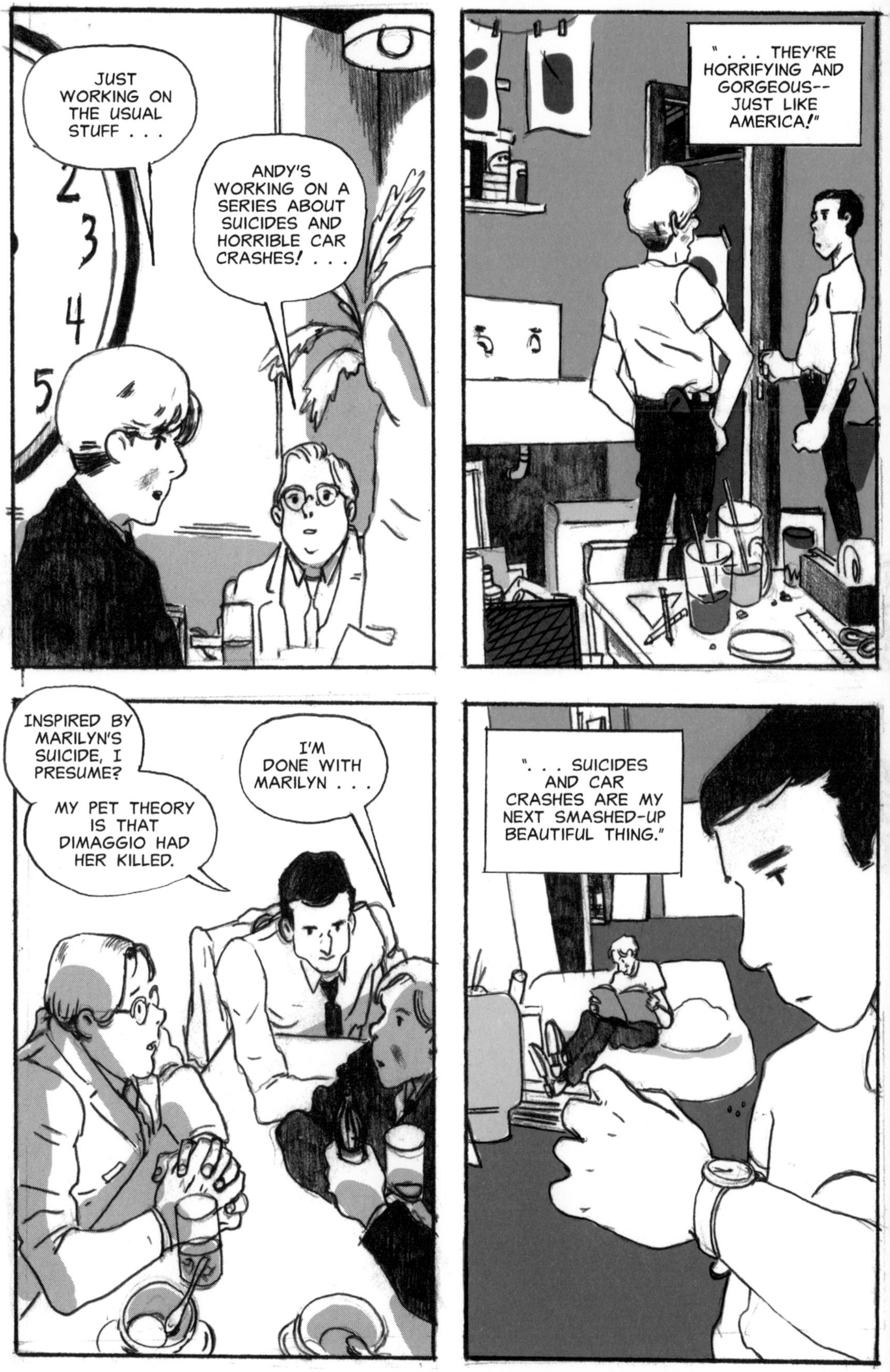
JUST WORKING ON THE USUAL STUFF . . .
ANDY'S WORKING ON A SERIES ABOUT SUICIDES AND HORRIBLE CAR CRASHES! . . .
" . . . THEY'RE HORRIFYING AND GORGEOUS-- JUST LIKE AMERICA!"
INSPIRED BY MARILYN'S SUICIDE, I PRESUME?
MY PET THEORY IS THAT DIMAGGIO HAD HER KILLED.
I'M DONE WITH MARILYN . . .
" . . . SUICIDES AND CAR CRASHES ARE MY NEXT SMASHED-UP BEAUTIFUL THING."

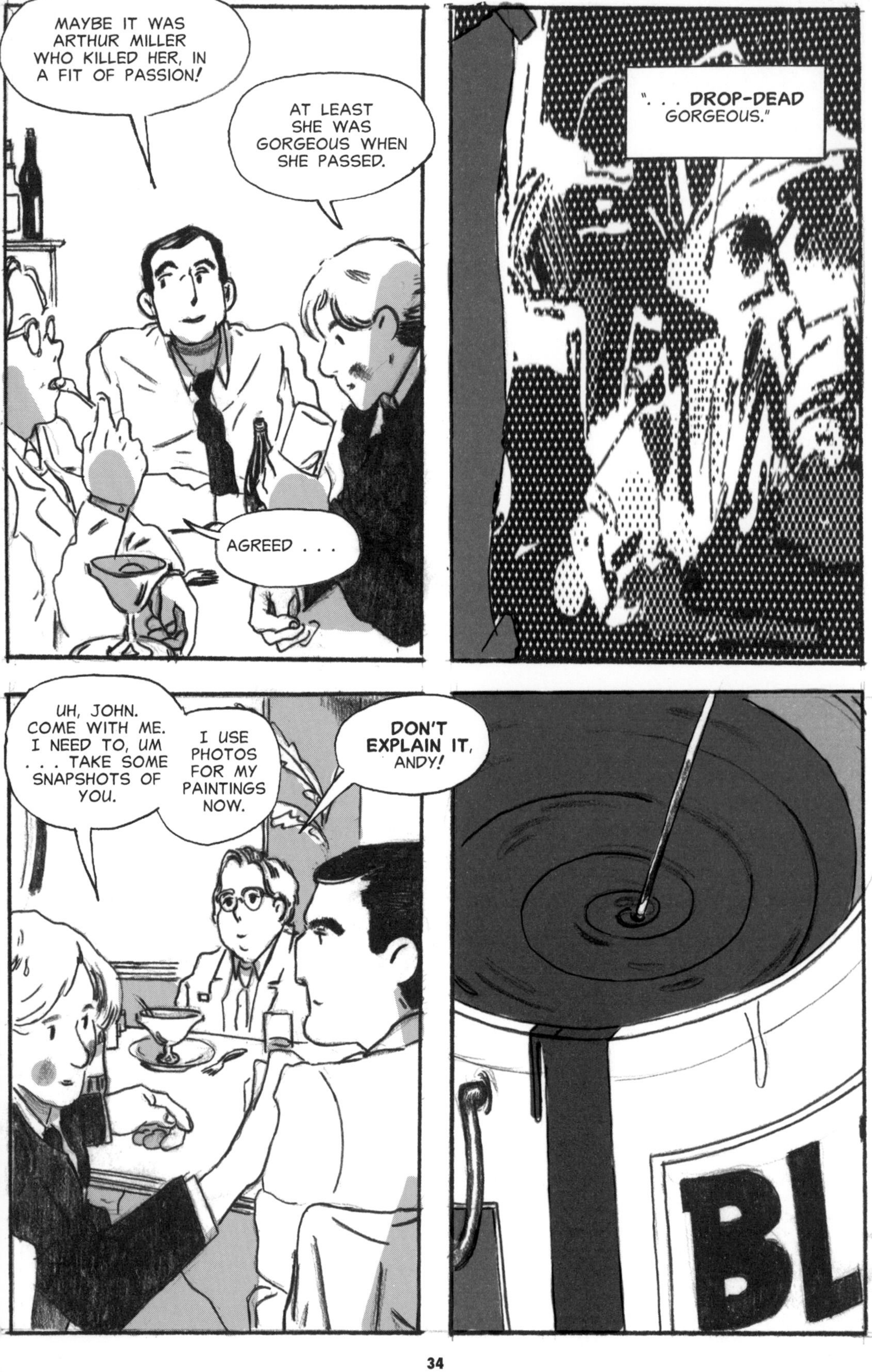

MAYBE IT WAS ARTHUR MILLER WHO KILLED HER, IN A FIT OF PASSION!
AT LEAST SHE WAS GORGEOUS WHEN SHE PASSED.
AGREED . . .
". . . DROP-DEAD GORGEOUS."
UH, JOHN. COME WITH ME. I NEED TO, UM . . . TAKE SOME SNAPSHOTS OF YOU.
I USE PHOTOS FOR MY PAINTINGS NOW.
DON'T EXPLAIN IT, ANDY!
BL

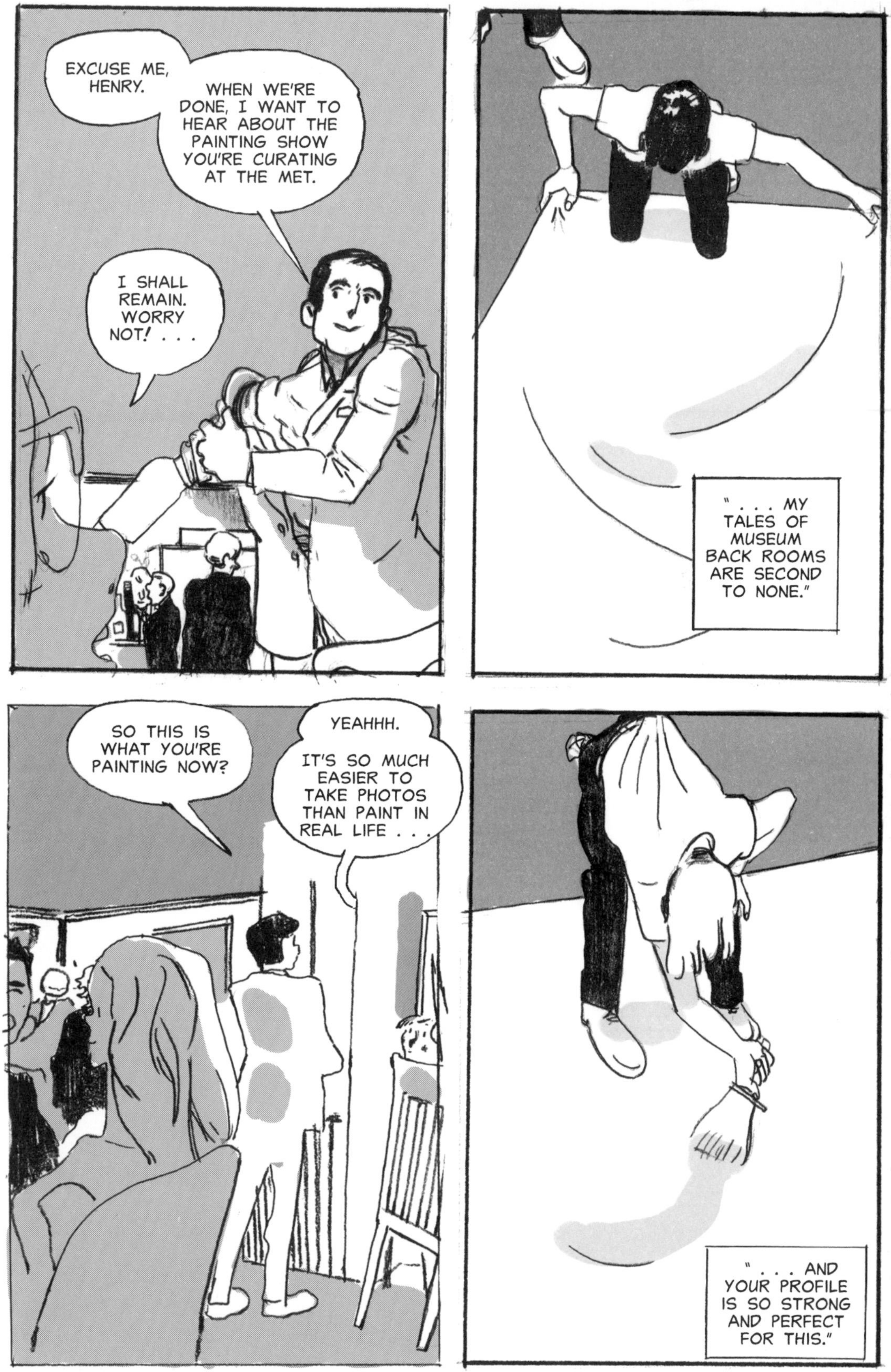
EXCUSE ME, HENRY.
WHEN WE'RE DONE, I WANT TO HEAR ABOUT THE PAINTING SHOW YOU'RE CURATING AT THE MET.
I SHALL REMAIN. WORRY NOT! . . .
" . . . MY TALES OF MUSEUM BACK ROOMS ARE SECOND TO NONE."
SO THIS IS WHAT YOU'RE PAINTING NOW?
YEAHHH.
IT'S SO MUCH EASIER TO TAKE PHOTOS THAN PAINT IN REAL LIFE . . .
" . . . AND YOUR PROFILE IS SO STRONG AND PERFECT FOR THIS."

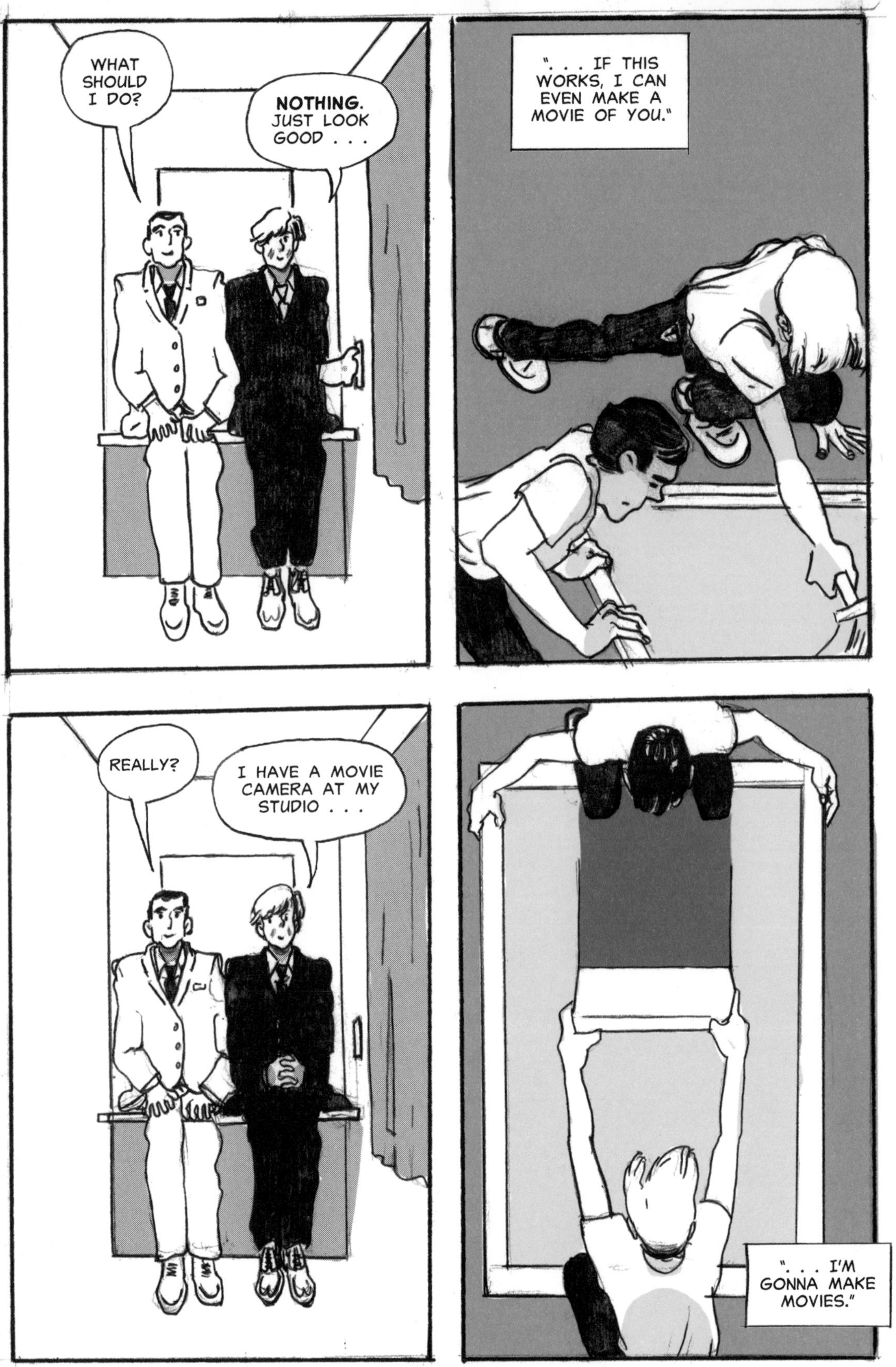
WHAT SHOULD I DO?
NOTHING. JUST LOOK GOOD . . .
". . . IF THIS WORKS, I CAN EVEN MAKE A MOVIE OF YOU."
REALLY?
I HAVE A MOVIE CAMERA AT MY STUDIO . . .
". . . I'M GONNA MAKE MOVIES."

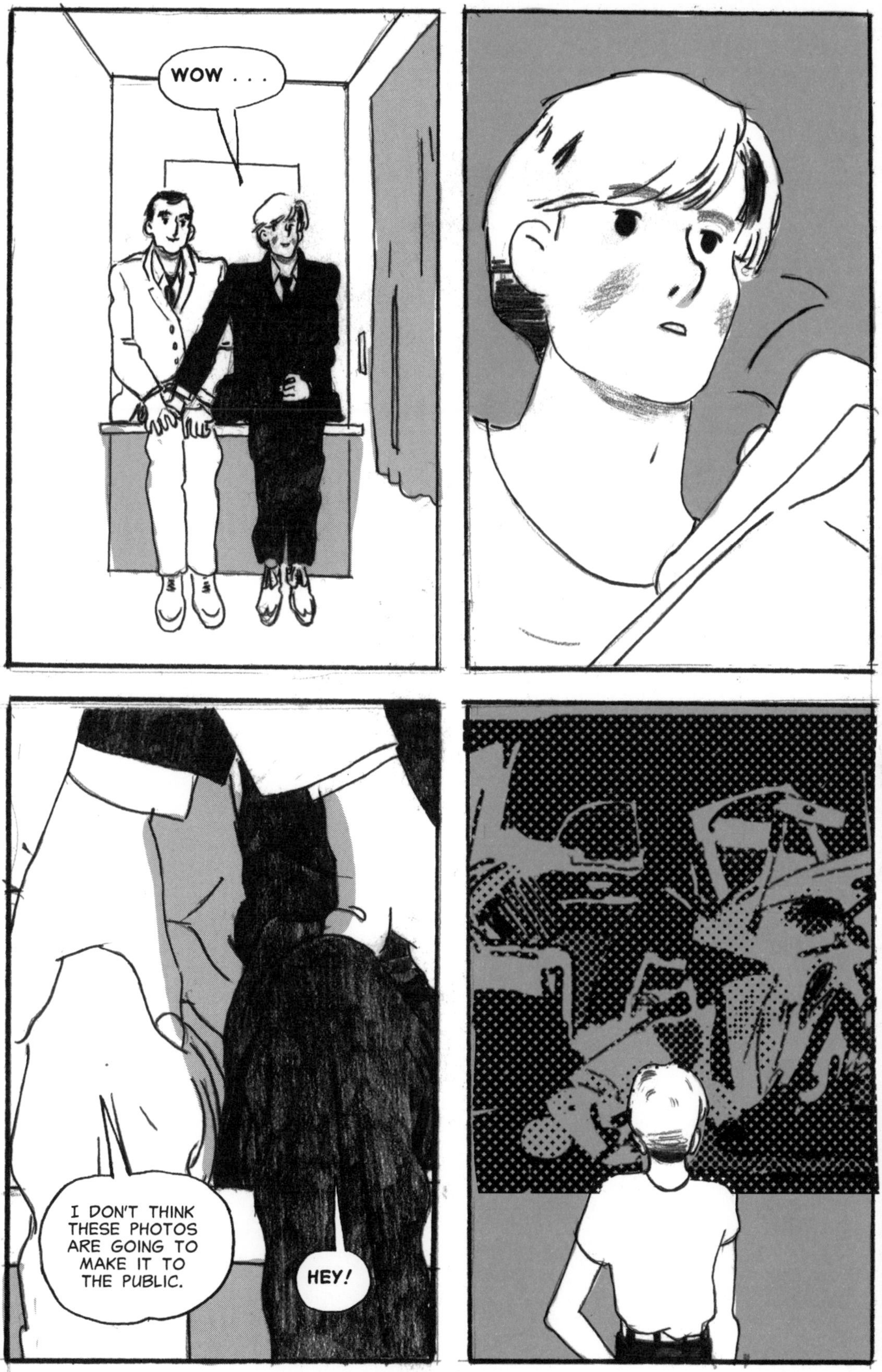
WOW . . .
I DON'T THINK THESE PHOTOS ARE GOING TO MAKE IT TO THE PUBLIC.
HEY!

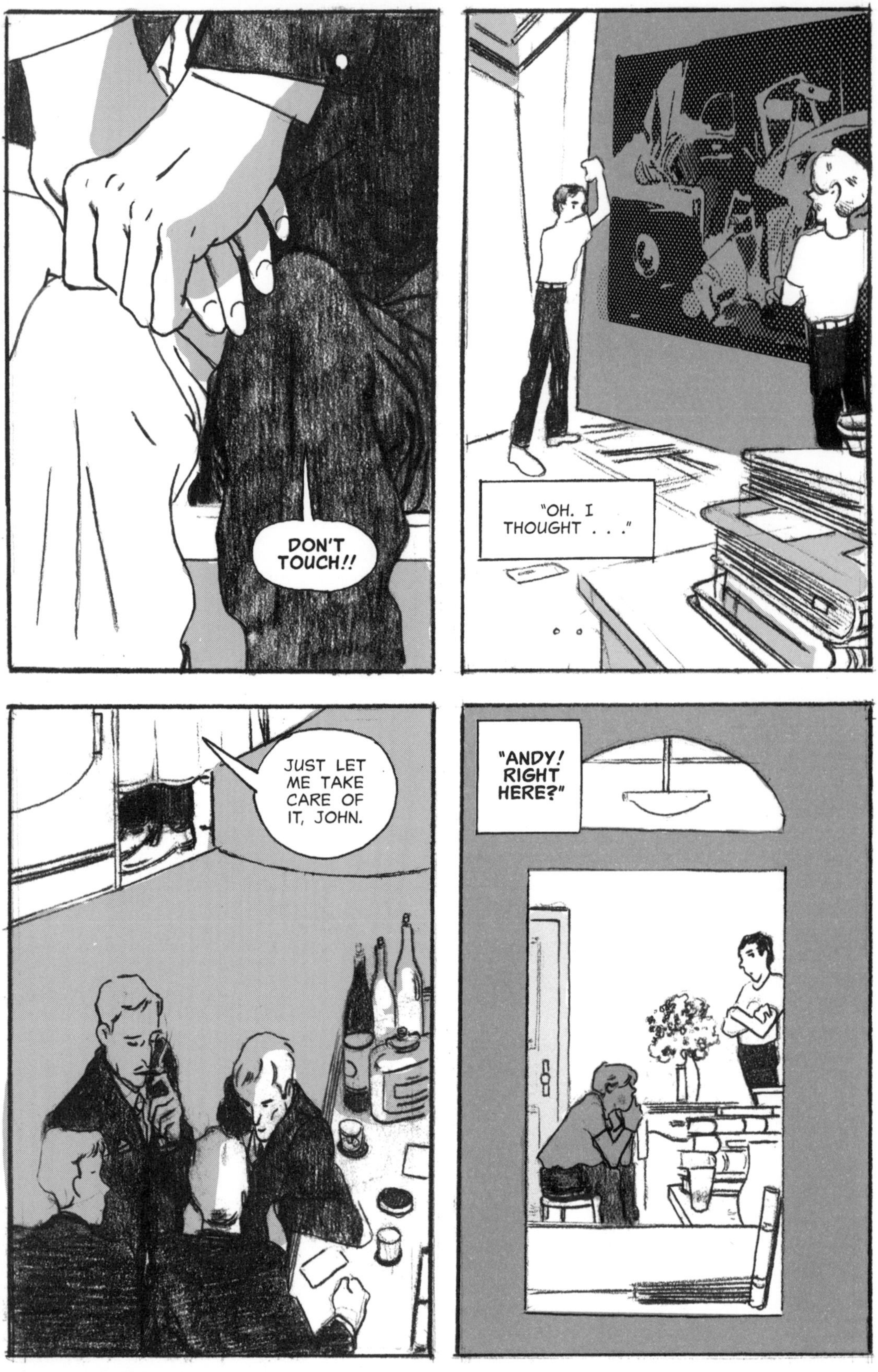
DON'T TOUCH!!
"OH. I THOUGHT . . ."
JUST LET ME TAKE CARE OF IT, JOHN.
"ANDY! RIGHT HERE?"

CHAPTER FIVE

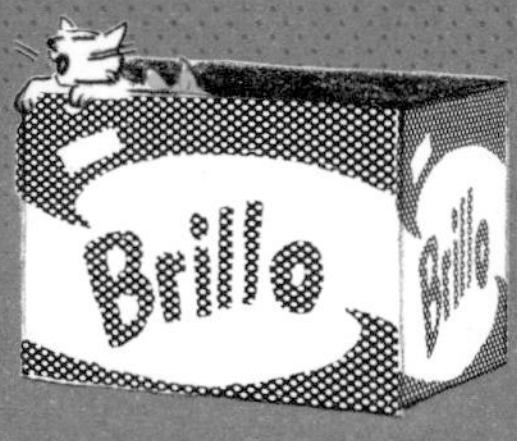
Brillo
Brillo

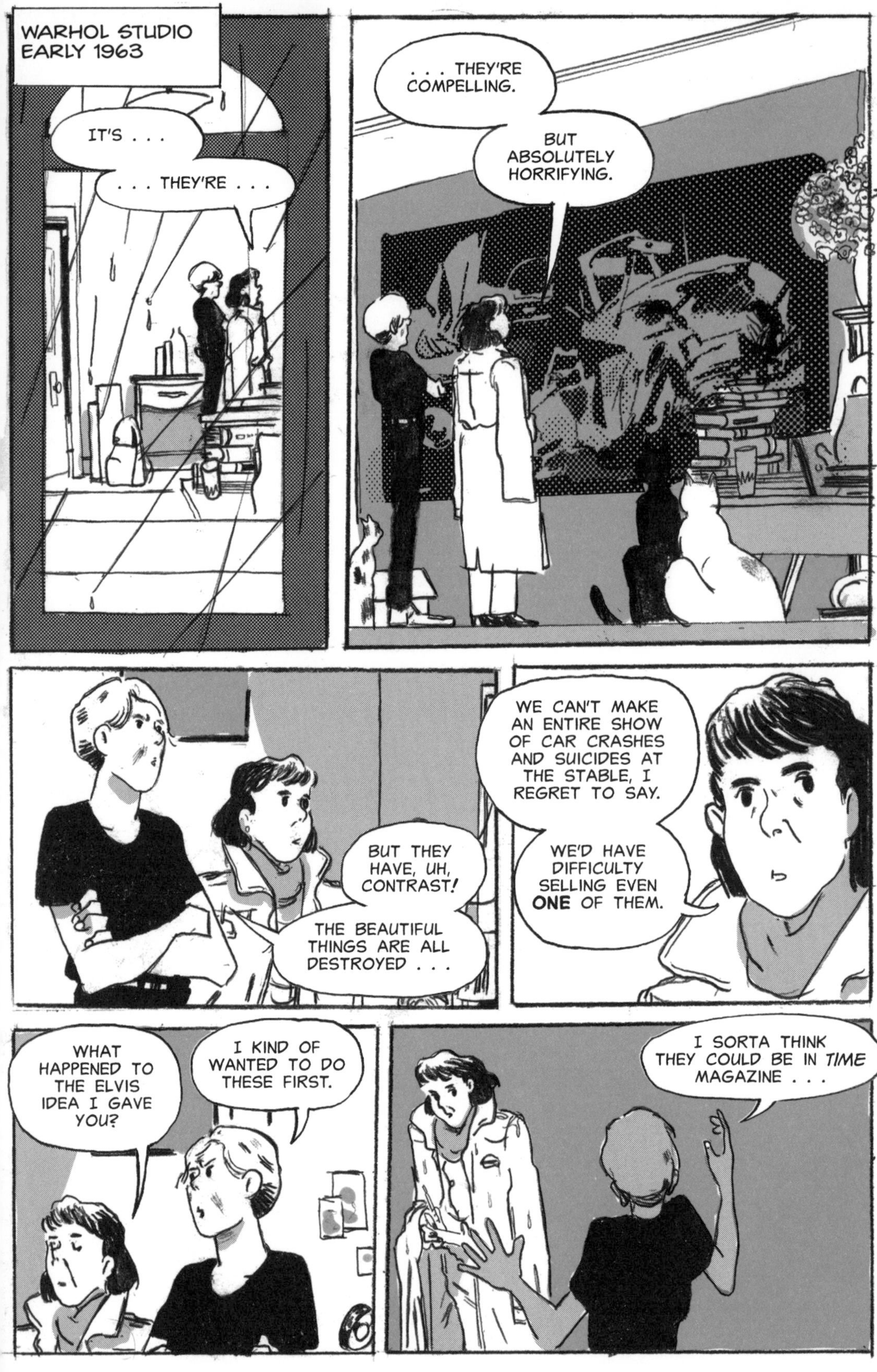

WARHOL STUDIO EARLY 1963
IT'S . . .
. . . THEY'RE . . .
. . . THEY'RE COMPELLING.
BUT ABSOLUTELY HORRIFYING.
BUT THEY HAVE, UH, CONTRAST!
THE BEAUTIFUL THINGS ARE ALL DESTROYED . . .
WE CAN'T MAKE AN ENTIRE SHOW OF CAR CRASHES AND SUICIDES AT THE STABLE, I REGRET TO SAY.
WE'D HAVE DIFFICULTY SELLING EVEN **ONE** OF THEM.
WHAT HAPPENED TO THE ELVIS IDEA I GAVE YOU?
I KIND OF WANTED TO DO THESE FIRST.
I SORTA THINK THEY COULD BE IN *TIME* MAGAZINE . . .

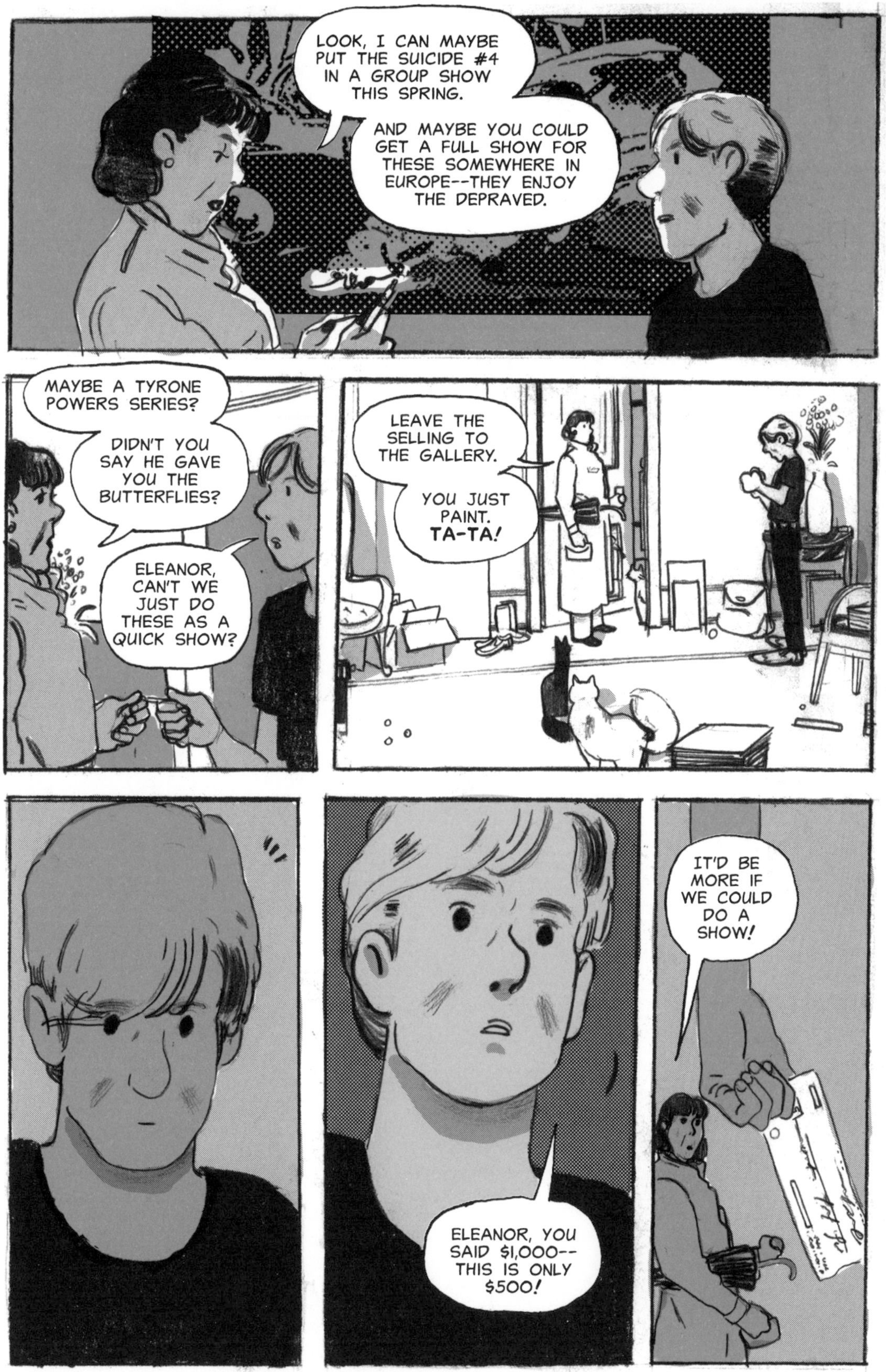
LOOK, I CAN MAYBE PUT THE SUICIDE #4 IN A GROUP SHOW THIS SPRING.
AND MAYBE YOU COULD GET A FULL SHOW FOR THESE SOMEWHERE IN EUROPE--THEY ENJOY THE DEPRAVED.
MAYBE A TYRONE POWERS SERIES?
DIDN'T YOU SAY HE GAVE YOU THE BUTTERFLIES?
ELEANOR, CAN'T WE JUST DO THESE AS A QUICK SHOW?
LEAVE THE SELLING TO THE GALLERY.
YOU JUST PAINT. **TA-TA!**
ELEANOR, YOU SAID $1,000-- THIS IS ONLY $500!
IT'D BE MORE IF WE COULD DO A SHOW!

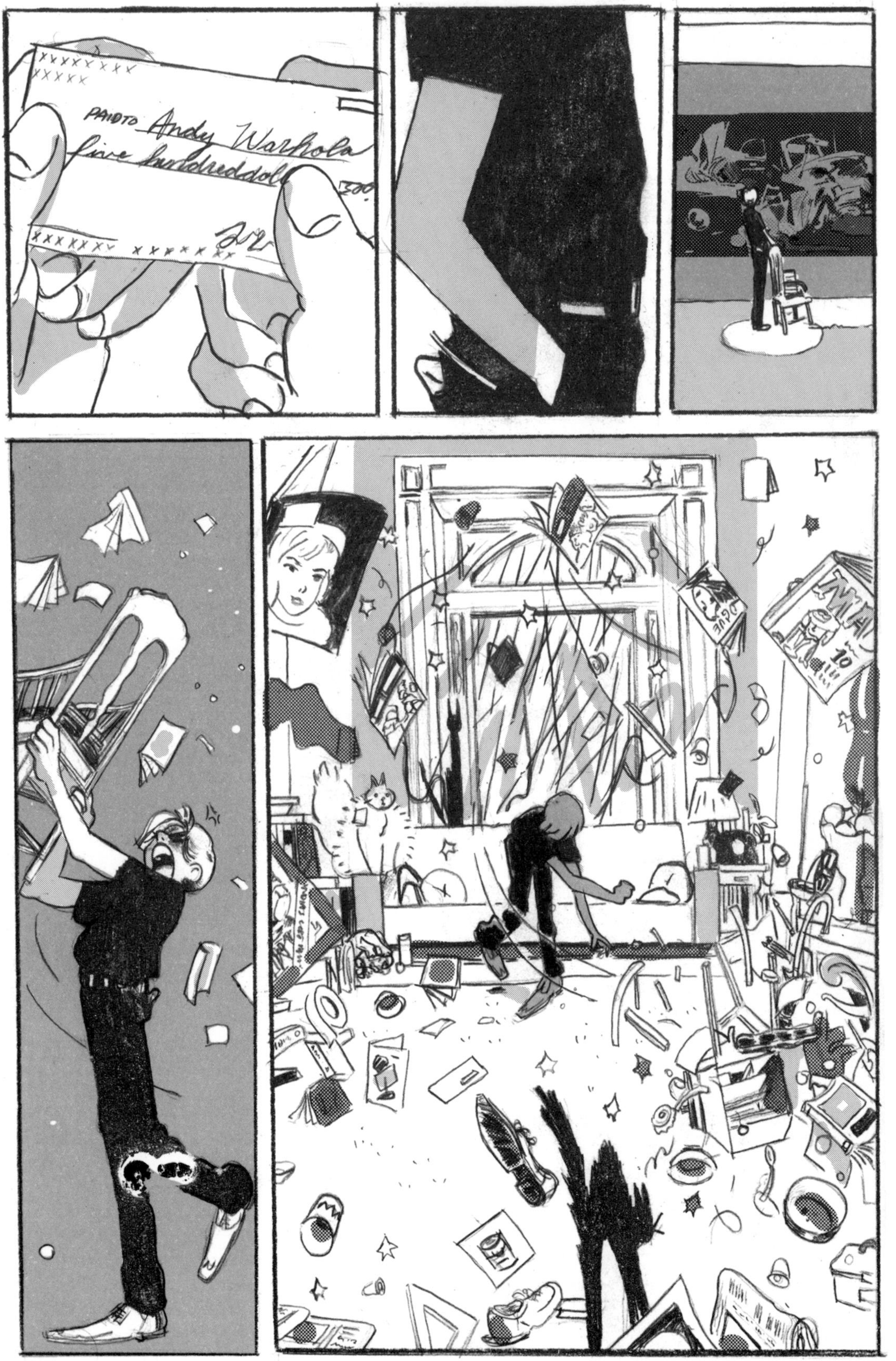
PAIDTO Andy Warhola
five hundreddoll

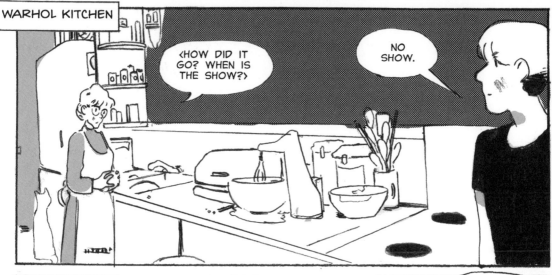

<HOW DID IT GO? WHEN IS THE SHOW?>

NO SHOW.

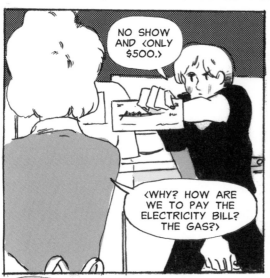

NO SHOW AND <ONLY $500.>

<WHY? HOW ARE WE TO PAY THE ELECTRICITY BILL? THE GAS?>

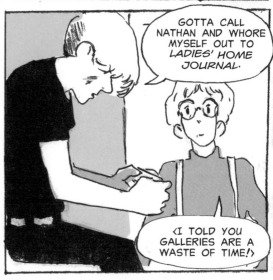

GOTTA CALL NATHAN AND WHORE MYSELF OUT TO *LADIES' HOME JOURNAL.*

<I TOLD YOU GALLERIES ARE A WASTE OF TIME!>

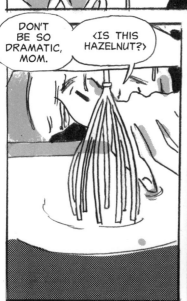

DON'T BE SO DRAMATIC, MOM.

<IS THIS HAZELNUT?>

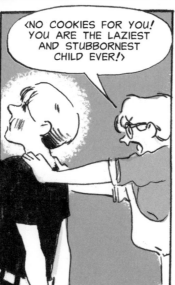

<NO COOKIES FOR YOU! YOU ARE THE LAZIEST AND STUBBORNEST CHILD EVER!>

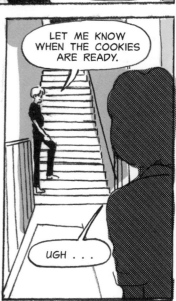

LET ME KNOW WHEN THE COOKIES ARE READY.

UGH . . .

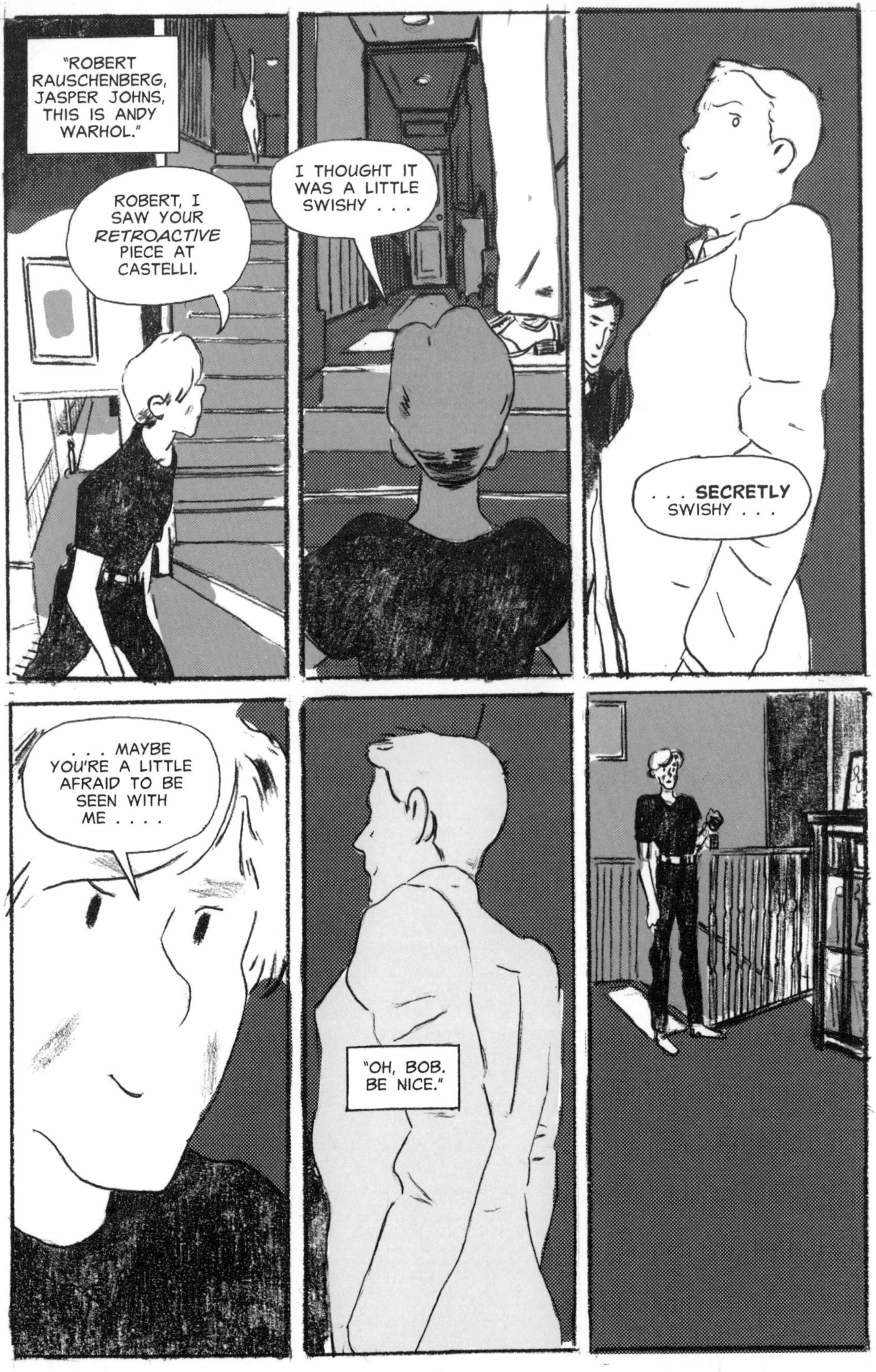
"ROBERT RAUSCHENBERG, JASPER JOHNS, THIS IS ANDY WARHOL."
ROBERT, I SAW YOUR *RETROACTIVE* PIECE AT CASTELLI.
I THOUGHT IT WAS A LITTLE SWISHY . . .
. . . **SECRETLY** SWISHY . . .
. . . MAYBE YOU'RE A LITTLE AFRAID TO BE SEEN WITH ME . . . .
"OH, BOB. BE NICE."

CHAPTER SIX

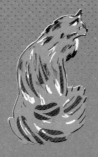

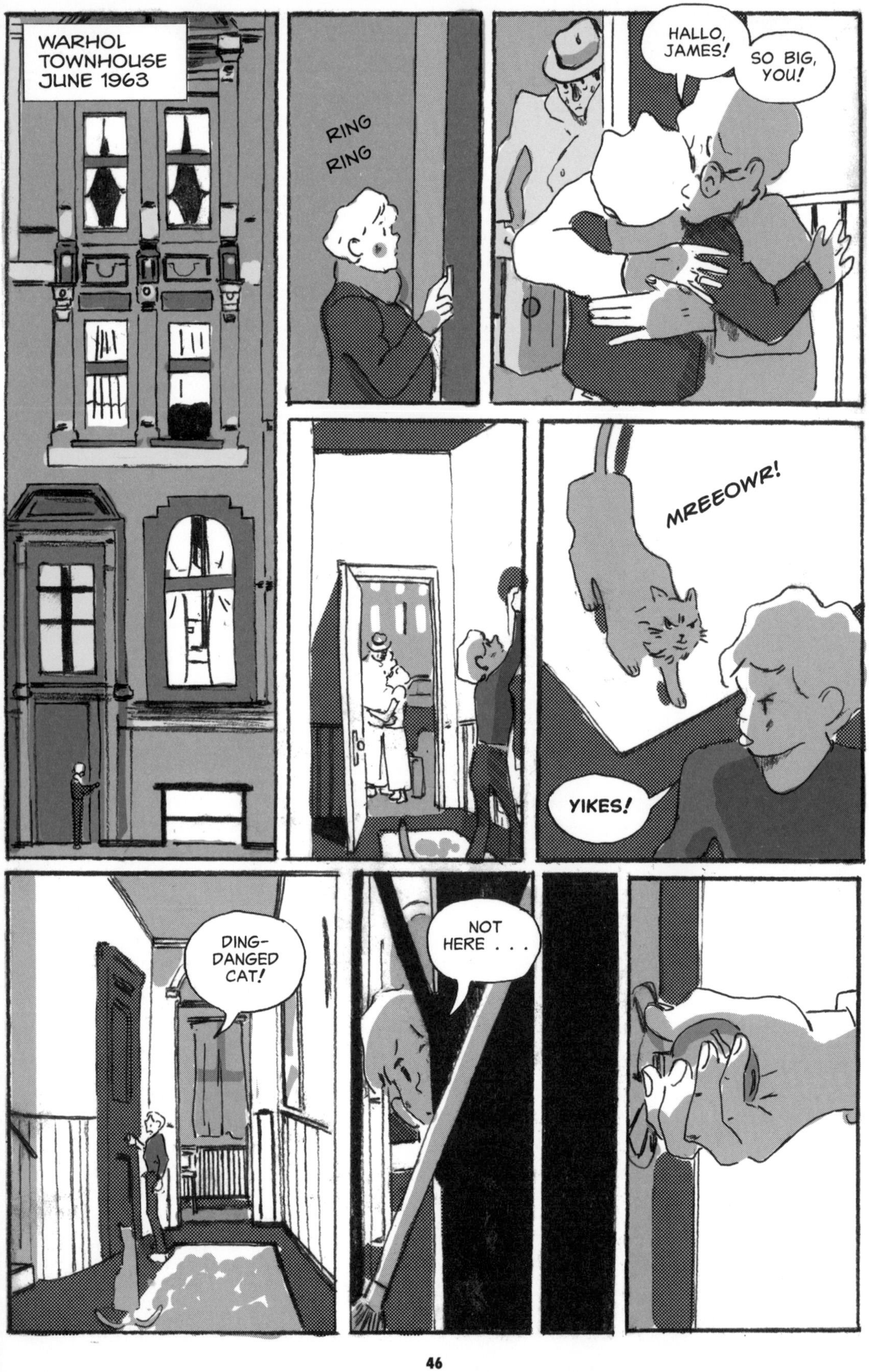
WARHOL TOWNHOUSE JUNE 1963
RING RING
HALLO, JAMES!
SO BIG, YOU!
MREEOWR!
YIKES!
DING-DANGED CAT!
NOT HERE . . .

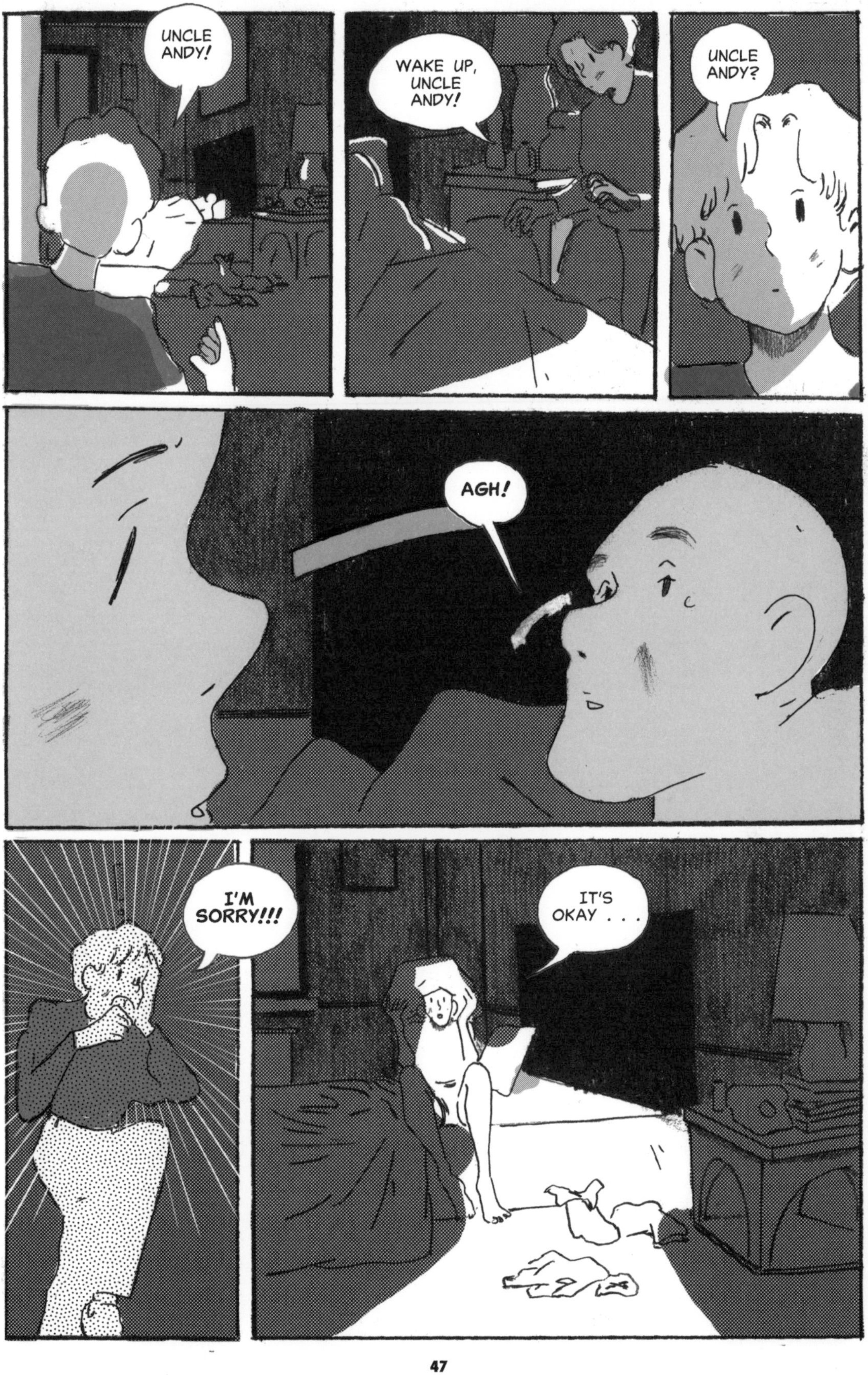
UNCLE ANDY!
WAKE UP, UNCLE ANDY!
UNCLE ANDY?
AGH!
I'M SORRY!!!
IT'S OKAY . . .

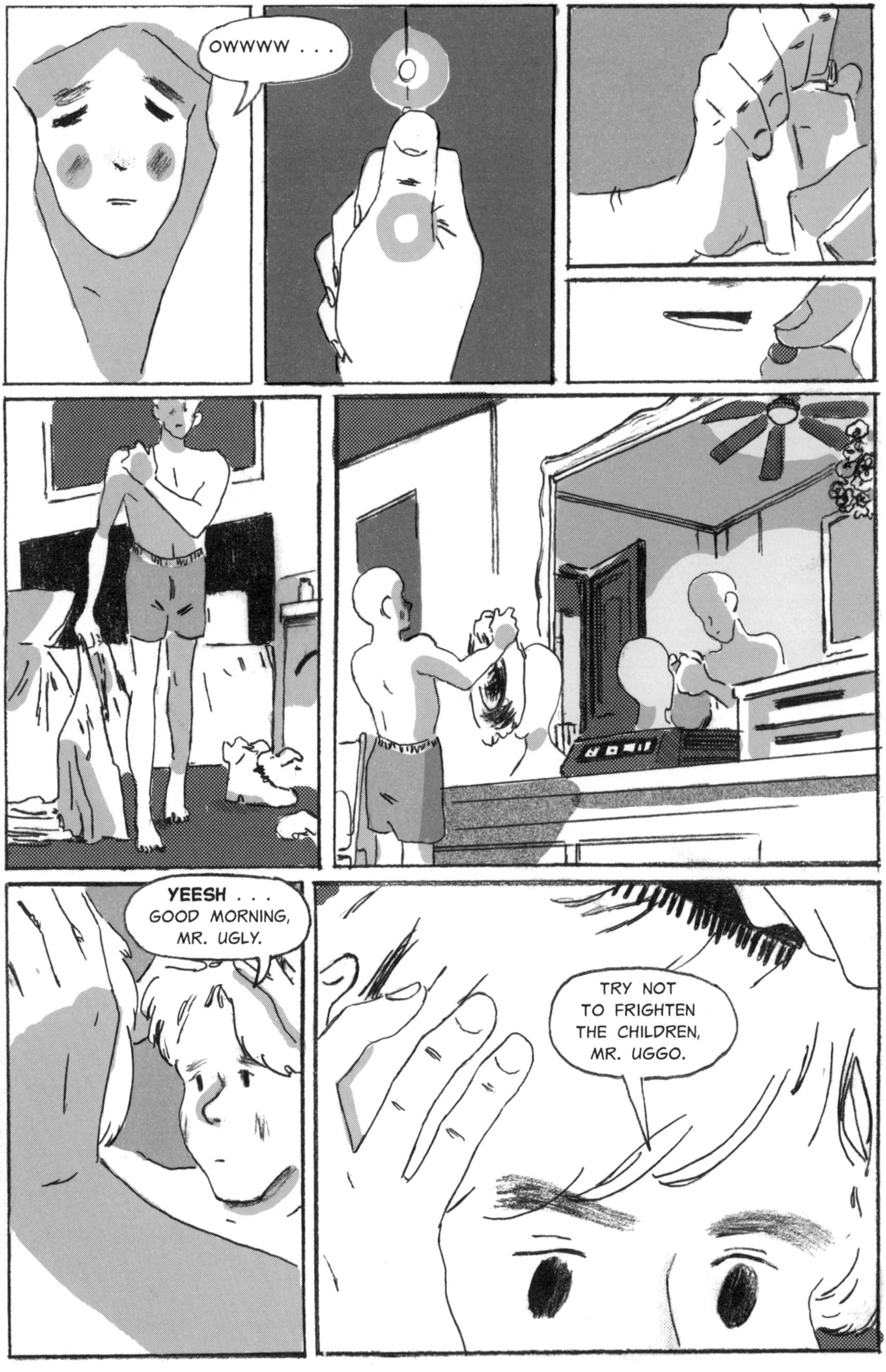
OWWWW . . .
YEESH . . .
GOOD MORNING,
MR. UGLY.
TRY NOT
TO FRIGHTEN
THE CHILDREN,
MR. UGGO.

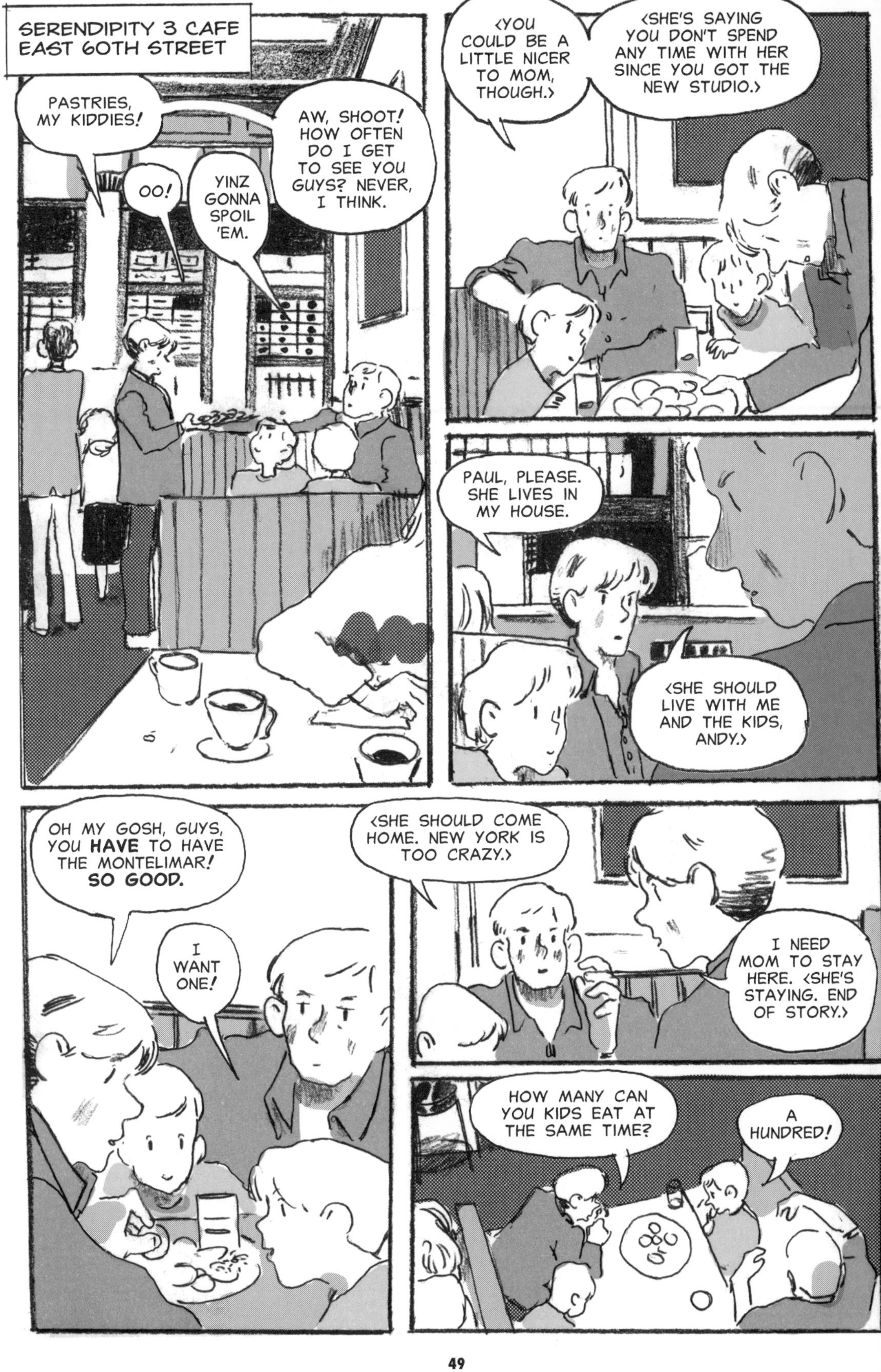
SERENDIPITY 3 CAFE EAST 60TH STREET
PASTRIES, MY KIDDIES!
OO!
YINZ GONNA SPOIL 'EM.
AW, SHOOT! HOW OFTEN DO I GET TO SEE YOU GUYS? NEVER, I THINK.
‹YOU COULD BE A LITTLE NICER TO MOM, THOUGH.›
‹SHE'S SAYING YOU DON'T SPEND ANY TIME WITH HER SINCE YOU GOT THE NEW STUDIO.›
PAUL, PLEASE. SHE LIVES IN MY HOUSE.
‹SHE SHOULD LIVE WITH ME AND THE KIDS, ANDY.›
OH MY GOSH, GUYS, YOU **HAVE** TO HAVE THE MONTELIMAR! **SO GOOD.**
I WANT ONE!
‹SHE SHOULD COME HOME. NEW YORK IS TOO CRAZY.›
I NEED MOM TO STAY HERE. ‹SHE'S STAYING. END OF STORY.›
HOW MANY CAN YOU KIDS EAT AT THE SAME TIME?
A HUNDRED!

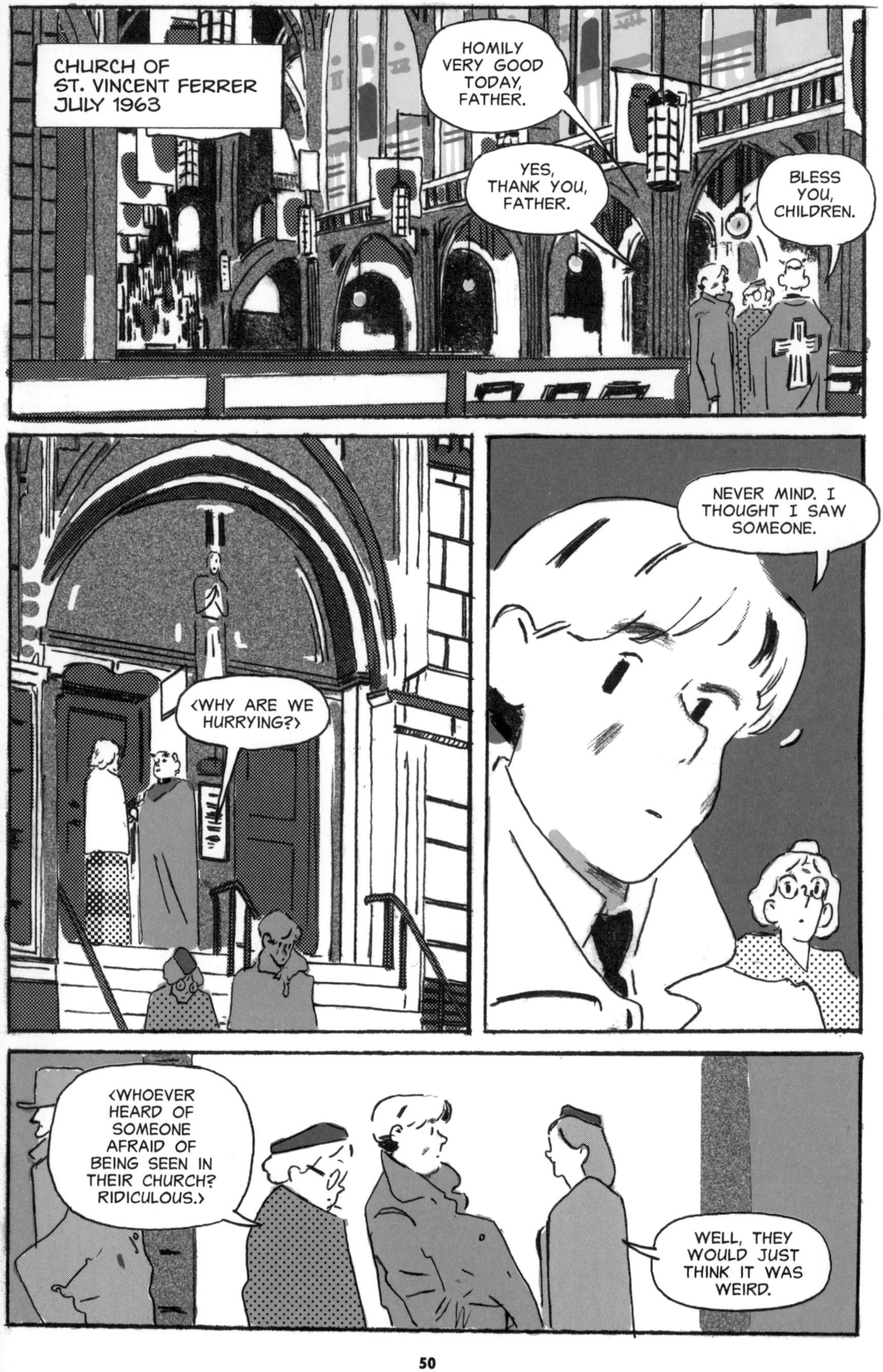
CHURCH OF ST. VINCENT FERRER JULY 1963
HOMILY VERY GOOD TODAY, FATHER.
YES, THANK YOU, FATHER.
BLESS YOU, CHILDREN.
<WHY ARE WE HURRYING?>
NEVER MIND. I THOUGHT I SAW SOMEONE.
<WHOEVER HEARD OF SOMEONE AFRAID OF BEING SEEN IN THEIR CHURCH? RIDICULOUS.>
WELL, THEY WOULD JUST THINK IT WAS WEIRD.

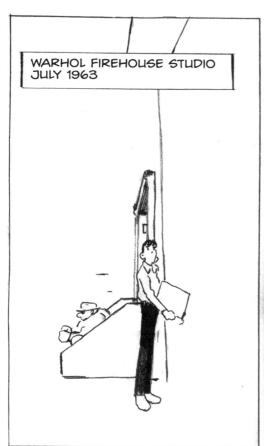

WARHOL FIREHOUSE STUDIO
JULY 1963

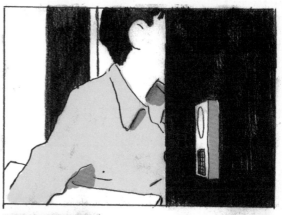

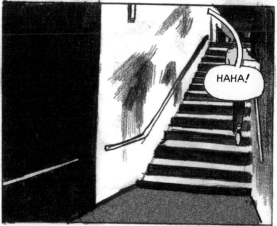

HAHA!

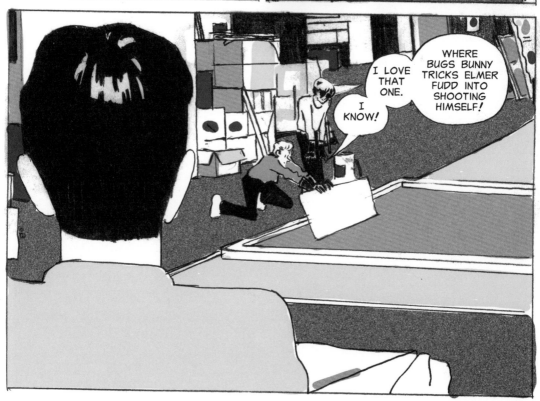

I LOVE THAT ONE.

I KNOW!

WHERE BUGS BUNNY TRICKS ELMER FUDD INTO SHOOTING HIMSELF!

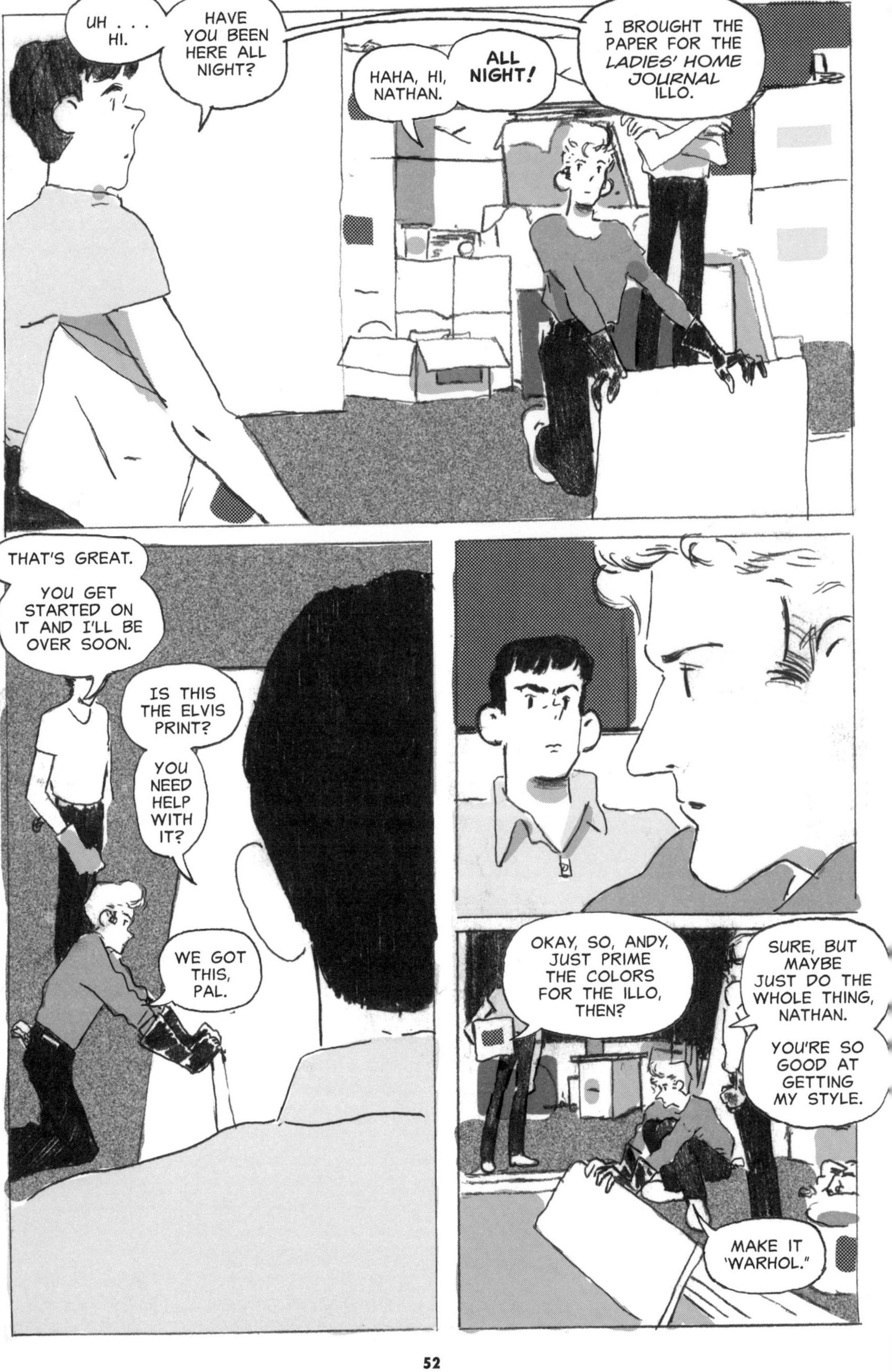
UH . . . HI.
HAVE YOU BEEN HERE ALL NIGHT?
HAHA, HI, NATHAN.
ALL NIGHT!
I BROUGHT THE PAPER FOR THE *LADIES' HOME JOURNAL* ILLO.
THAT'S GREAT.
YOU GET STARTED ON IT AND I'LL BE OVER SOON.
IS THIS THE ELVIS PRINT?
YOU NEED HELP WITH IT?
WE GOT THIS, PAL.
OKAY, SO, ANDY, JUST PRIME THE COLORS FOR THE ILLO, THEN?
SURE, BUT MAYBE JUST DO THE WHOLE THING, NATHAN.
YOU'RE SO GOOD AT GETTING MY STYLE.
MAKE IT 'WARHOL.'"

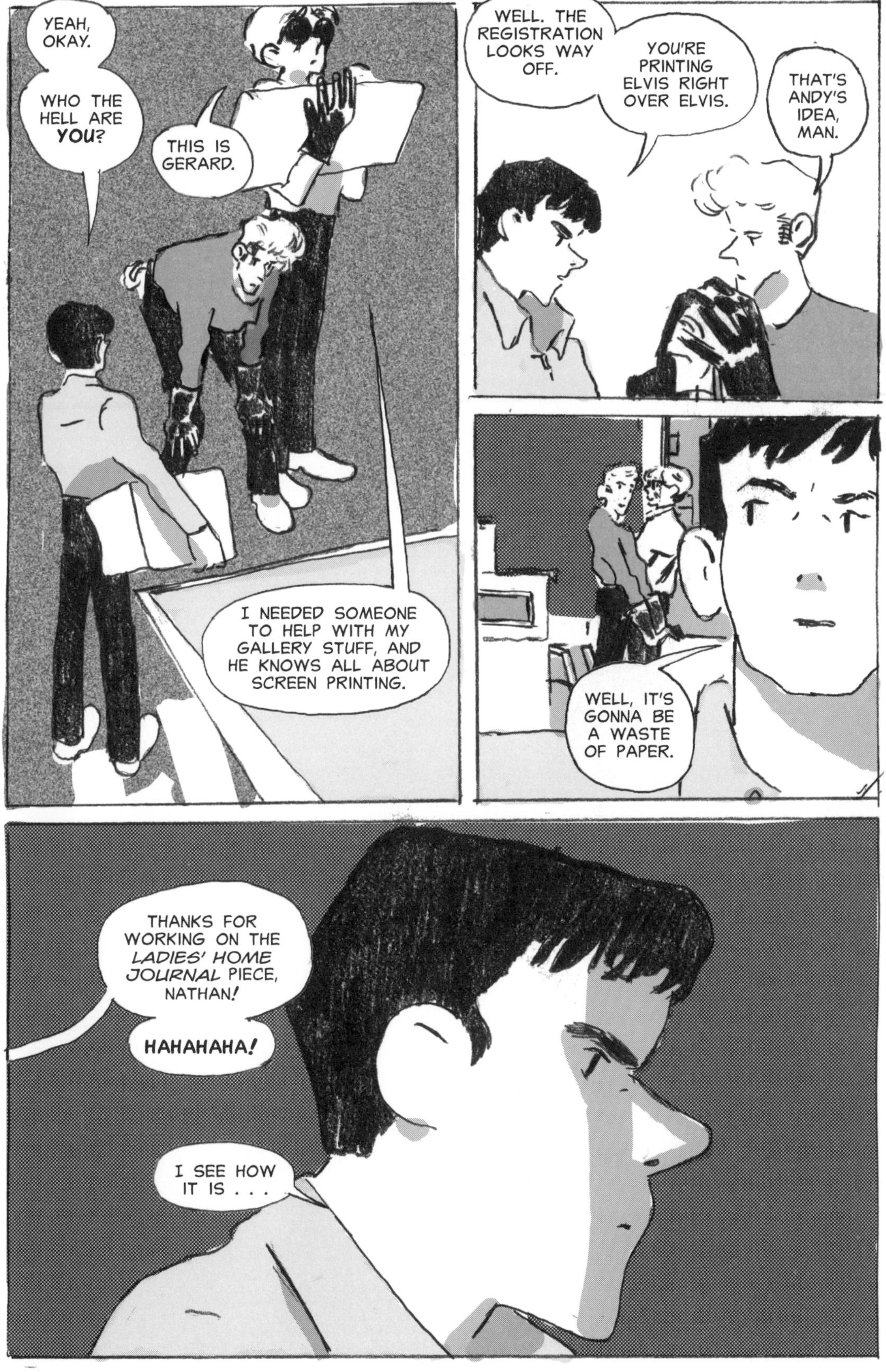
YEAH, OKAY.
WHO THE HELL ARE **YOU**?
THIS IS GERARD.
I NEEDED SOMEONE TO HELP WITH MY GALLERY STUFF, AND HE KNOWS ALL ABOUT SCREEN PRINTING.
WELL. THE REGISTRATION LOOKS WAY OFF.
YOU'RE PRINTING ELVIS RIGHT OVER ELVIS.
THAT'S ANDY'S IDEA, MAN.
WELL, IT'S GONNA BE A WASTE OF PAPER.
THANKS FOR WORKING ON THE *LADIES' HOME JOURNAL* PIECE, NATHAN!
HAHAHAHA!
I SEE HOW IT IS . . .

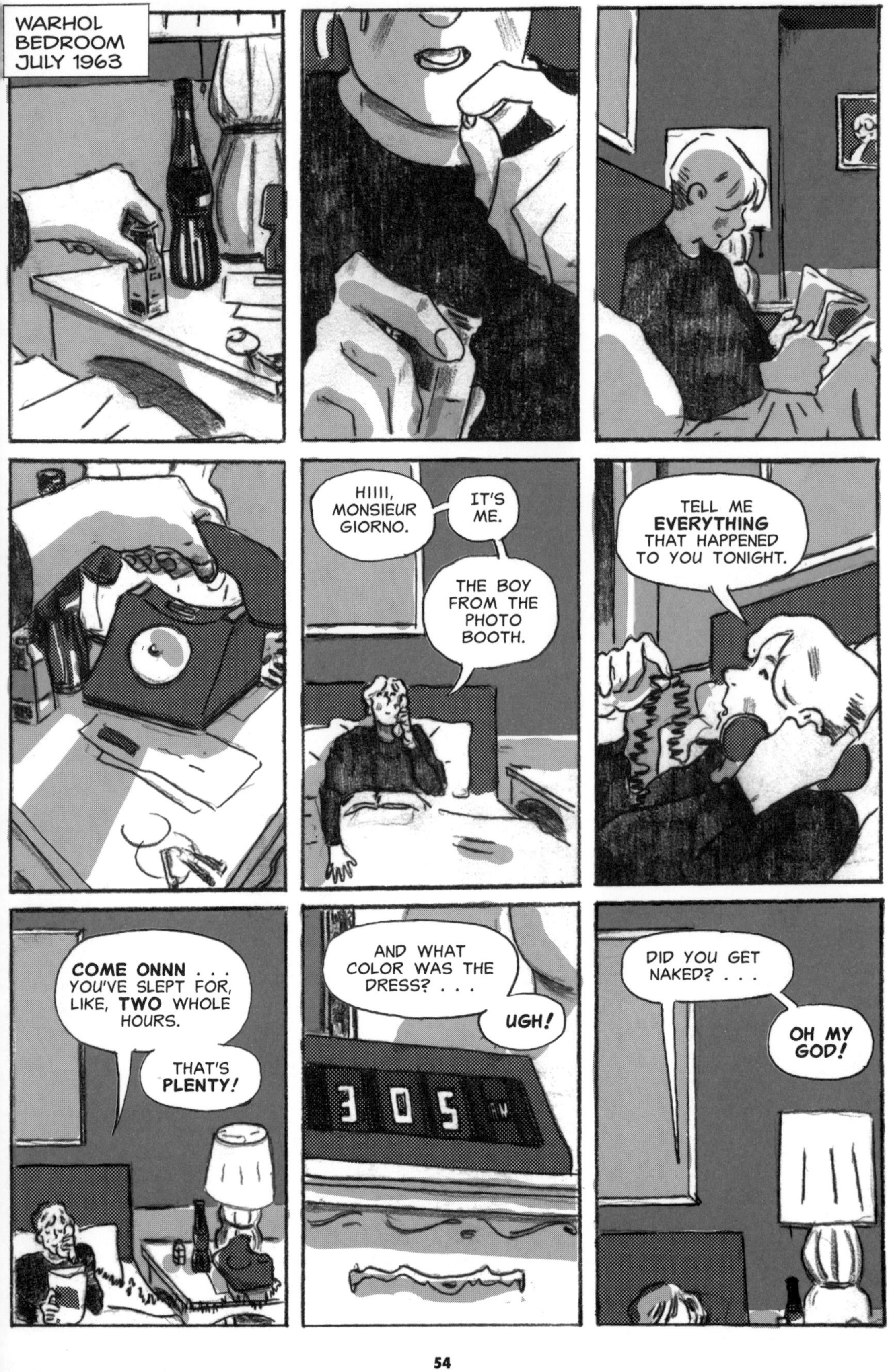
WARHOL BEDROOM JULY 1963
HIIII, MONSIEUR GIORNO.
IT'S ME.
THE BOY FROM THE PHOTO BOOTH.
TELL ME **EVERYTHING** THAT HAPPENED TO YOU TONIGHT.
COME ONNN . . . YOU'VE SLEPT FOR, LIKE, **TWO** WHOLE HOURS.
THAT'S **PLENTY!**
AND WHAT COLOR WAS THE DRESS? . . .
UGH!
DID YOU GET NAKED? . . .
OH MY GOD!

CHAPTER SEVEN

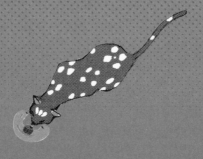

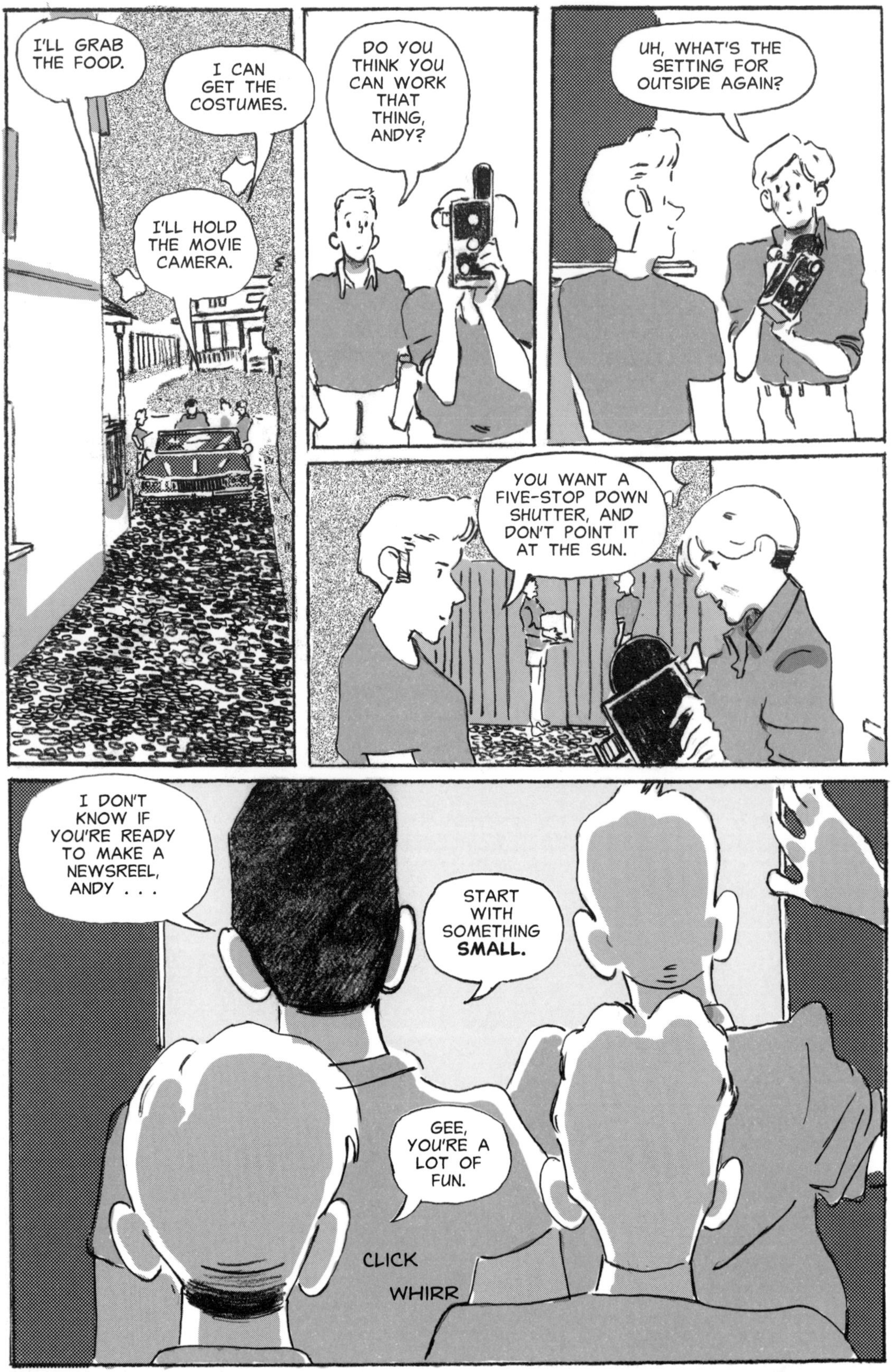
I'LL GRAB THE FOOD.
I CAN GET THE COSTUMES.
I'LL HOLD THE MOVIE CAMERA.
DO YOU THINK YOU CAN WORK THAT THING, ANDY?
UH, WHAT'S THE SETTING FOR OUTSIDE AGAIN?
YOU WANT A FIVE-STOP DOWN SHUTTER, AND DON'T POINT IT AT THE SUN.
I DON'T KNOW IF YOU'RE READY TO MAKE A NEWSREEL, ANDY . . .
START WITH SOMETHING **SMALL.**
GEE, YOU'RE A LOT OF FUN.
CLICK
WHIRR

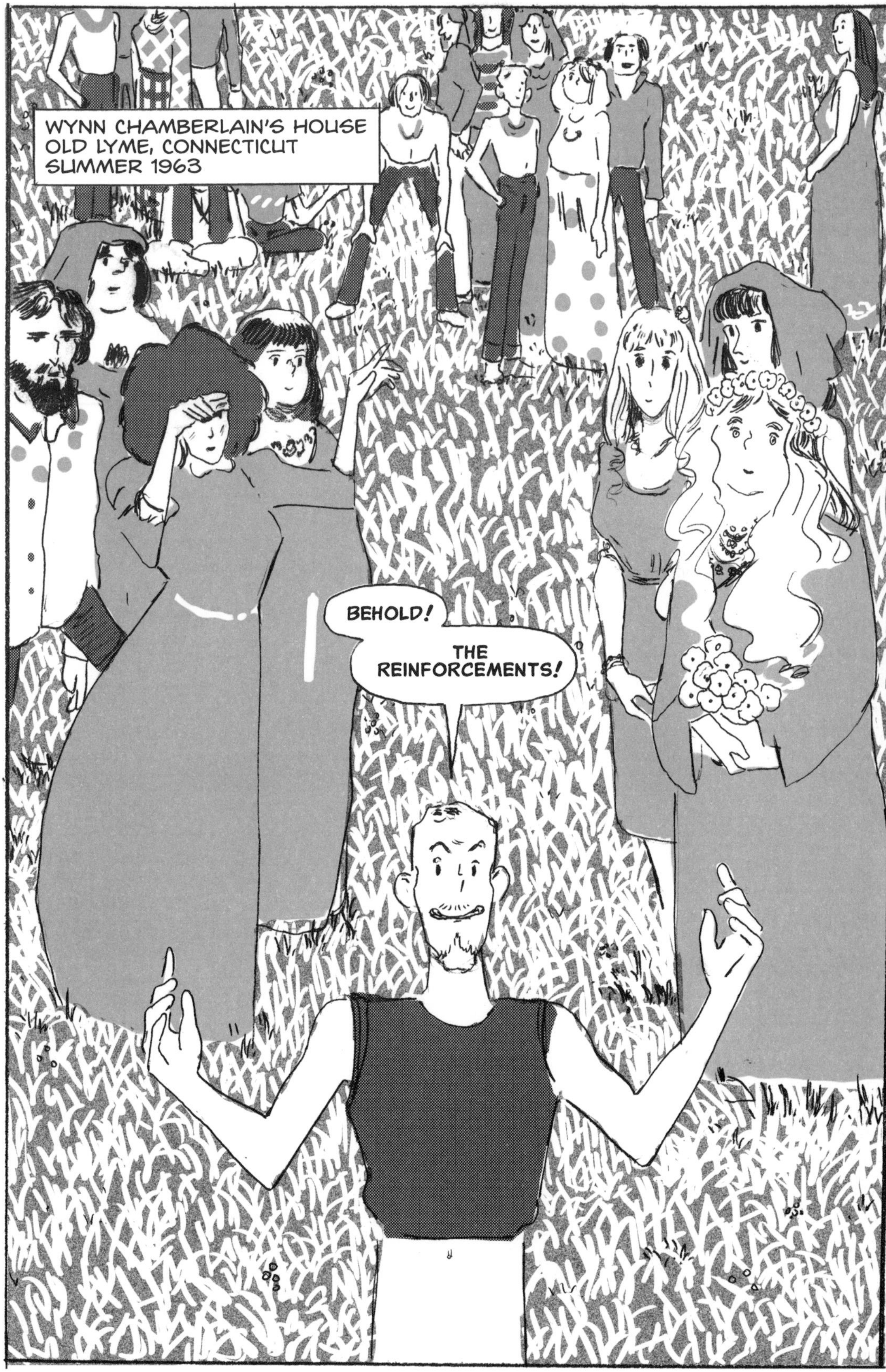
WYNN CHAMBERLAIN'S HOUSE
OLD LYME, CONNECTICUT
SUMMER 1963
BEHOLD!
THE REINFORCEMENTS!

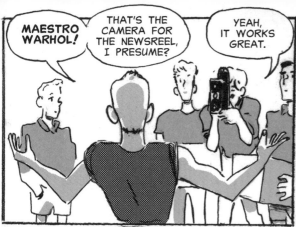

MAESTRO WARHOL!

THAT'S THE CAMERA FOR THE NEWSREEL, I PRESUME?

YEAH, IT WORKS GREAT.

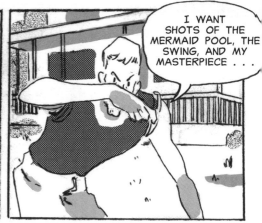

I WANT SHOTS OF THE MERMAID POOL, THE SWING, AND MY MASTERPIECE . . .

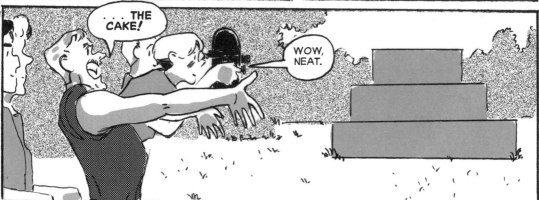

. . . THE CAKE!

WOW, NEAT.

AND WHEN YOU'RE DONE, ANDY, I WANT YOU AS ONE OF MY MARILYNS.

THERE ARE BRAS AND DRESSES BY THE TREE.

WHAT?

UM, THAT'S NOT REALLY--

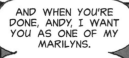

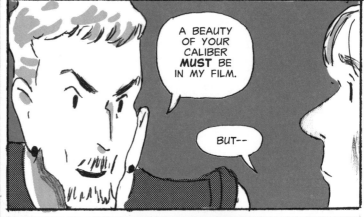

A BEAUTY OF YOUR CALIBER **MUST** BE IN MY FILM.

BUT--

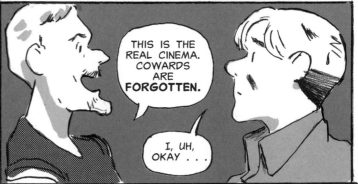

THIS IS THE REAL CINEMA. COWARDS ARE **FORGOTTEN.**

I, UH, OKAY . . .

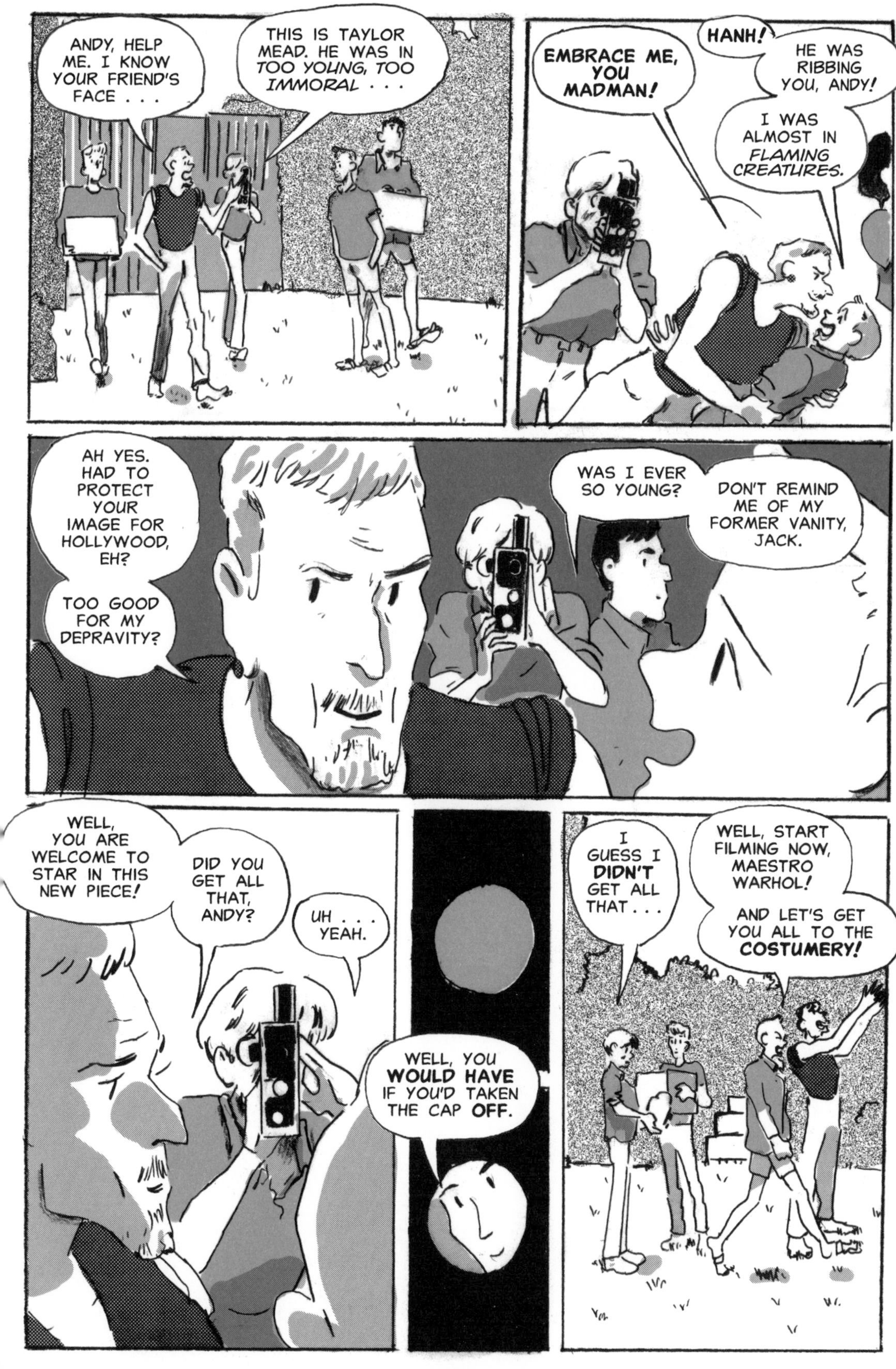
ANDY, HELP ME. I KNOW YOUR FRIEND'S FACE . . .
THIS IS TAYLOR MEAD. HE WAS IN *TOO YOUNG, TOO IMMORAL* . . .
EMBRACE ME, YOU MADMAN!
HANH!
HE WAS RIBBING YOU, ANDY!
I WAS ALMOST IN *FLAMING CREATURES.*
AH YES. HAD TO PROTECT YOUR IMAGE FOR HOLLYWOOD, EH?
TOO GOOD FOR MY DEPRAVITY?
WAS I EVER SO YOUNG?
DON'T REMIND ME OF MY FORMER VANITY, JACK.
WELL, YOU ARE WELCOME TO STAR IN THIS NEW PIECE!
DID YOU GET ALL THAT, ANDY?
UH . . . YEAH.
WELL, YOU **WOULD HAVE** IF YOU'D TAKEN THE CAP **OFF**.
I GUESS I **DIDN'T** GET ALL THAT . . .
WELL, START FILMING NOW, MAESTRO WARHOL!
AND LET'S GET YOU ALL TO THE **COSTUMERY!**

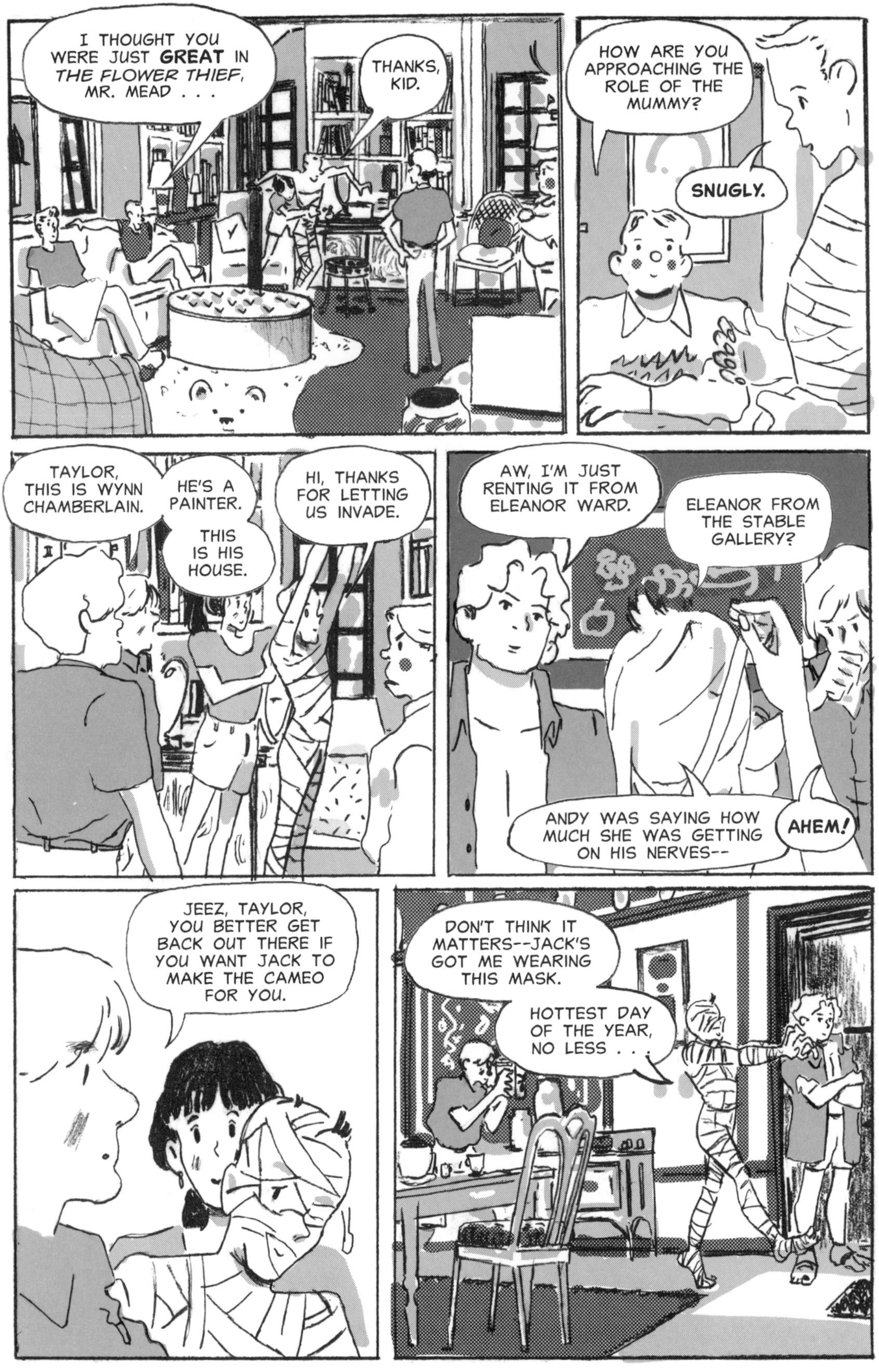

I THOUGHT YOU WERE JUST GREAT IN THE FLOWER THIEF, MR. MEAD . . .
THANKS, KID.
HOW ARE YOU APPROACHING THE ROLE OF THE MUMMY?
SNUGLY.
TAYLOR, THIS IS WYNN CHAMBERLAIN.
HE'S A PAINTER.
THIS IS HIS HOUSE.
HI, THANKS FOR LETTING US INVADE.
AW, I'M JUST RENTING IT FROM ELEANOR WARD.
ELEANOR FROM THE STABLE GALLERY?
ANDY WAS SAYING HOW MUCH SHE WAS GETTING ON HIS NERVES--
AHEM!
JEEZ, TAYLOR, YOU BETTER GET BACK OUT THERE IF YOU WANT JACK TO MAKE THE CAMEO FOR YOU.
DON'T THINK IT MATTERS--JACK'S GOT ME WEARING THIS MASK.
HOTTEST DAY OF THE YEAR, NO LESS . . .

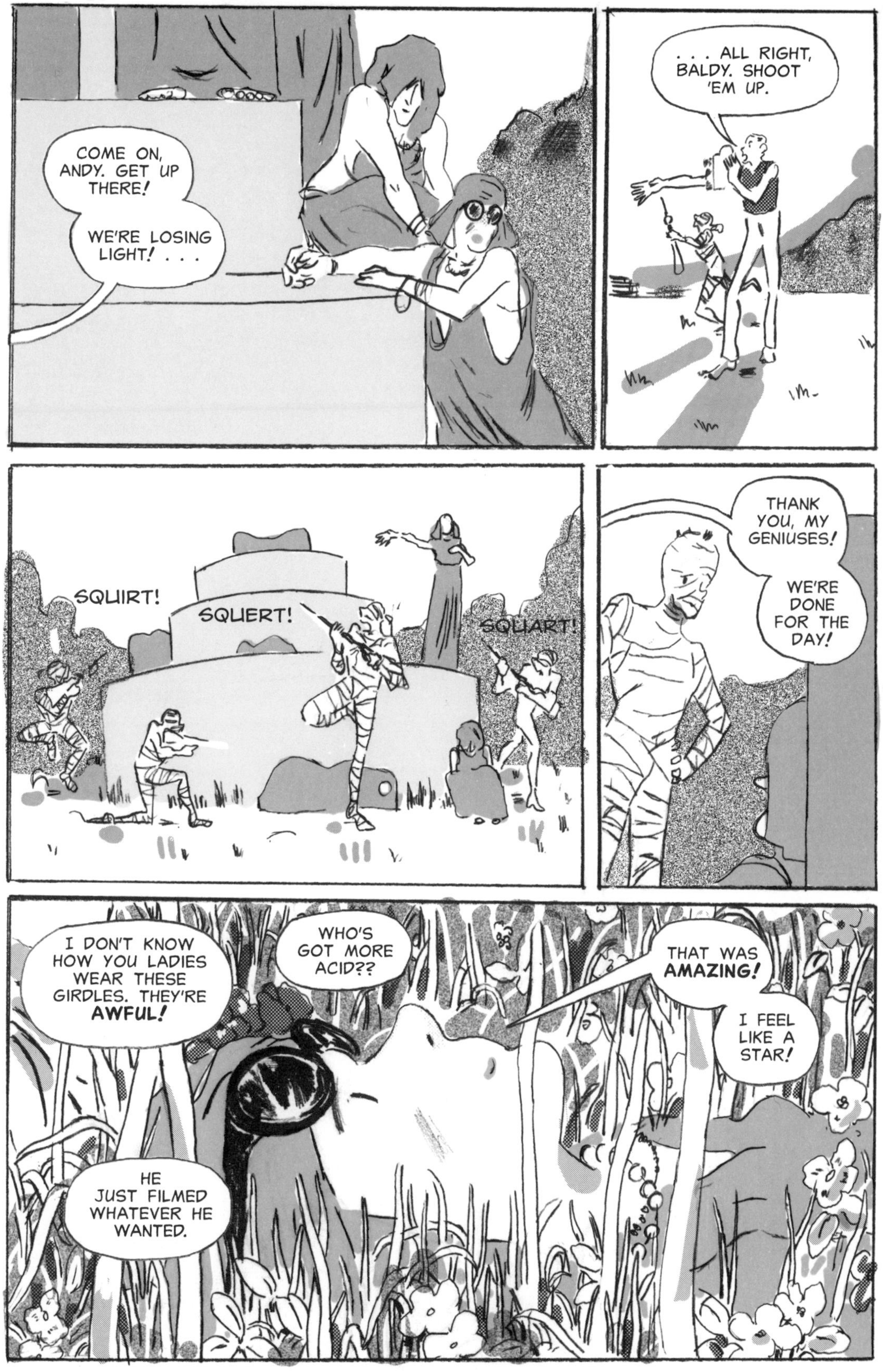
COME ON, ANDY. GET UP THERE!
WE'RE LOSING LIGHT! . . .
. . . ALL RIGHT, BALDY. SHOOT 'EM UP.
SQUIRT!
SQUERT!
SQUART!
THANK YOU, MY GENIUSES!
WE'RE DONE FOR THE DAY!
I DON'T KNOW HOW YOU LADIES WEAR THESE GIRDLES. THEY'RE **AWFUL!**
WHO'S GOT MORE ACID??
THAT WAS **AMAZING!**
I FEEL LIKE A STAR!
HE JUST FILMED WHATEVER HE WANTED.

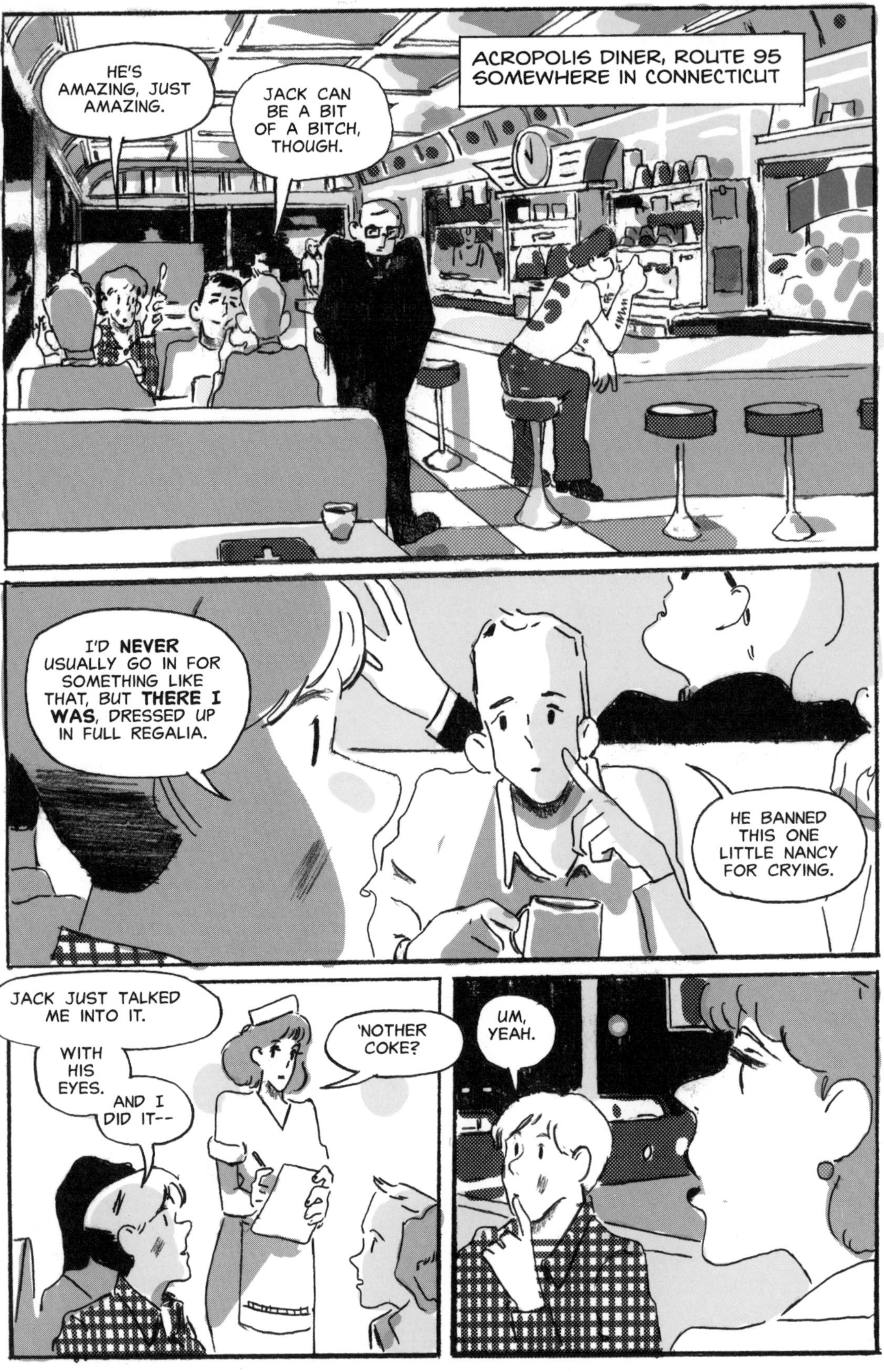
ACROPOLIS DINER, ROUTE 95 SOMEWHERE IN CONNECTICUT
HE'S AMAZING, JUST AMAZING.
JACK CAN BE A BIT OF A BITCH, THOUGH.
I'D **NEVER** USUALLY GO IN FOR SOMETHING LIKE THAT, BUT **THERE I WAS**, DRESSED UP IN FULL REGALIA.
HE BANNED THIS ONE LITTLE NANCY FOR CRYING.
JACK JUST TALKED ME INTO IT.
WITH HIS EYES.
AND I DID IT--
'NOTHER COKE?
UM, YEAH.

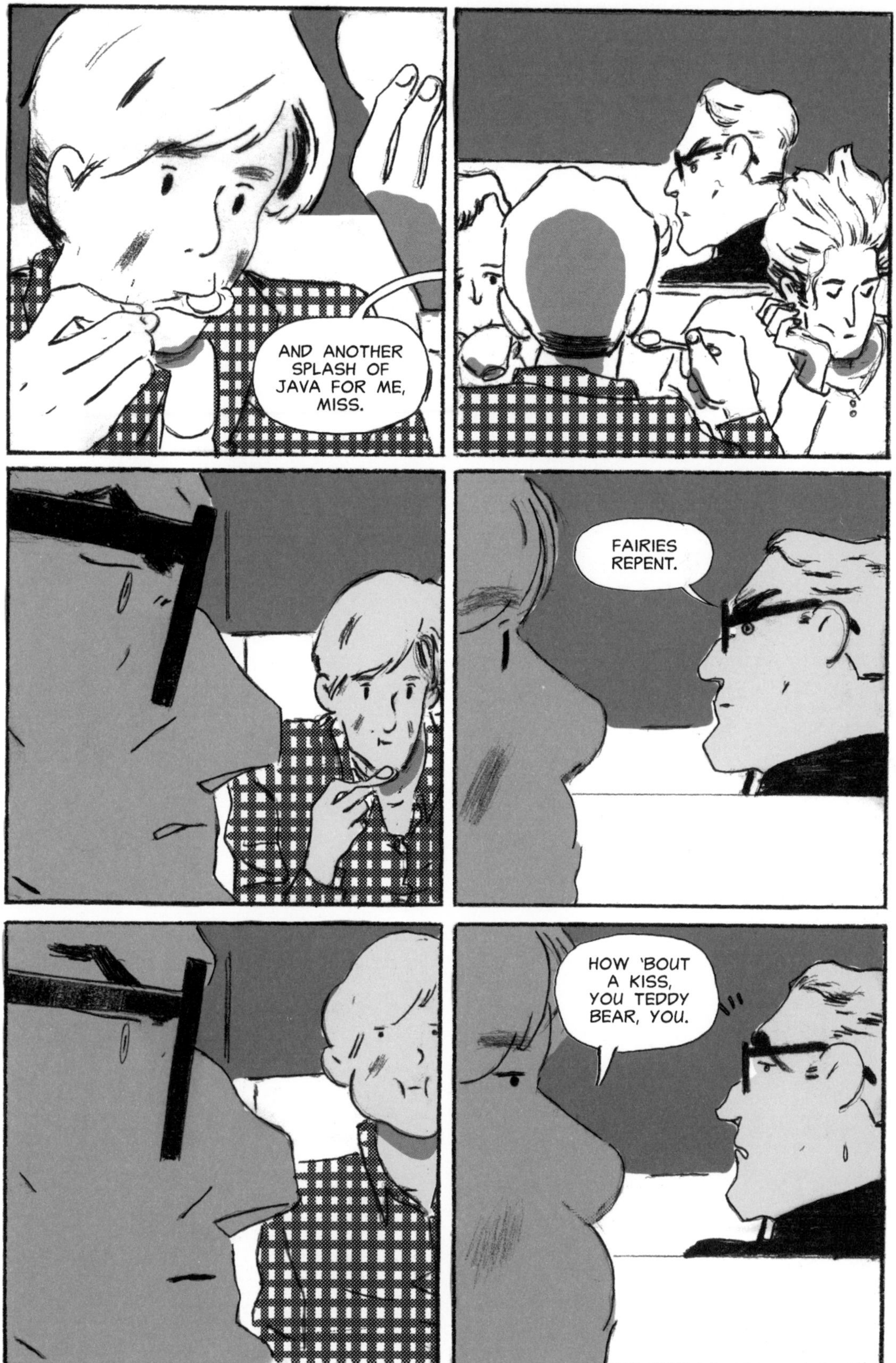
AND ANOTHER SPLASH OF JAVA FOR ME, MISS.
FAIRIES REPENT.
HOW 'BOUT A KISS, YOU TEDDY BEAR, YOU.

CHAPTER EIGHT

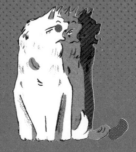

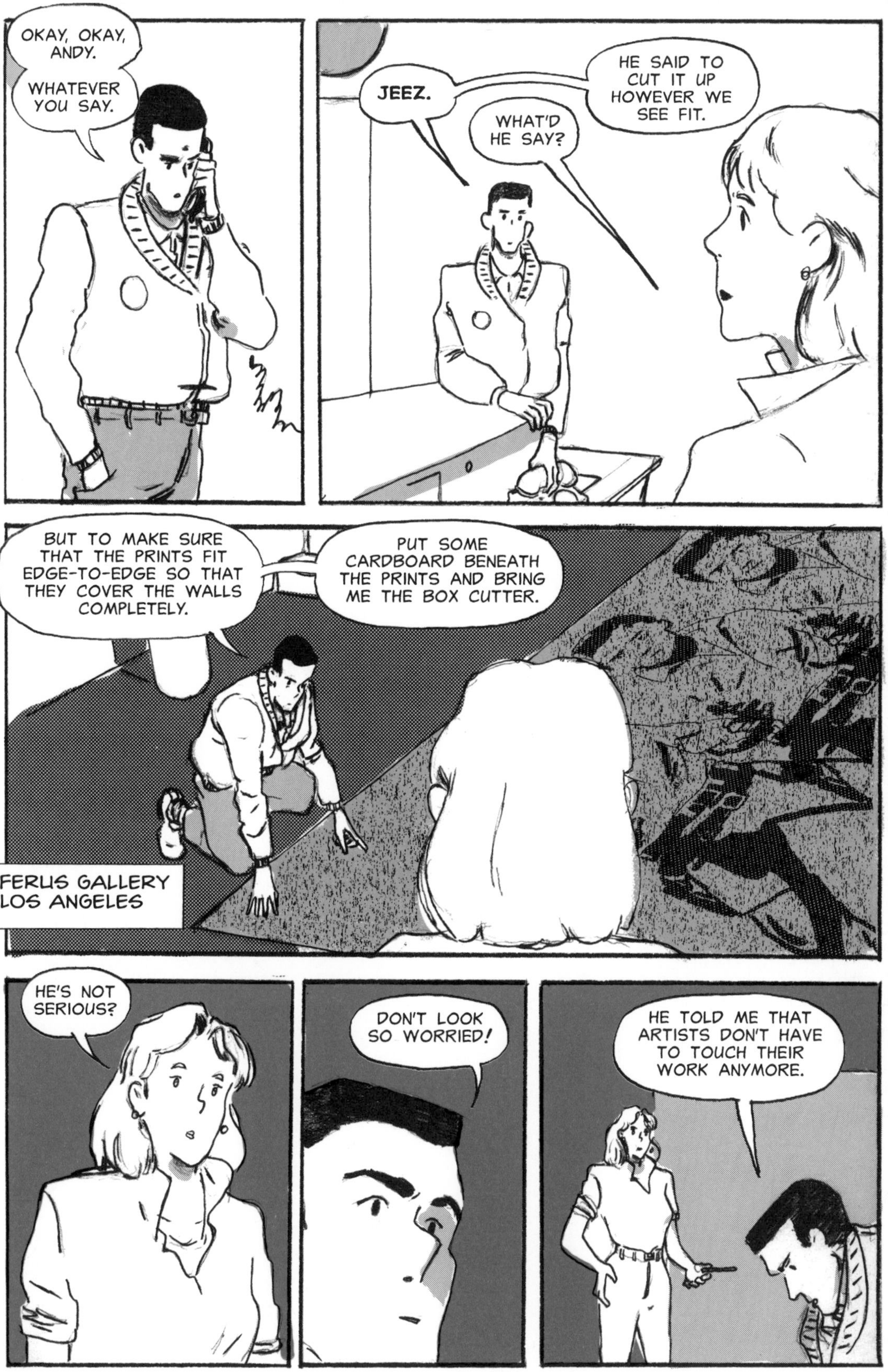
OKAY, OKAY, ANDY.
WHATEVER YOU SAY.
JEEZ.
HE SAID TO CUT IT UP HOWEVER WE SEE FIT.
WHAT'D HE SAY?
BUT TO MAKE SURE THAT THE PRINTS FIT EDGE-TO-EDGE SO THAT THEY COVER THE WALLS COMPLETELY.
PUT SOME CARDBOARD BENEATH THE PRINTS AND BRING ME THE BOX CUTTER.
FERUS GALLERY LOS ANGELES
HE'S NOT SERIOUS?
DON'T LOOK SO WORRIED!
HE TOLD ME THAT ARTISTS DON'T HAVE TO TOUCH THEIR WORK ANYMORE.

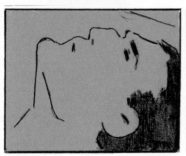

WHIRRR

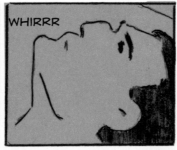

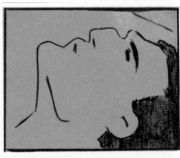

WHIRRR

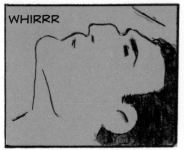

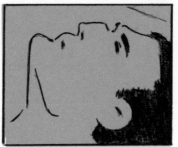

WHIRRR

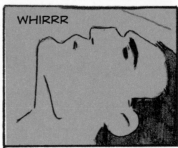

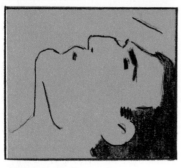

WHIRRR

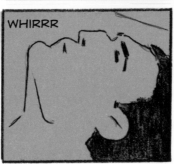

WHIRRR

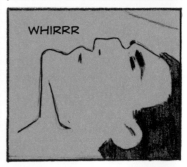

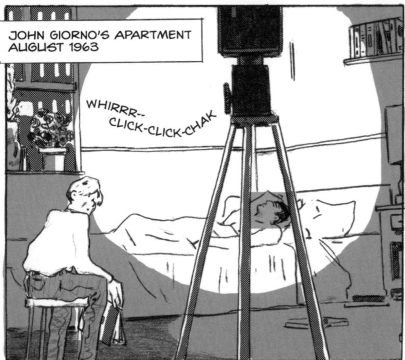

JOHN GIORNO'S APARTMENT AUGUST 1963

WHIRRR-- CLICK-CLICK-CHAK

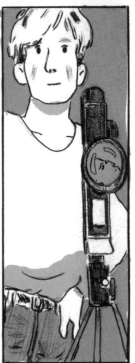

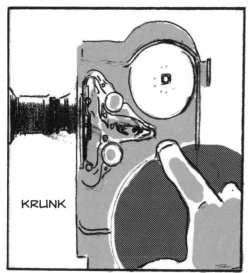

KRUNK

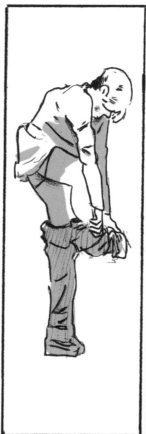

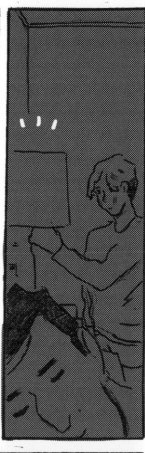

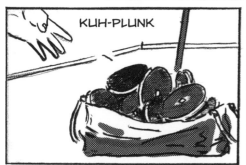

KUH-PLUNK

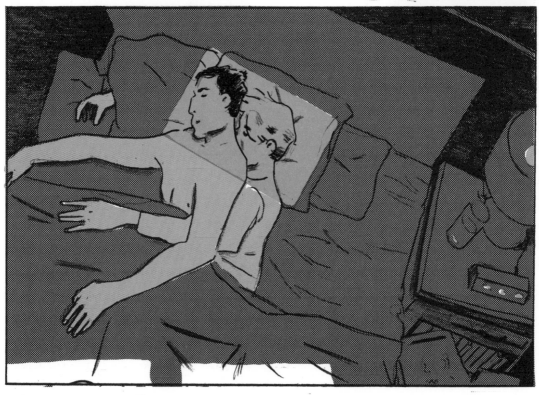

CHAPTER NINE

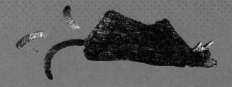

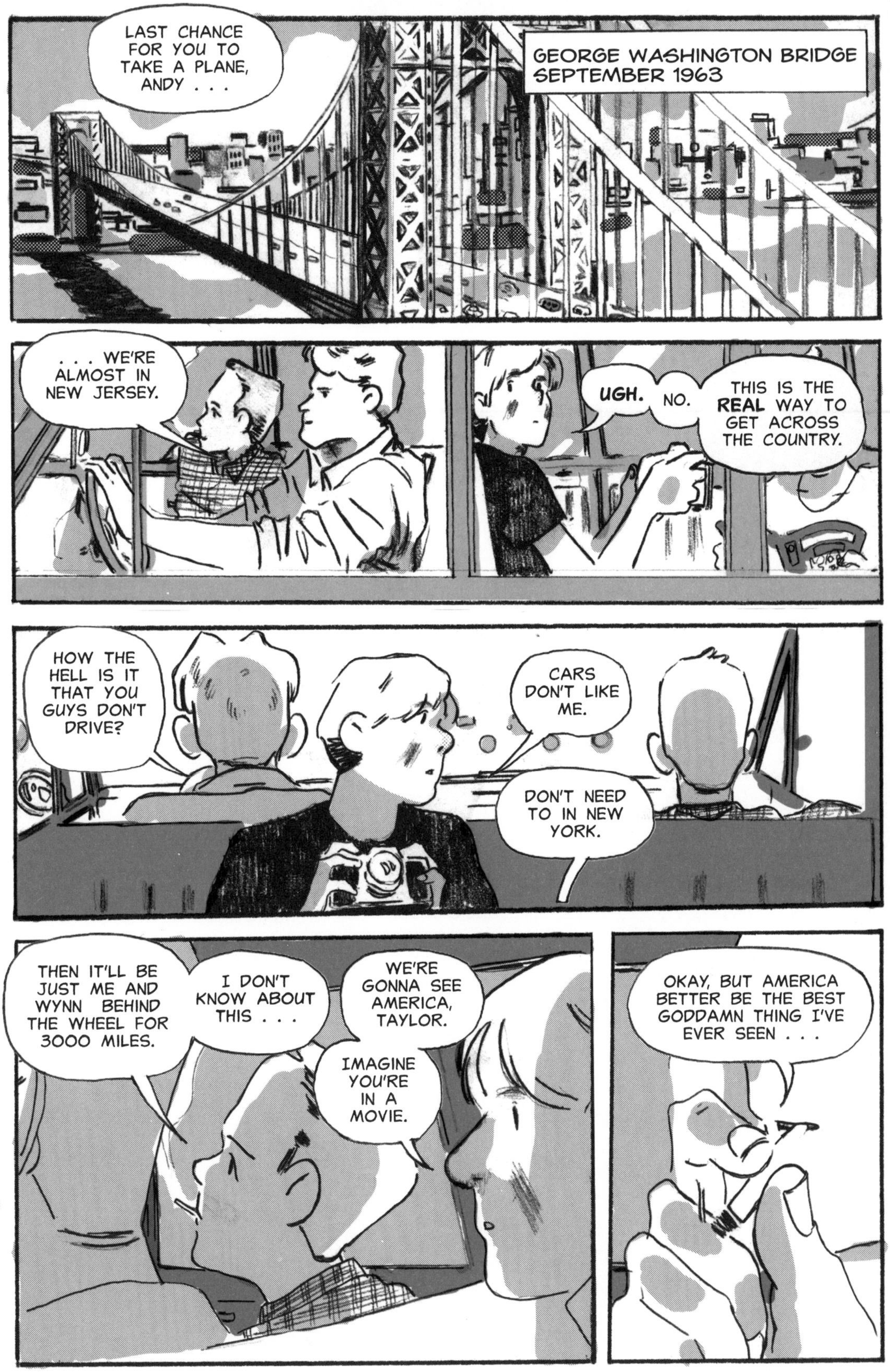
LAST CHANCE FOR YOU TO TAKE A PLANE, ANDY . . .
GEORGE WASHINGTON BRIDGE SEPTEMBER 1963
. . . WE'RE ALMOST IN NEW JERSEY.
UGH.
NO.
THIS IS THE REAL WAY TO GET ACROSS THE COUNTRY.
HOW THE HELL IS IT THAT YOU GUYS DON'T DRIVE?
CARS DON'T LIKE ME.
DON'T NEED TO IN NEW YORK.
THEN IT'LL BE JUST ME AND WYNN BEHIND THE WHEEL FOR 3000 MILES.
I DON'T KNOW ABOUT THIS . . .
WE'RE GONNA SEE AMERICA, TAYLOR.
IMAGINE YOU'RE IN A MOVIE.
OKAY, BUT AMERICA BETTER BE THE BEST GODDAMN THING I'VE EVER SEEN . . .

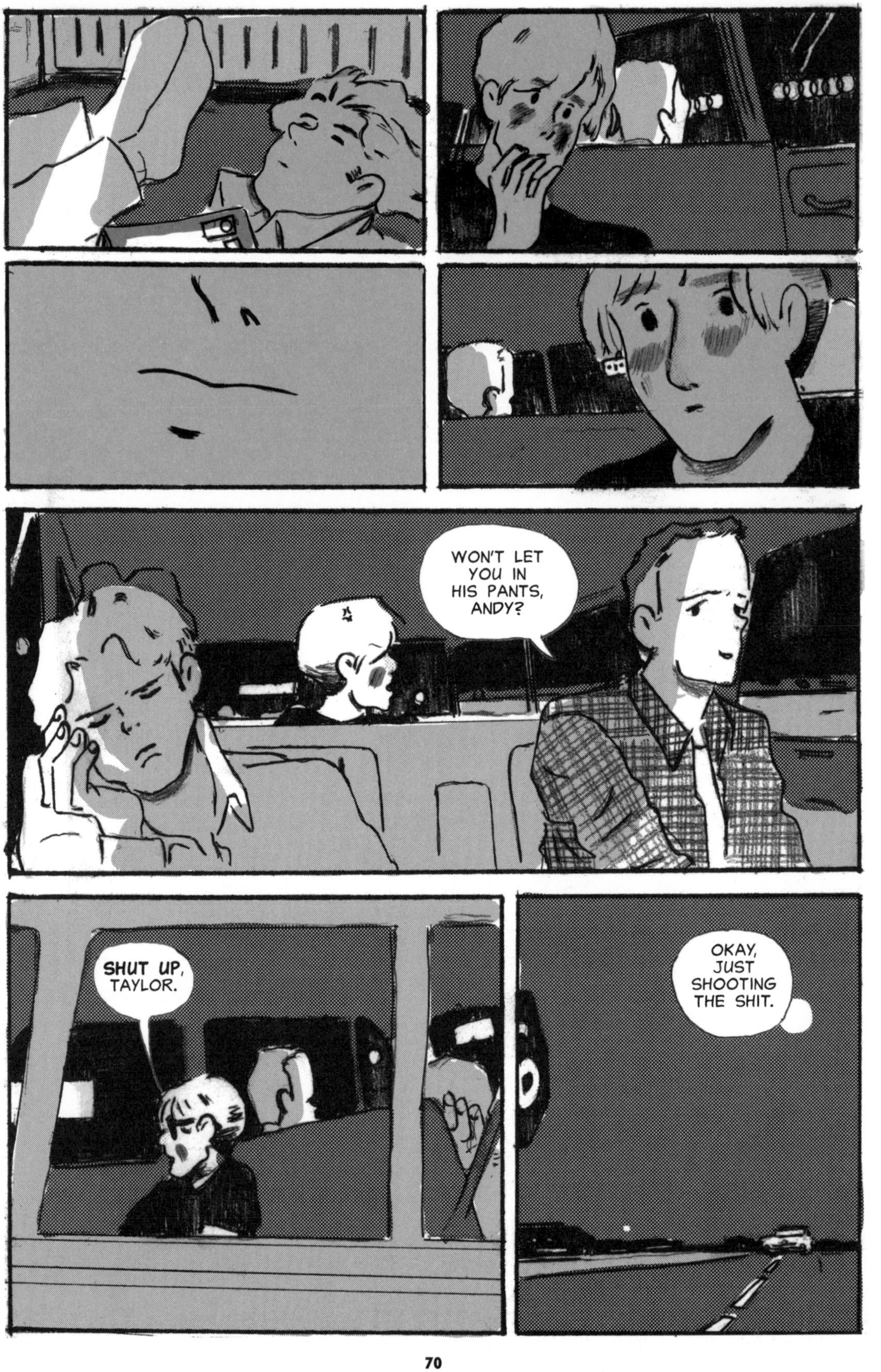
WON'T LET YOU IN HIS PANTS, ANDY?
SHUT UP, TAYLOR.
OKAY, JUST SHOOTING THE SHIT.

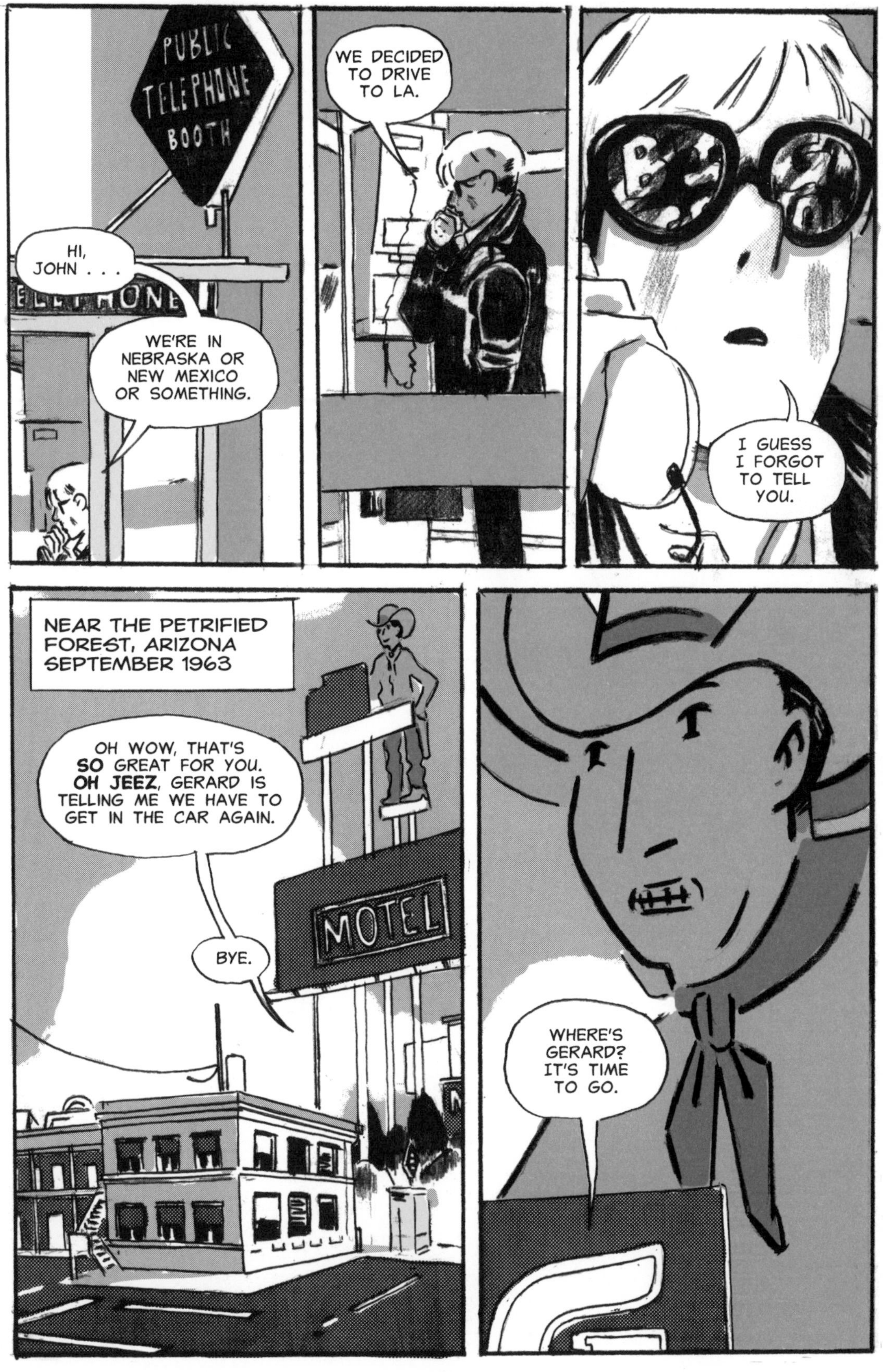
PUBLIC TELEPHONE BOOTH
HI, JOHN . . .
WE'RE IN NEBRASKA OR NEW MEXICO OR SOMETHING.
WE DECIDED TO DRIVE TO LA.
I GUESS I FORGOT TO TELL YOU.
NEAR THE PETRIFIED FOREST, ARIZONA SEPTEMBER 1963
OH WOW, THAT'S **SO** GREAT FOR YOU. **OH JEEZ**, GERARD IS TELLING ME WE HAVE TO GET IN THE CAR AGAIN.
BYE.
MOTEL
WHERE'S GERARD? IT'S TIME TO GO.

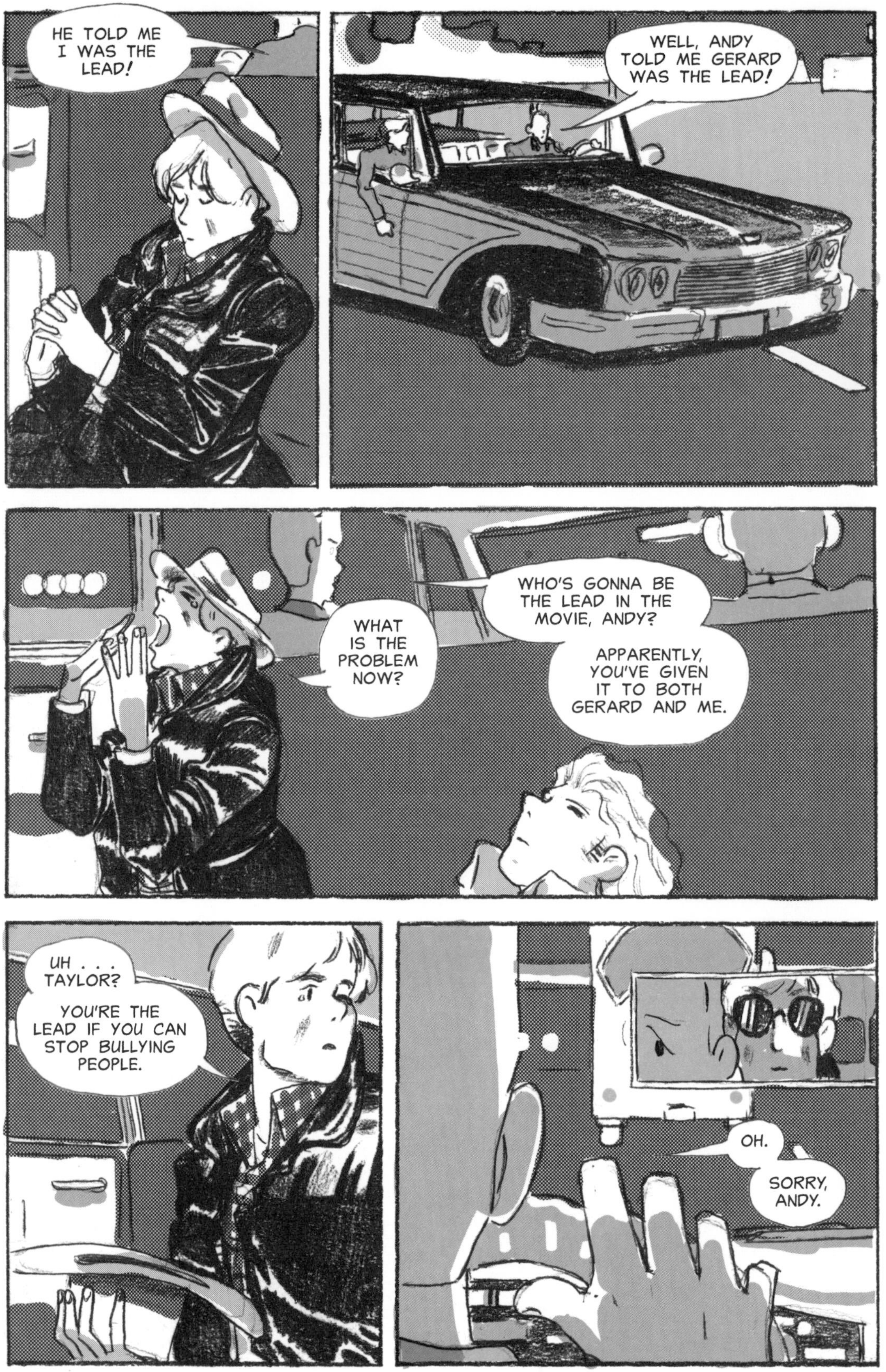
HE TOLD ME I WAS THE LEAD!
WELL, ANDY TOLD ME GERARD WAS THE LEAD!
WHO'S GONNA BE THE LEAD IN THE MOVIE, ANDY?
APPARENTLY, YOU'VE GIVEN IT TO BOTH GERARD AND ME.
WHAT IS THE PROBLEM NOW?
UH . . . TAYLOR?
YOU'RE THE LEAD IF YOU CAN STOP BULLYING PEOPLE.
OH.
SORRY, ANDY.

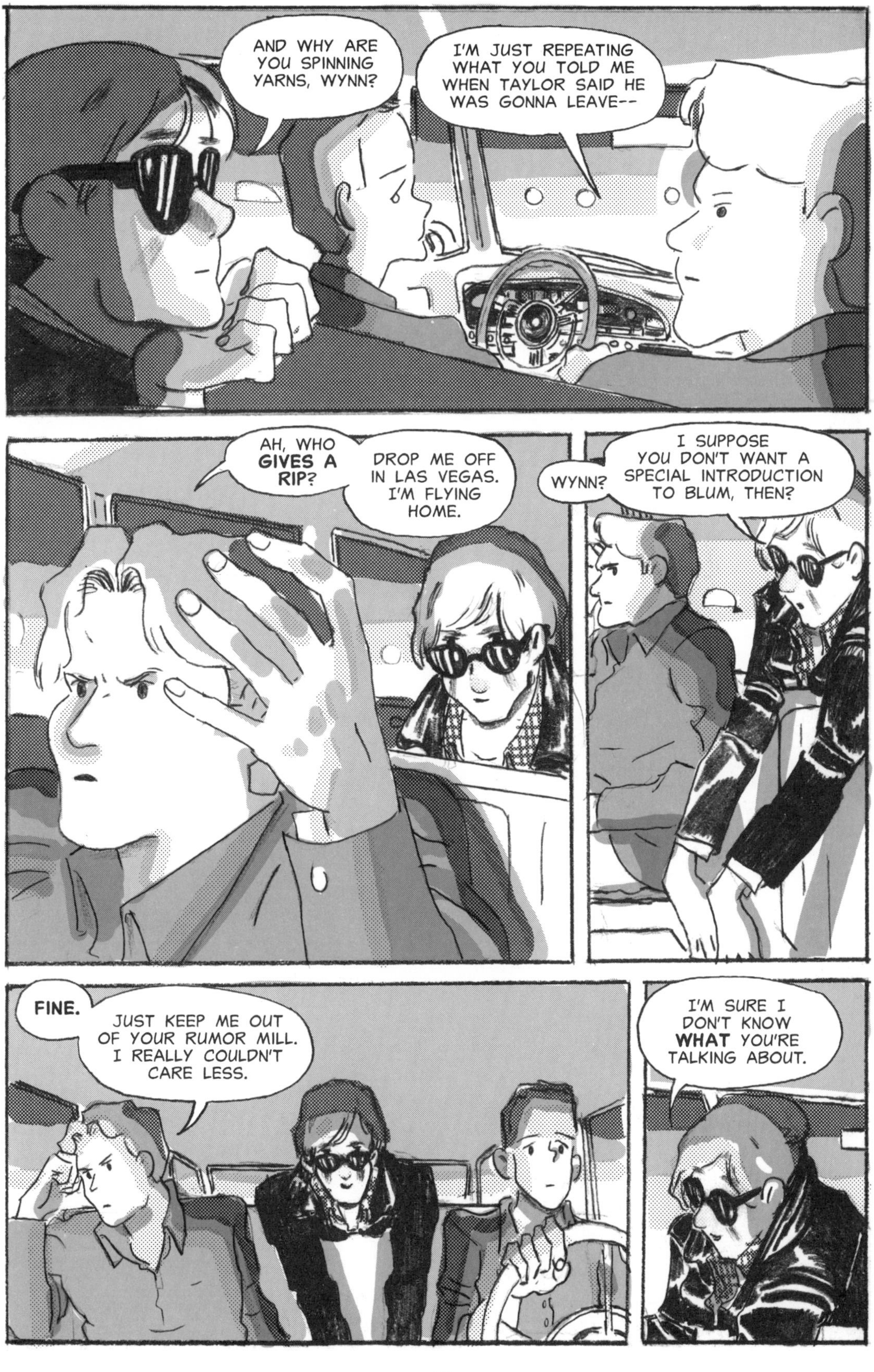
AND WHY ARE YOU SPINNING YARNS, WYNN?
I'M JUST REPEATING WHAT YOU TOLD ME WHEN TAYLOR SAID HE WAS GONNA LEAVE--
AH, WHO **GIVES A RIP**?
DROP ME OFF IN LAS VEGAS. I'M FLYING HOME.
WYNN?
I SUPPOSE YOU DON'T WANT A SPECIAL INTRODUCTION TO BLUM, THEN?
FINE.
JUST KEEP ME OUT OF YOUR RUMOR MILL. I REALLY COULDN'T CARE LESS.
I'M SURE I DON'T KNOW **WHAT** YOU'RE TALKING ABOUT.

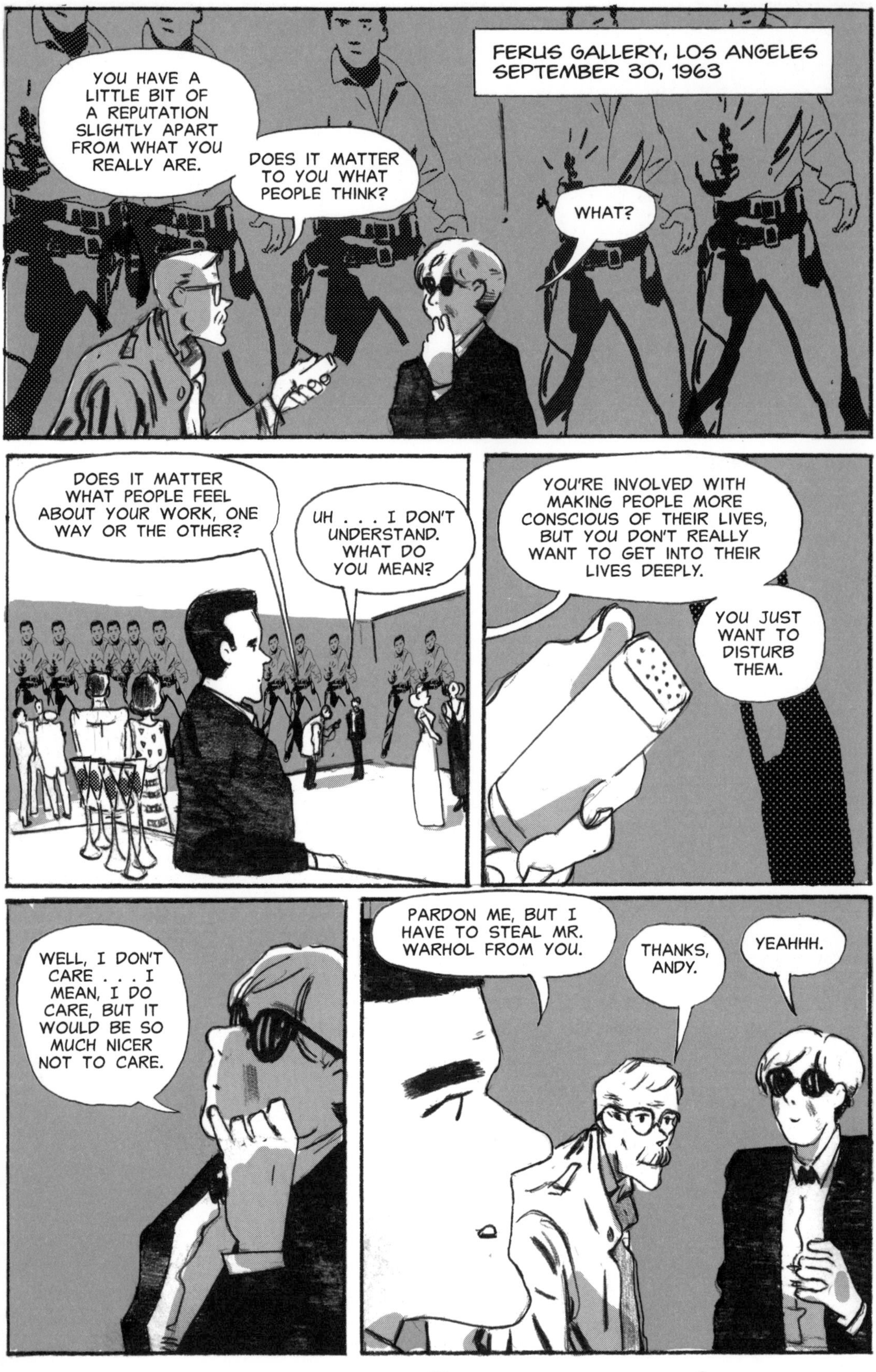
FERUS GALLERY, LOS ANGELES SEPTEMBER 30, 1963
YOU HAVE A LITTLE BIT OF A REPUTATION SLIGHTLY APART FROM WHAT YOU REALLY ARE.
DOES IT MATTER TO YOU WHAT PEOPLE THINK?
WHAT?
DOES IT MATTER WHAT PEOPLE FEEL ABOUT YOUR WORK, ONE WAY OR THE OTHER?
UH . . . I DON'T UNDERSTAND. WHAT DO YOU MEAN?
YOU'RE INVOLVED WITH MAKING PEOPLE MORE CONSCIOUS OF THEIR LIVES, BUT YOU DON'T REALLY WANT TO GET INTO THEIR LIVES DEEPLY.
YOU JUST WANT TO DISTURB THEM.
WELL, I DON'T CARE . . . I MEAN, I DO CARE, BUT IT WOULD BE SO MUCH NICER NOT TO CARE.
PARDON ME, BUT I HAVE TO STEAL MR. WARHOL FROM YOU.
THANKS, ANDY.
YEAHHH.

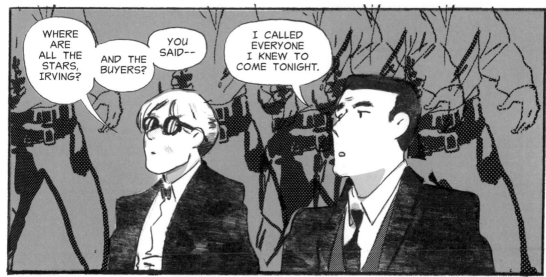

WHERE ARE ALL THE STARS, IRVING?

AND THE BUYERS?

YOU SAID--

I CALLED EVERYONE I KNEW TO COME TONIGHT.

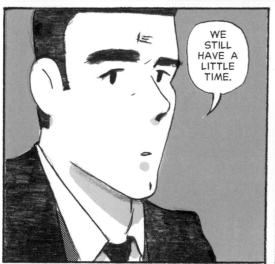

WE STILL HAVE A LITTLE TIME.

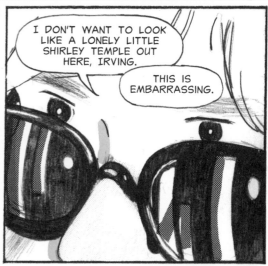

I DON'T WANT TO LOOK LIKE A LONELY LITTLE SHIRLEY TEMPLE OUT HERE, IRVING.

THIS IS EMBARRASSING.

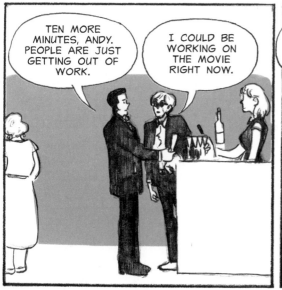

TEN MORE MINUTES, ANDY. PEOPLE ARE JUST GETTING OUT OF WORK.

I COULD BE WORKING ON THE MOVIE RIGHT NOW.

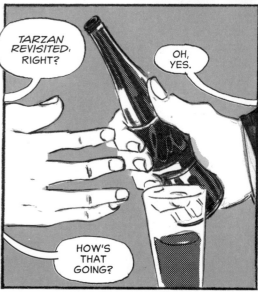

TARZAN REVISITED, RIGHT?

OH, YES.

HOW'S THAT GOING?

75

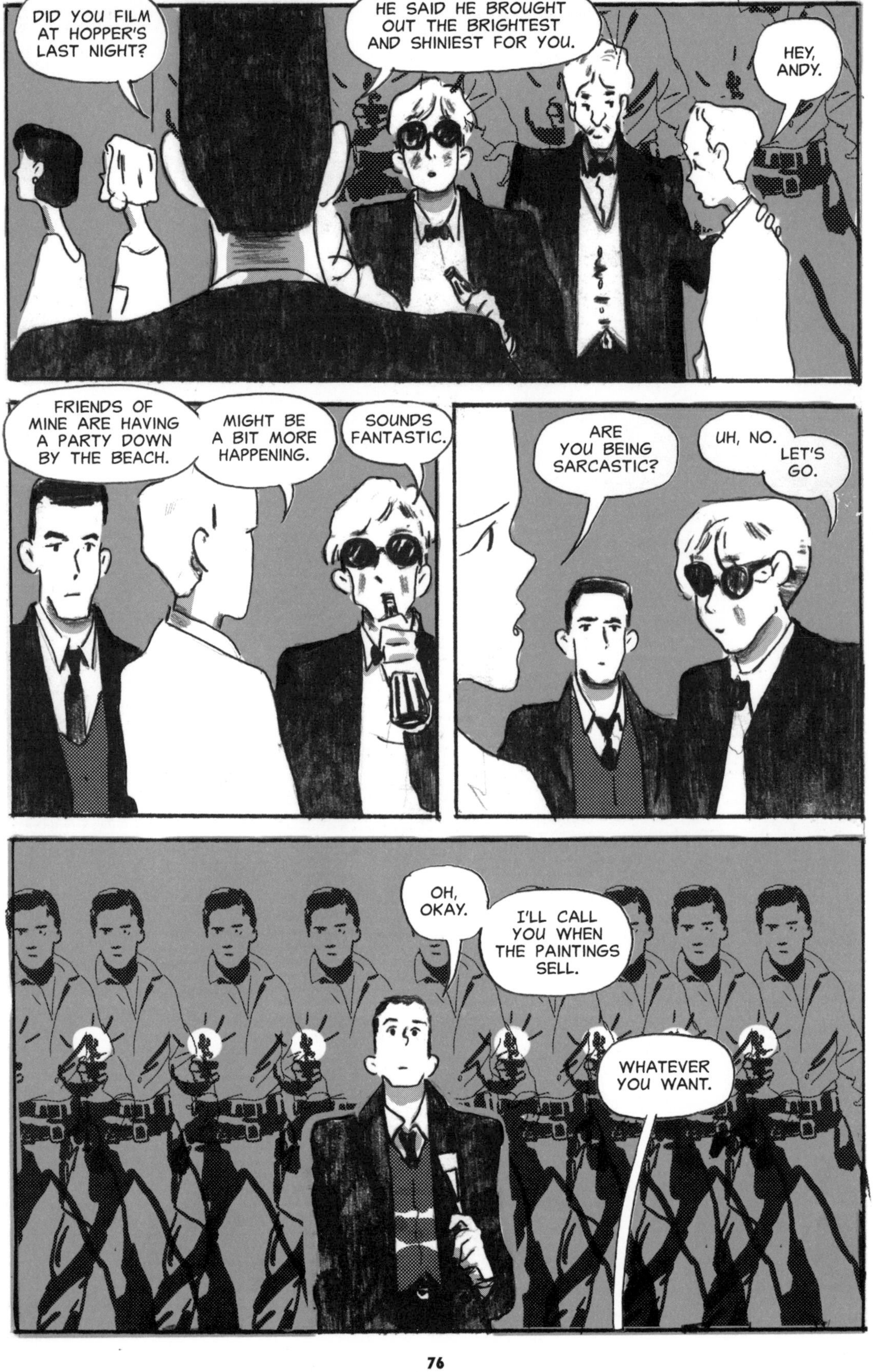
DID YOU FILM AT HOPPER'S LAST NIGHT?
HE SAID HE BROUGHT OUT THE BRIGHTEST AND SHINIEST FOR YOU.
HEY, ANDY.
FRIENDS OF MINE ARE HAVING A PARTY DOWN BY THE BEACH.
MIGHT BE A BIT MORE HAPPENING.
SOUNDS FANTASTIC.
ARE YOU BEING SARCASTIC?
UH, NO.
LET'S GO.
OH, OKAY.
I'LL CALL YOU WHEN THE PAINTINGS SELL.
WHATEVER YOU WANT.

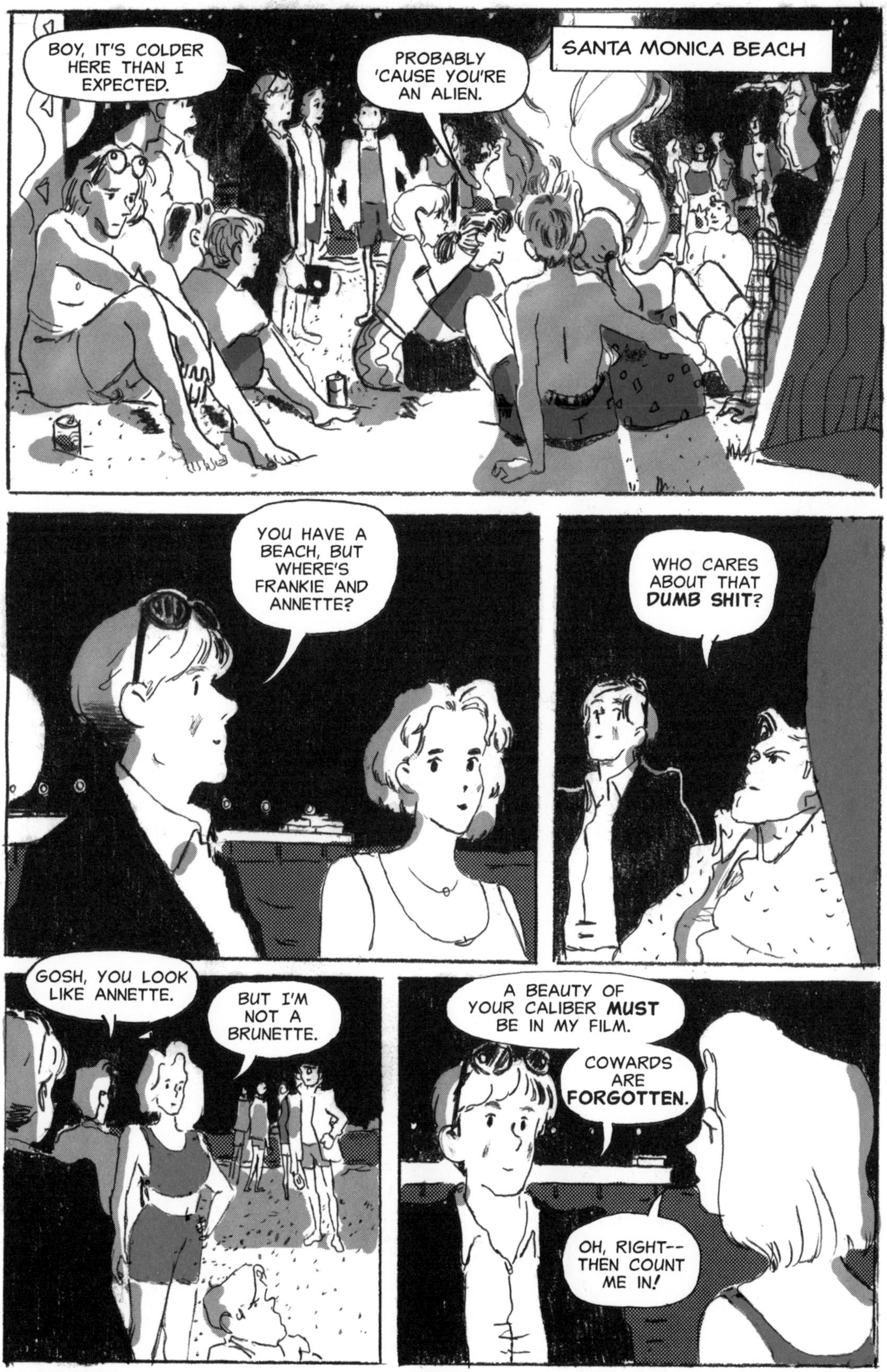
SANTA MONICA BEACH
BOY, IT'S COLDER HERE THAN I EXPECTED.
PROBABLY 'CAUSE YOU'RE AN ALIEN.
YOU HAVE A BEACH, BUT WHERE'S FRANKIE AND ANNETTE?
WHO CARES ABOUT THAT DUMB SHIT?
GOSH, YOU LOOK LIKE ANNETTE.
BUT I'M NOT A BRUNETTE.
A BEAUTY OF YOUR CALIBER MUST BE IN MY FILM.
COWARDS ARE FORGOTTEN.
OH, RIGHT-- THEN COUNT ME IN!

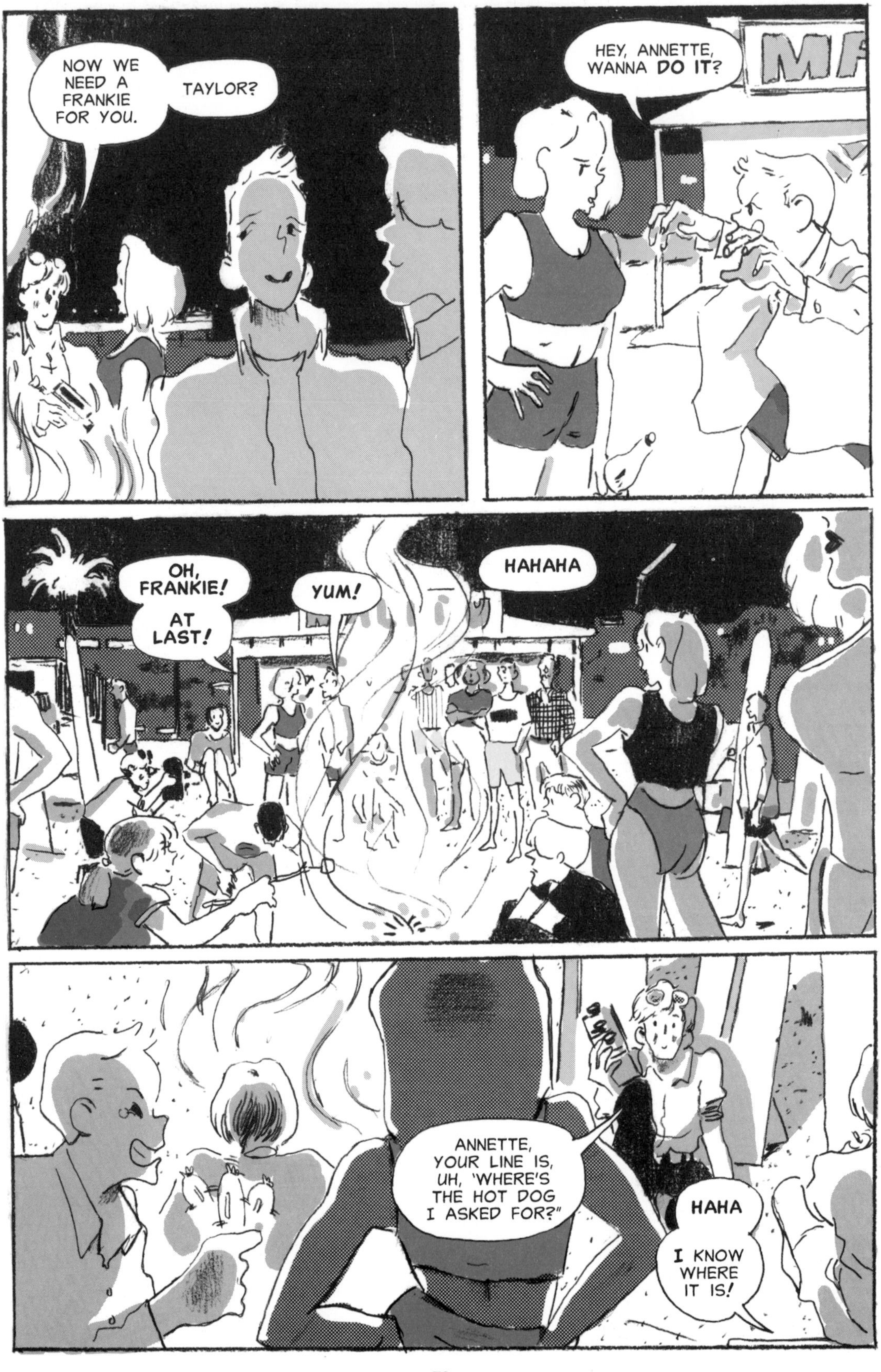
NOW WE NEED A FRANKIE FOR YOU.
TAYLOR?
HEY, ANNETTE, WANNA **DO IT**?
OH, FRANKIE!
AT LAST!
YUM!
HAHAHA
ANNETTE, YOUR LINE IS, UH, 'WHERE'S THE HOT DOG I ASKED FOR?"
HAHA
I KNOW WHERE IT IS!

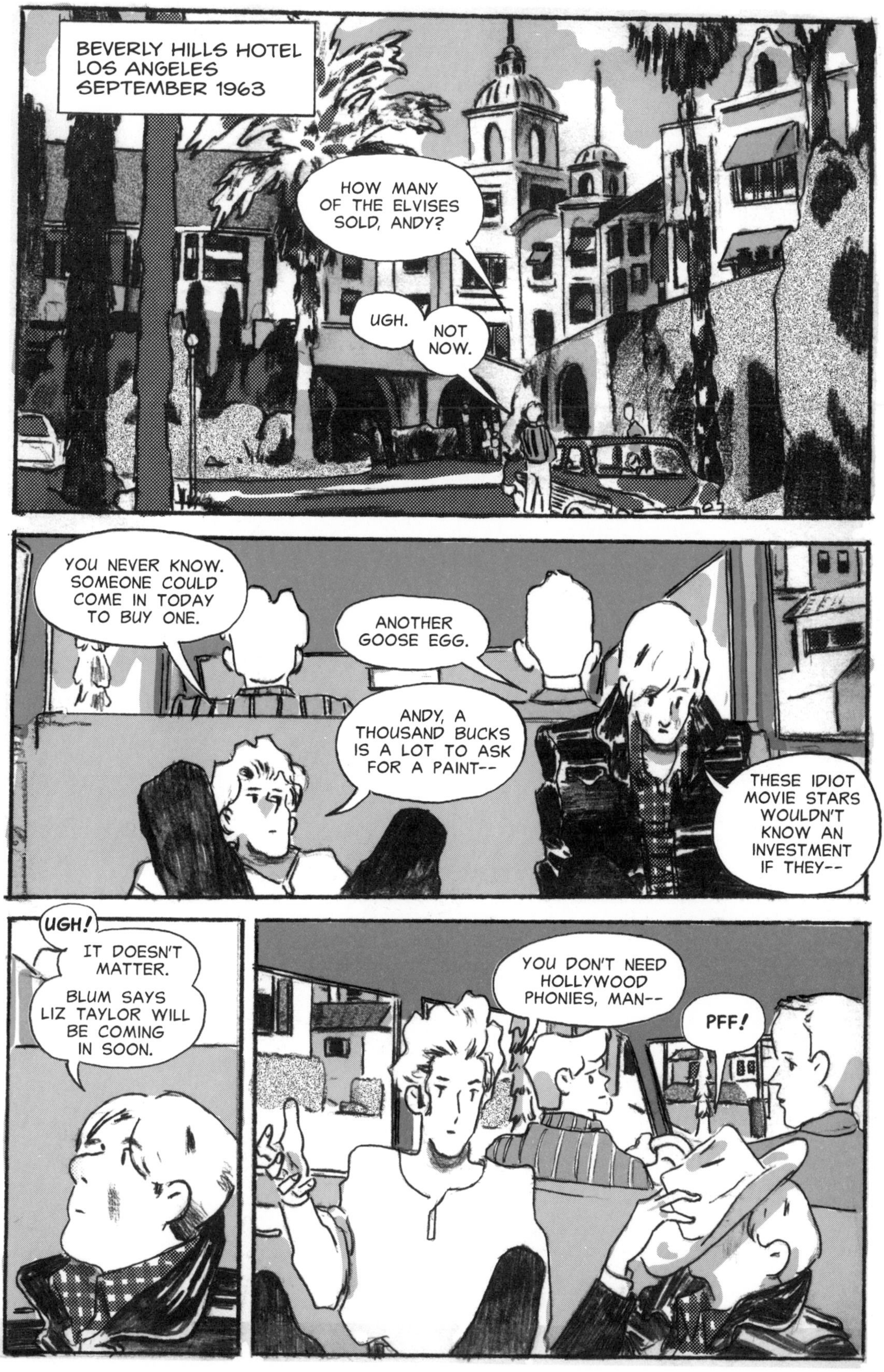
BEVERLY HILLS HOTEL
LOS ANGELES
SEPTEMBER 1963
HOW MANY OF THE ELVISES SOLD, ANDY?
UGH.
NOT NOW.
YOU NEVER KNOW. SOMEONE COULD COME IN TODAY TO BUY ONE.
ANOTHER GOOSE EGG.
ANDY, A THOUSAND BUCKS IS A LOT TO ASK FOR A PAINT--
THESE IDIOT MOVIE STARS WOULDN'T KNOW AN INVESTMENT IF THEY--
UGH!
IT DOESN'T MATTER.
BLUM SAYS LIZ TAYLOR WILL BE COMING IN SOON.
YOU DON'T NEED HOLLYWOOD PHONIES, MAN--
PFF!

CHAPTER TEN

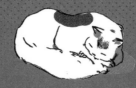

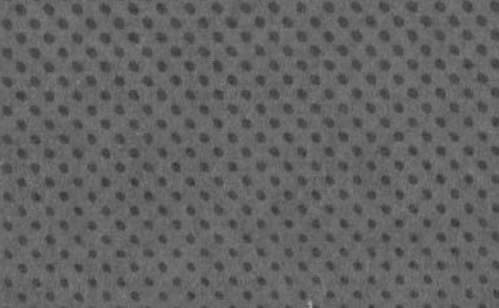

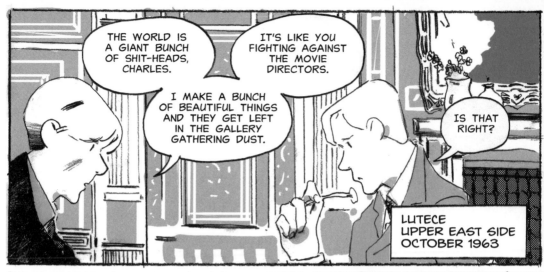

THE WORLD IS A GIANT BUNCH OF SHIT-HEADS, CHARLES.

IT'S LIKE YOU FIGHTING AGAINST THE MOVIE DIRECTORS.

I MAKE A BUNCH OF BEAUTIFUL THINGS AND THEY GET LEFT IN THE GALLERY GATHERING DUST.

IS THAT RIGHT?

LUTECE
UPPER EAST SIDE
OCTOBER 1963

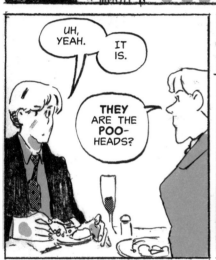

UH, YEAH.

IT IS.

THEY ARE THE POO-HEADS?

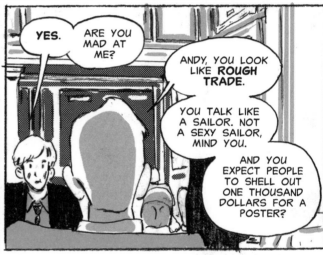

YES.

ARE YOU MAD AT ME?

ANDY, YOU LOOK LIKE **ROUGH TRADE.**

YOU TALK LIKE A SAILOR. NOT A SEXY SAILOR, MIND YOU.

AND YOU EXPECT PEOPLE TO SHELL OUT ONE THOUSAND DOLLARS FOR A POSTER?

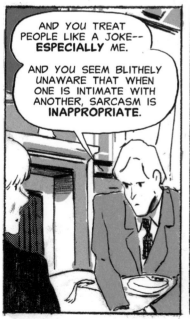

AND YOU TREAT PEOPLE LIKE A JOKE-- **ESPECIALLY** ME.

AND YOU SEEM BLITHELY UNAWARE THAT WHEN ONE IS INTIMATE WITH ANOTHER, SARCASM IS **INAPPROPRIATE.**

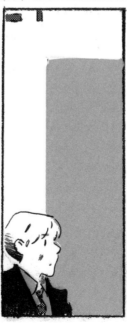

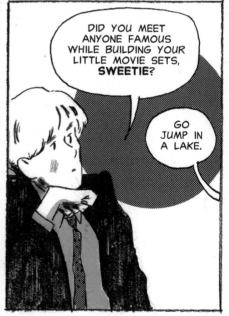

DID YOU MEET ANYONE FAMOUS WHILE BUILDING YOUR LITTLE MOVIE SETS, **SWEETIE?**

GO JUMP IN A LAKE.

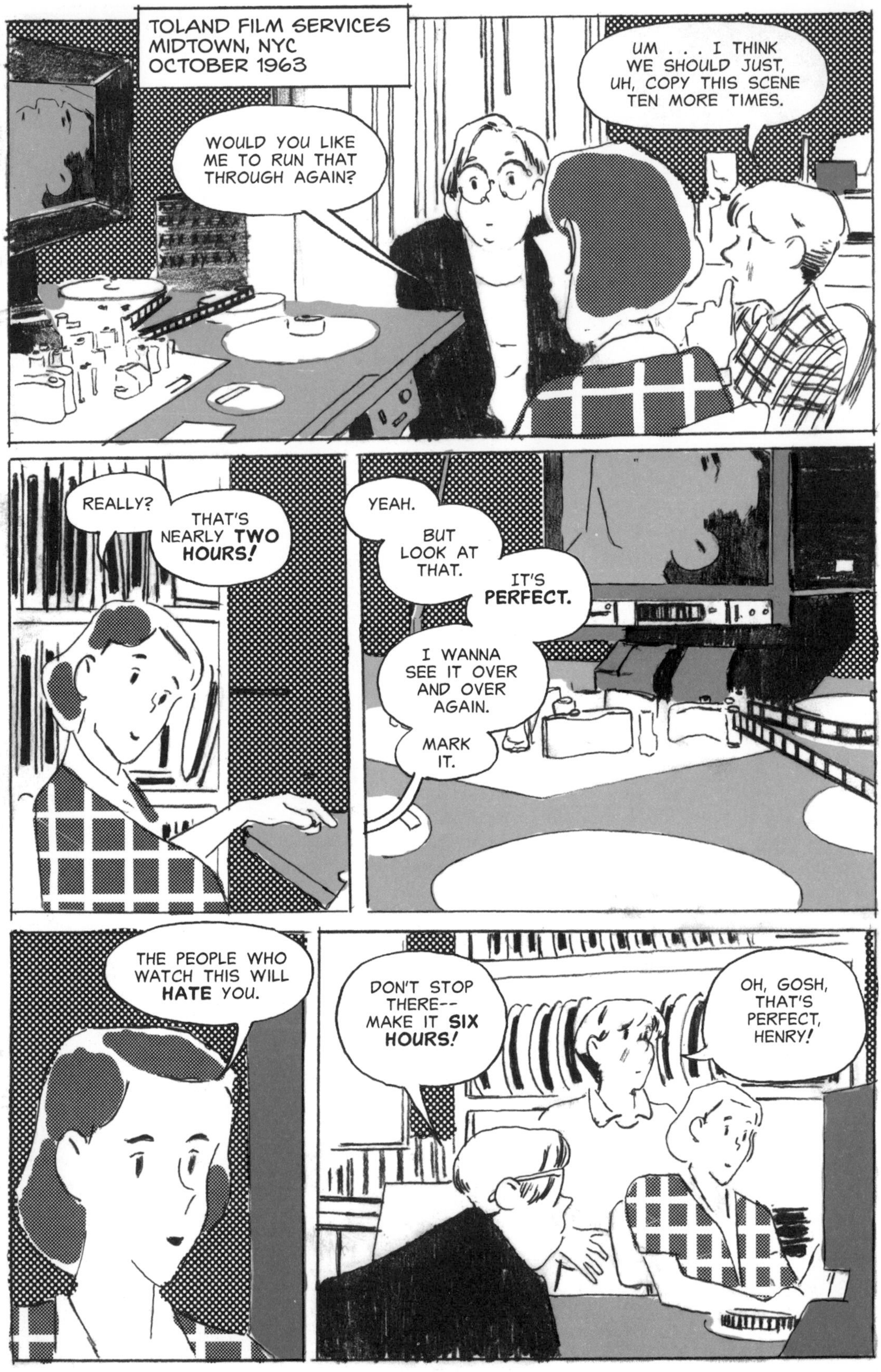
TOLAND FILM SERVICES
MIDTOWN, NYC
OCTOBER 1963
WOULD YOU LIKE ME TO RUN THAT THROUGH AGAIN?
UM . . . I THINK WE SHOULD JUST, UH, COPY THIS SCENE TEN MORE TIMES.
REALLY?
THAT'S NEARLY **TWO HOURS!**
YEAH.
BUT LOOK AT THAT.
IT'S **PERFECT.**
I WANNA SEE IT OVER AND OVER AGAIN.
MARK IT.
THE PEOPLE WHO WATCH THIS WILL **HATE** YOU.
DON'T STOP THERE-- MAKE IT **SIX HOURS!**
OH, GOSH, THAT'S PERFECT, HENRY!

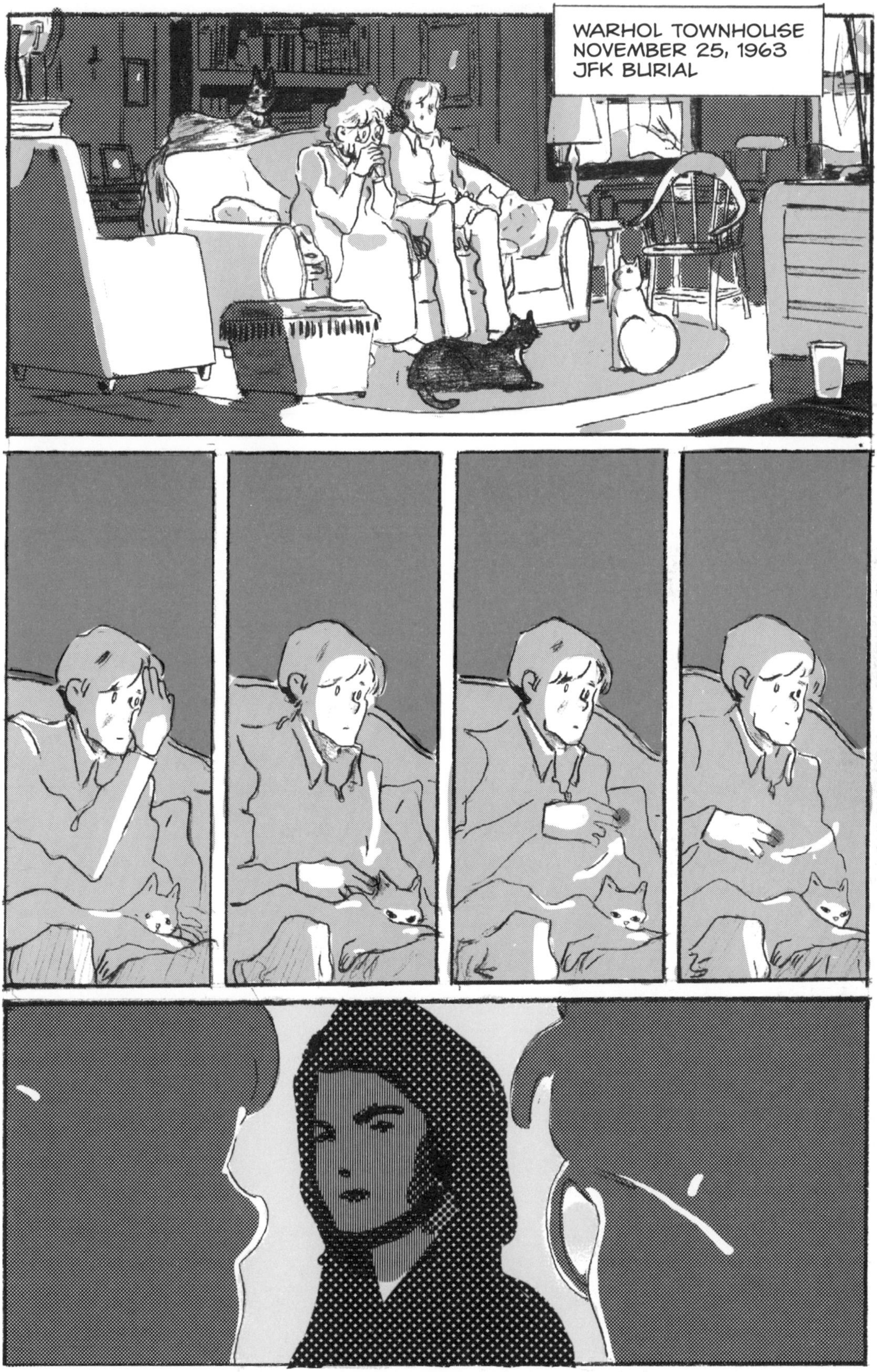
WARHOL TOWNHOUSE
NOVEMBER 25, 1963
JFK BURIAL

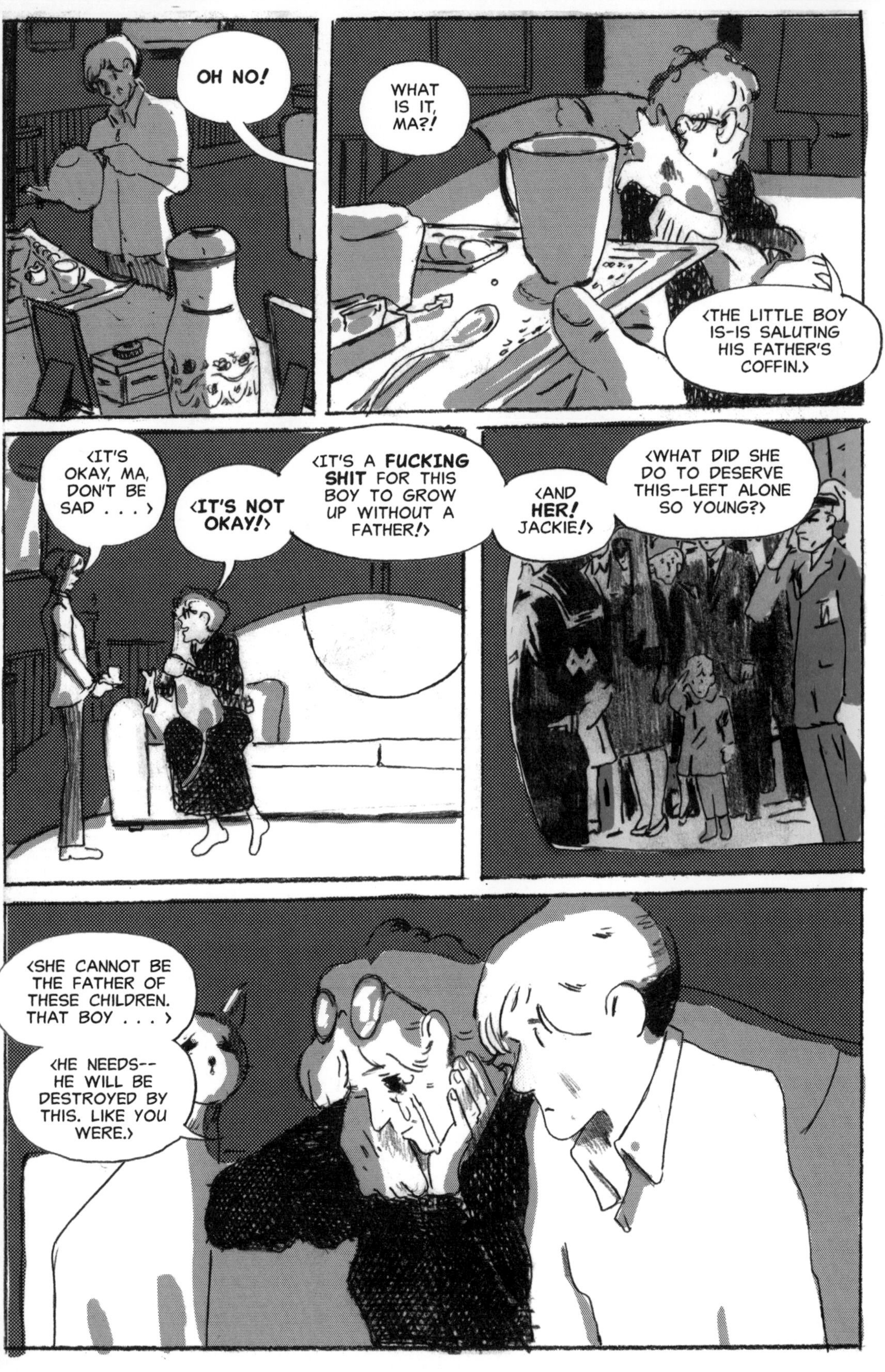
OH NO!
WHAT IS IT, MA?!
<THE LITTLE BOY IS-IS SALUTING HIS FATHER'S COFFIN.>
<IT'S OKAY, MA, DON'T BE SAD . . . >
<IT'S NOT OKAY!>
<IT'S A FUCKING SHIT FOR THIS BOY TO GROW UP WITHOUT A FATHER!>
<AND HER! JACKIE!>
<WHAT DID SHE DO TO DESERVE THIS--LEFT ALONE SO YOUNG?>
<SHE CANNOT BE THE FATHER OF THESE CHILDREN. THAT BOY . . . >
<HE NEEDS-- HE WILL BE DESTROYED BY THIS. LIKE YOU WERE.>

CHAPTER ELEVEN

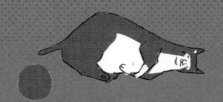

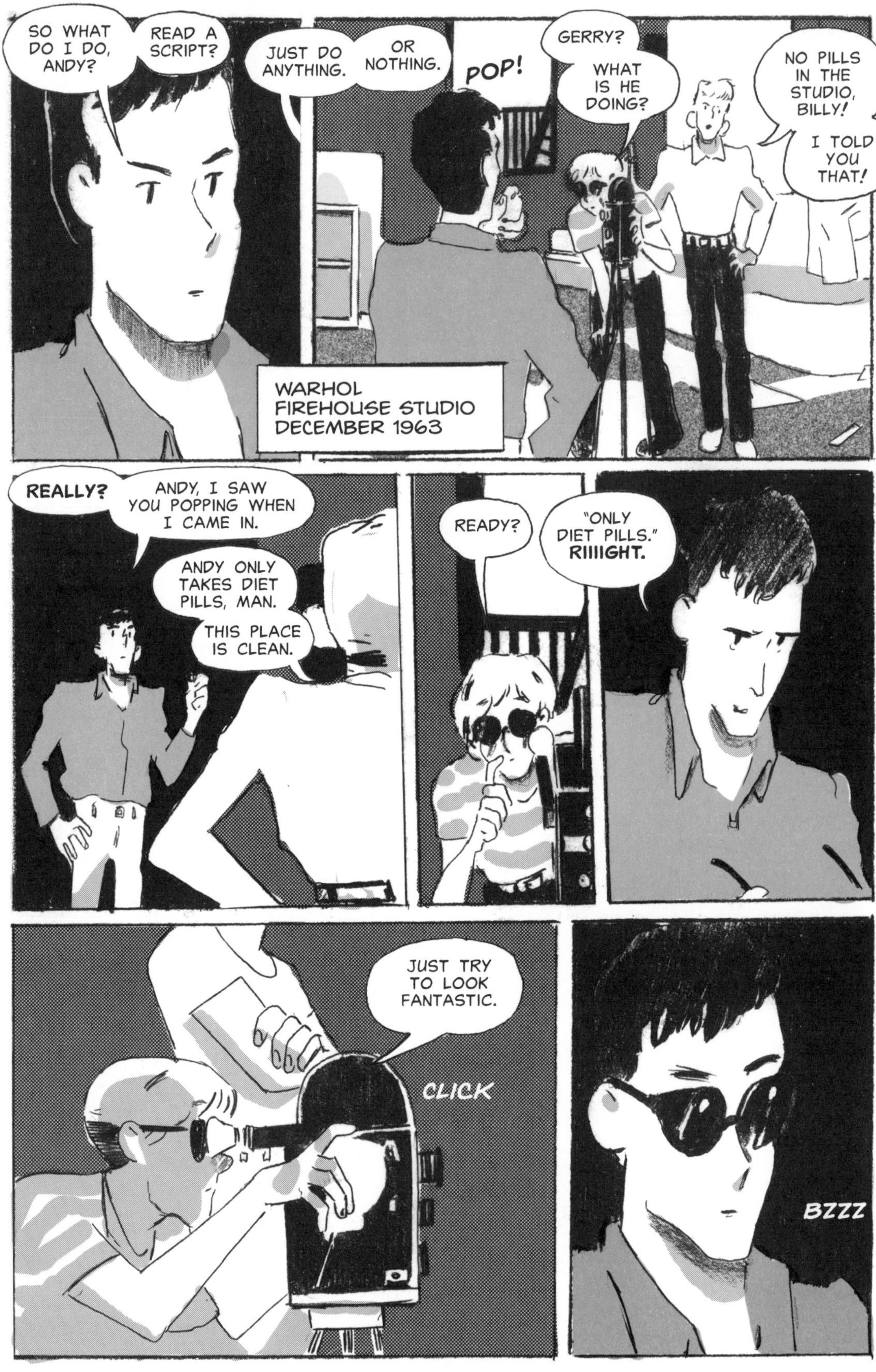
SO WHAT DO I DO, ANDY?
READ A SCRIPT?
JUST DO ANYTHING.
OR NOTHING.
WARHOL FIREHOUSE STUDIO DECEMBER 1963
POP!
GERRY?
WHAT IS HE DOING?
NO PILLS IN THE STUDIO, BILLY!
I TOLD YOU THAT!
REALLY?
ANDY, I SAW YOU POPPING WHEN I CAME IN.
ANDY ONLY TAKES DIET PILLS, MAN.
THIS PLACE IS CLEAN.
READY?
"ONLY DIET PILLS." RIIIIGHT.
JUST TRY TO LOOK FANTASTIC.
CLICK
BZZZ

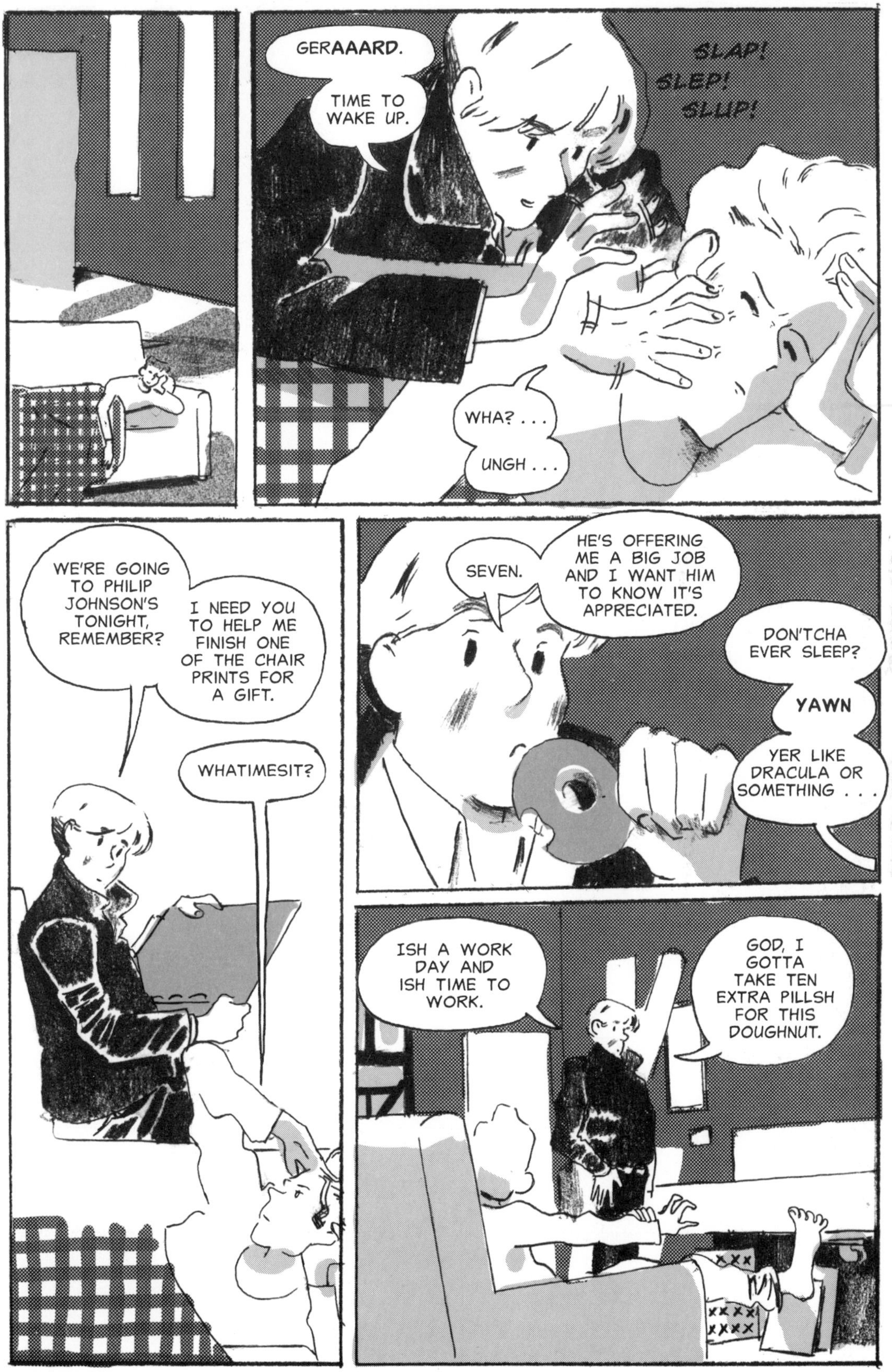
GERAAARD.
TIME TO WAKE UP.
SLAP! SLEP! SLUP!
WHA? . . .
UNGH . . .
WE'RE GOING TO PHILIP JOHNSON'S TONIGHT, REMEMBER?
I NEED YOU TO HELP ME FINISH ONE OF THE CHAIR PRINTS FOR A GIFT.
WHATIMESIT?
SEVEN.
HE'S OFFERING ME A BIG JOB AND I WANT HIM TO KNOW IT'S APPRECIATED.
DON'TCHA EVER SLEEP?
YAWN
YER LIKE DRACULA OR SOMETHING . . .
ISH A WORK DAY AND ISH TIME TO WORK.
GOD, I GOTTA TAKE TEN EXTRA PILLSH FOR THIS DOUGHNUT.

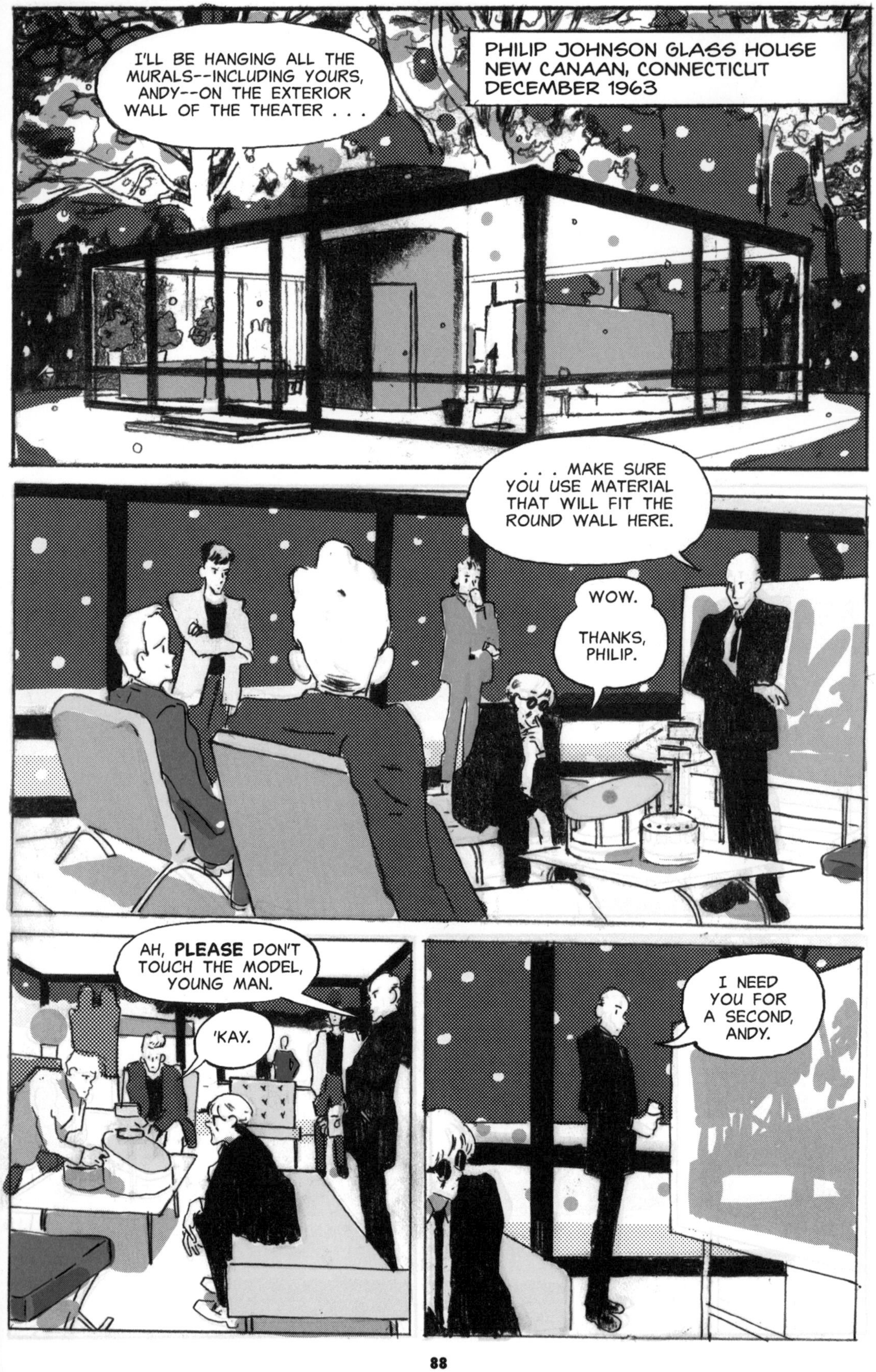
PHILIP JOHNSON GLASS HOUSE
NEW CANAAN, CONNECTICUT
DECEMBER 1963
I'LL BE HANGING ALL THE MURALS--INCLUDING YOURS, ANDY--ON THE EXTERIOR WALL OF THE THEATER . . .
. . . MAKE SURE YOU USE MATERIAL THAT WILL FIT THE ROUND WALL HERE.
WOW.
THANKS, PHILIP.
AH, **PLEASE** DON'T TOUCH THE MODEL, YOUNG MAN.
'KAY.
I NEED YOU FOR A SECOND, ANDY.

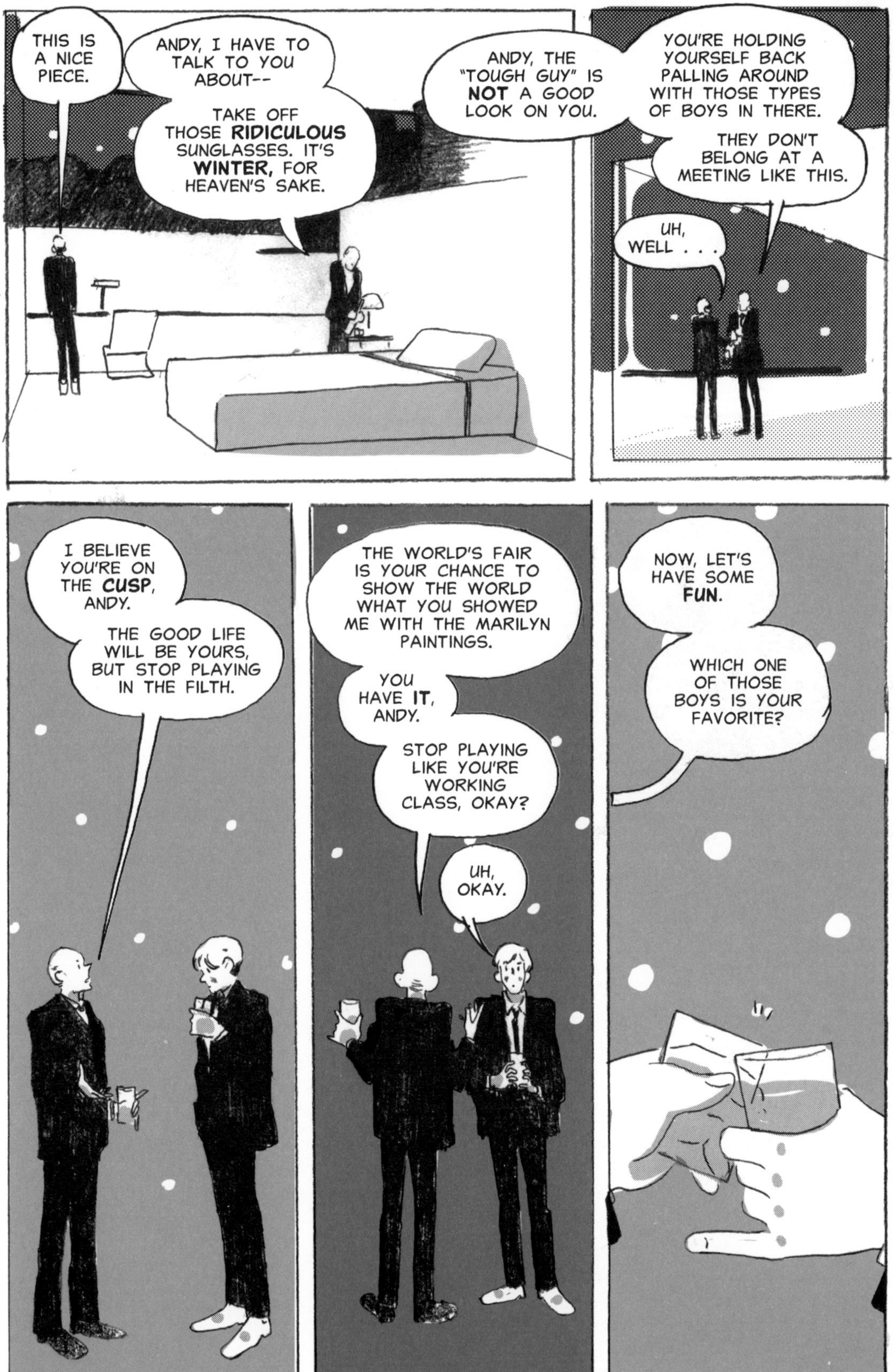
THIS IS A NICE PIECE.
ANDY, I HAVE TO TALK TO YOU ABOUT--
TAKE OFF THOSE **RIDICULOUS** SUNGLASSES. IT'S **WINTER,** FOR HEAVEN'S SAKE.
ANDY, THE "TOUGH GUY" IS **NOT** A GOOD LOOK ON YOU.
YOU'RE HOLDING YOURSELF BACK PALLING AROUND WITH THOSE TYPES OF BOYS IN THERE.
THEY DON'T BELONG AT A MEETING LIKE THIS.
UH, WELL . . .
I BELIEVE YOU'RE ON THE **CUSP**, ANDY.
THE GOOD LIFE WILL BE YOURS, BUT STOP PLAYING IN THE FILTH.
THE WORLD'S FAIR IS YOUR CHANCE TO SHOW THE WORLD WHAT YOU SHOWED ME WITH THE MARILYN PAINTINGS.
YOU HAVE **IT**, ANDY.
STOP PLAYING LIKE YOU'RE WORKING CLASS, OKAY?
UH, OKAY.
NOW, LET'S HAVE SOME **FUN**.
WHICH ONE OF THOSE BOYS IS YOUR FAVORITE?

CHAPTER TWELVE

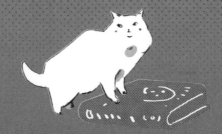

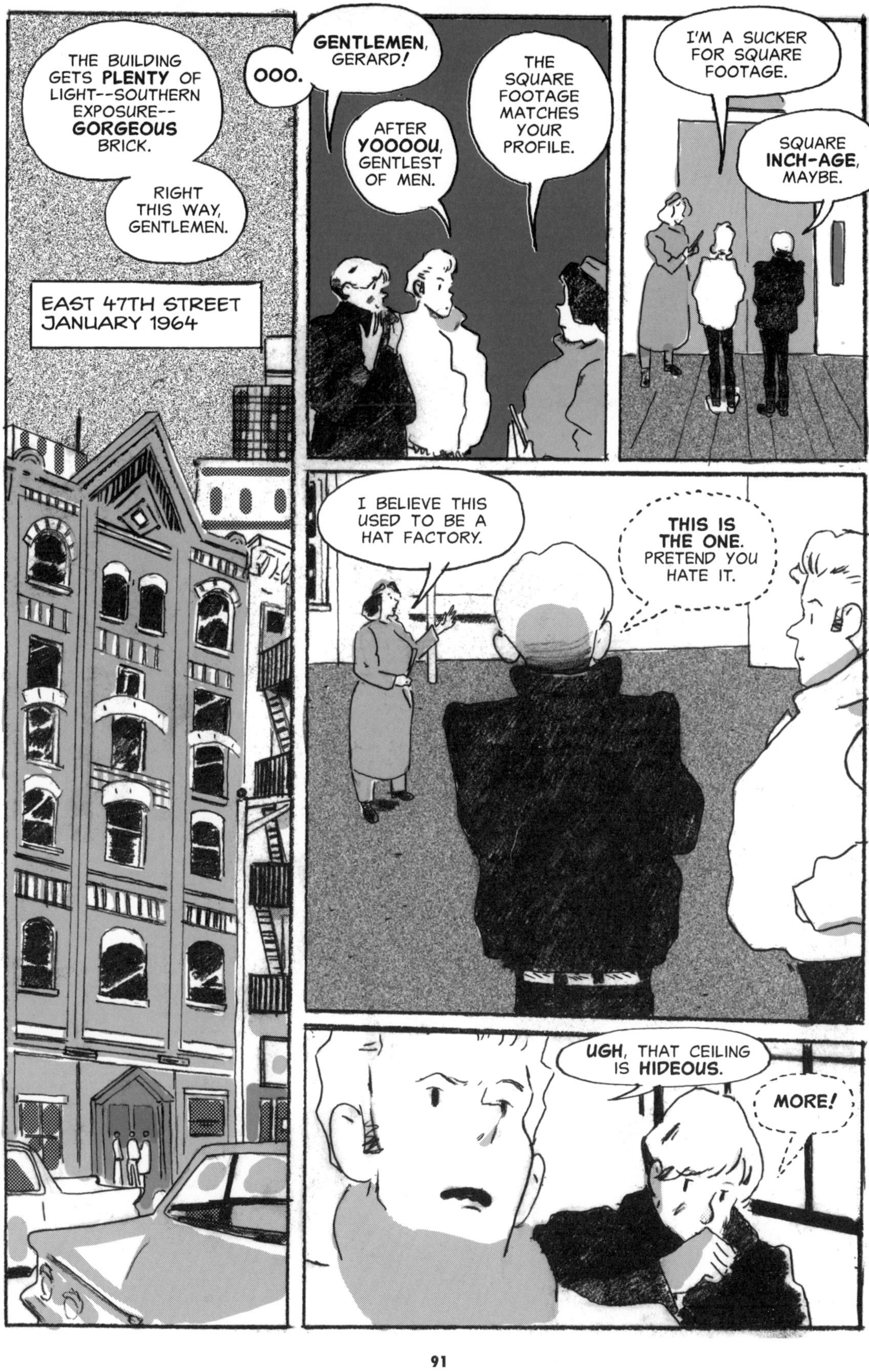

THE BUILDING GETS **PLENTY** OF LIGHT--SOUTHERN EXPOSURE--**GORGEOUS** BRICK.
RIGHT THIS WAY, GENTLEMEN.
EAST 47TH STREET JANUARY 1964
OOO.
GENTLEMEN, GERARD!
AFTER **YOOOOU,** GENTLEST OF MEN.
THE SQUARE FOOTAGE MATCHES YOUR PROFILE.
I'M A SUCKER FOR SQUARE FOOTAGE.
SQUARE **INCH-AGE,** MAYBE.
I BELIEVE THIS USED TO BE A HAT FACTORY.
THIS IS THE ONE. PRETEND YOU HATE IT.
UGH, THAT CEILING IS **HIDEOUS.**
MORE!

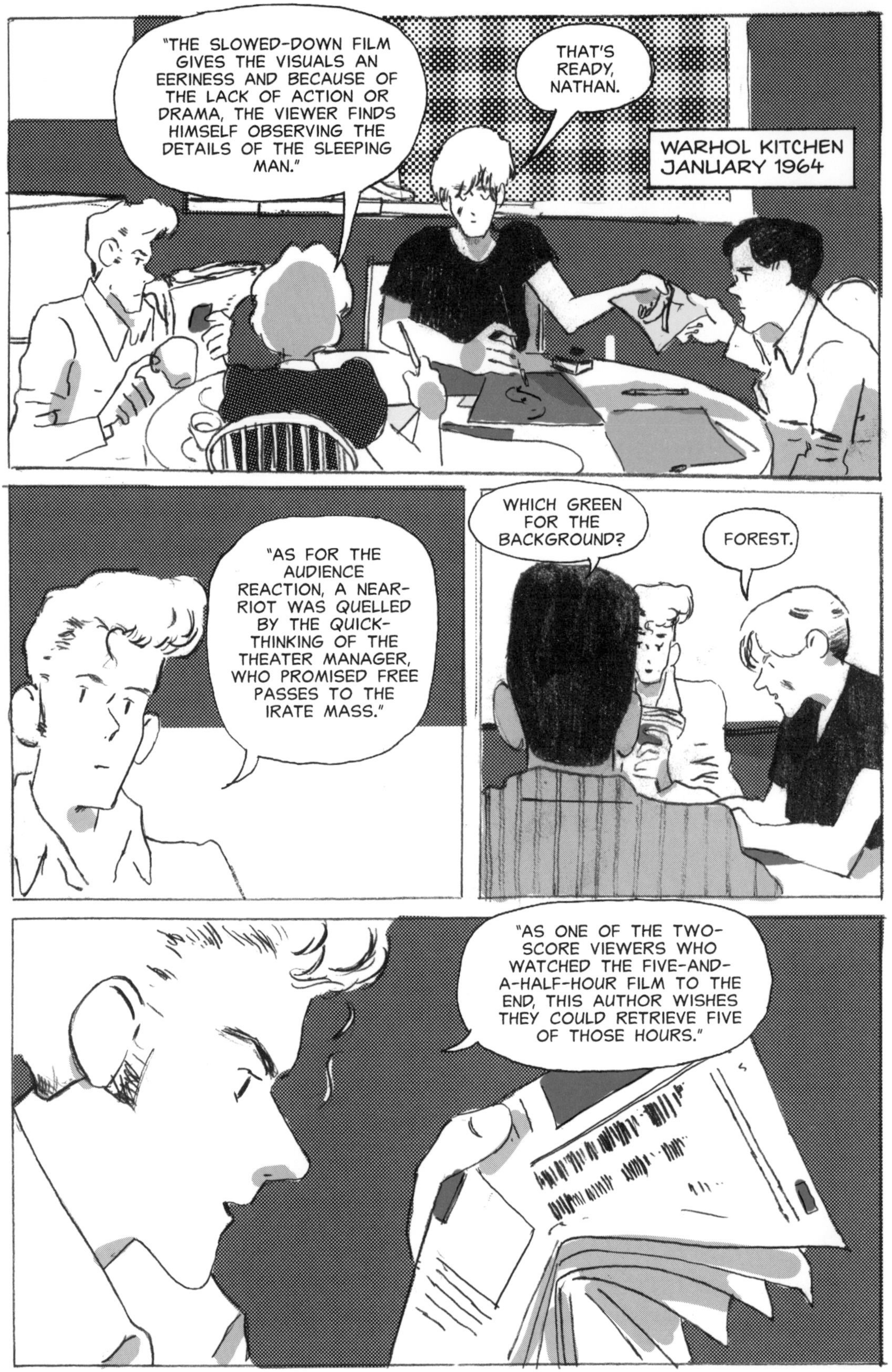
"THE SLOWED-DOWN FILM GIVES THE VISUALS AN EERINESS AND BECAUSE OF THE LACK OF ACTION OR DRAMA, THE VIEWER FINDS HIMSELF OBSERVING THE DETAILS OF THE SLEEPING MAN."
THAT'S READY, NATHAN.
WARHOL KITCHEN JANUARY 1964
"AS FOR THE AUDIENCE REACTION, A NEAR-RIOT WAS QUELLED BY THE QUICK-THINKING OF THE THEATER MANAGER, WHO PROMISED FREE PASSES TO THE IRATE MASS."
WHICH GREEN FOR THE BACKGROUND?
FOREST.
"AS ONE OF THE TWO-SCORE VIEWERS WHO WATCHED THE FIVE-AND-A-HALF-HOUR FILM TO THE END, THIS AUTHOR WISHES THEY COULD RETRIEVE FIVE OF THOSE HOURS."

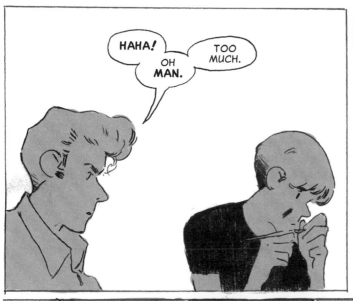

HAHA! OH MAN. TOO MUCH.

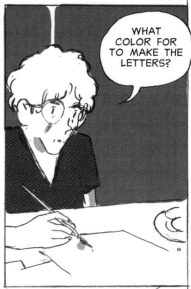

WHAT COLOR FOR TO MAKE THE LETTERS?

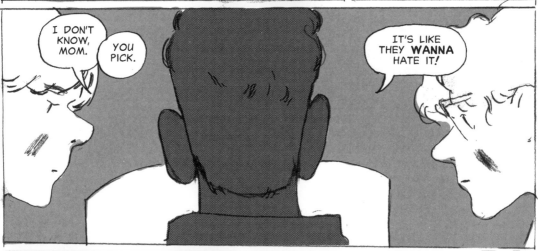

I DON'T KNOW, MOM. YOU PICK.

IT'S LIKE THEY **WANNA** HATE IT!

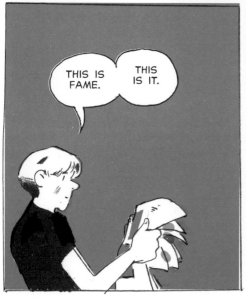

THIS IS FAME. THIS IS IT.

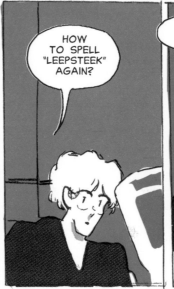

HOW TO SPELL "LEEPSTEEK" AGAIN?

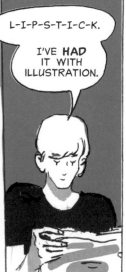

L-I-P-S-T-I-C-K.

I'VE **HAD** IT WITH ILLUSTRATION.

93

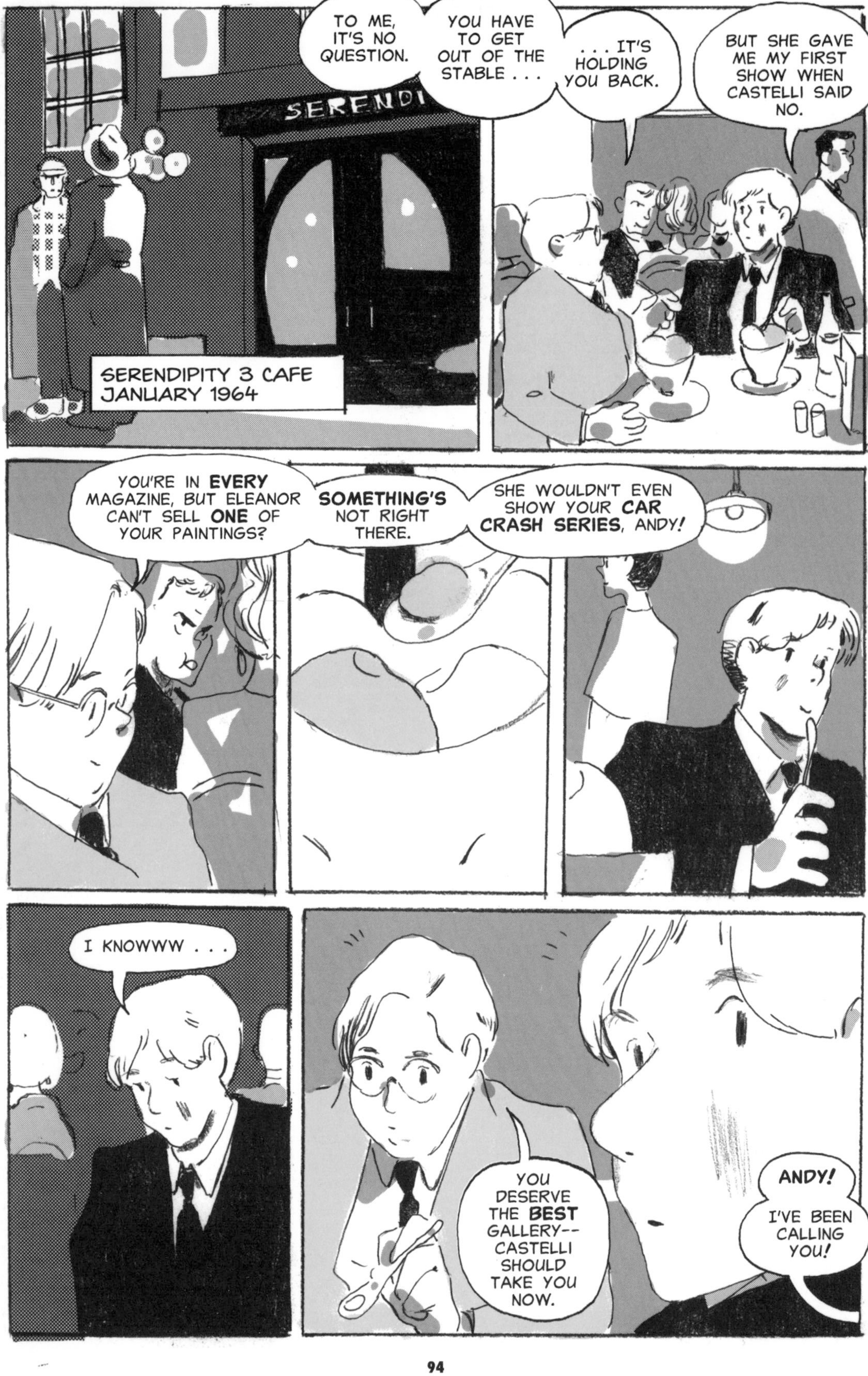

SERENDI
SERENDIPITY 3 CAFE JANUARY 1964
TO ME, IT'S NO QUESTION.
YOU HAVE TO GET OUT OF THE STABLE . . .
. . . IT'S HOLDING YOU BACK.
BUT SHE GAVE ME MY FIRST SHOW WHEN CASTELLI SAID NO.
YOU'RE IN **EVERY** MAGAZINE, BUT ELEANOR CAN'T SELL **ONE** OF YOUR PAINTINGS?
SOMETHING'S NOT RIGHT THERE.
SHE WOULDN'T EVEN SHOW YOUR **CAR CRASH SERIES**, ANDY!
I KNOWWW . . .
YOU DESERVE THE **BEST** GALLERY-- CASTELLI SHOULD TAKE YOU NOW.
ANDY!
I'VE BEEN CALLING YOU!

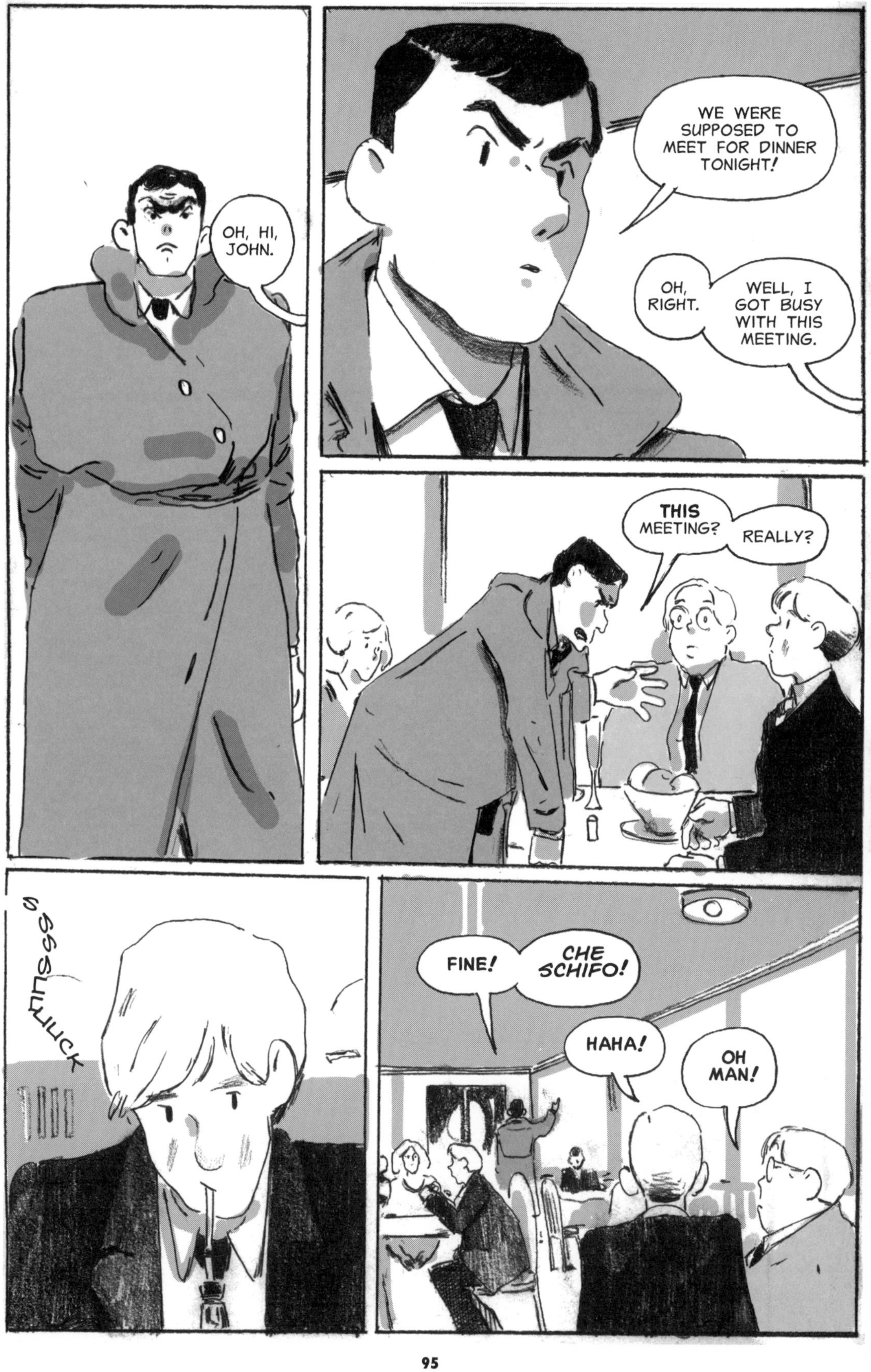
OH, HI, JOHN.
WE WERE SUPPOSED TO MEET FOR DINNER TONIGHT!
OH, RIGHT.
WELL, I GOT BUSY WITH THIS MEETING.
THIS MEETING?
REALLY?
SSSSLLLLLICK
FINE!
CHE SCHIFO!
HAHA!
OH MAN!

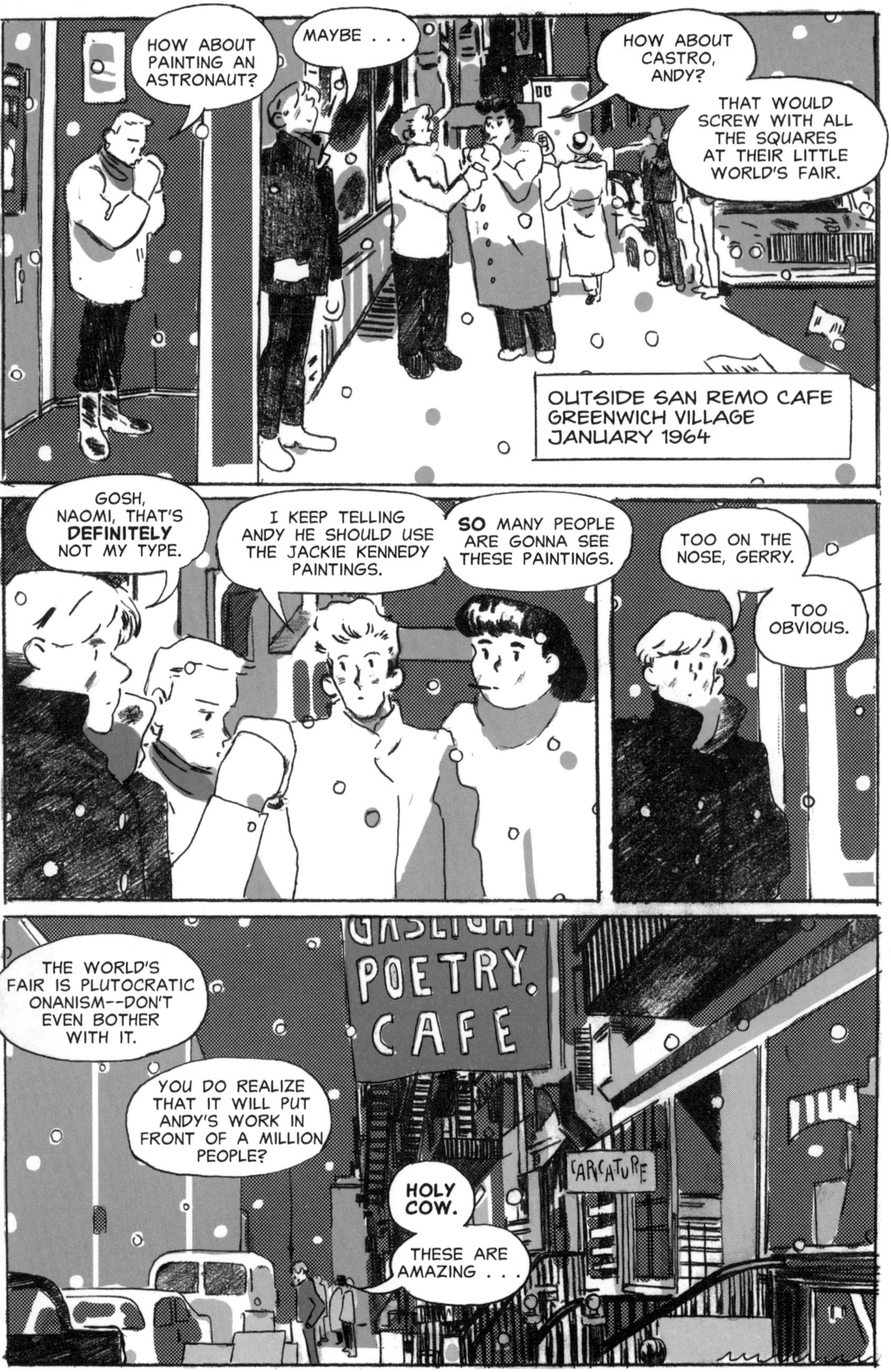
HOW ABOUT PAINTING AN ASTRONAUT?
MAYBE . . .
HOW ABOUT CASTRO, ANDY?
THAT WOULD SCREW WITH ALL THE SQUARES AT THEIR LITTLE WORLD'S FAIR.
OUTSIDE SAN REMO CAFE
GREENWICH VILLAGE
JANUARY 1964
GOSH, NAOMI, THAT'S **DEFINITELY** NOT MY TYPE.
I KEEP TELLING ANDY HE SHOULD USE THE JACKIE KENNEDY PAINTINGS.
SO MANY PEOPLE ARE GONNA SEE THESE PAINTINGS.
TOO ON THE NOSE, GERRY.
TOO OBVIOUS.
POETRY CAFE
THE WORLD'S FAIR IS PLUTOCRATIC ONANISM--DON'T EVEN BOTHER WITH IT.
YOU DO REALIZE THAT IT WILL PUT ANDY'S WORK IN FRONT OF A MILLION PEOPLE?
CARICATURE
HOLY COW.
THESE ARE AMAZING . . .

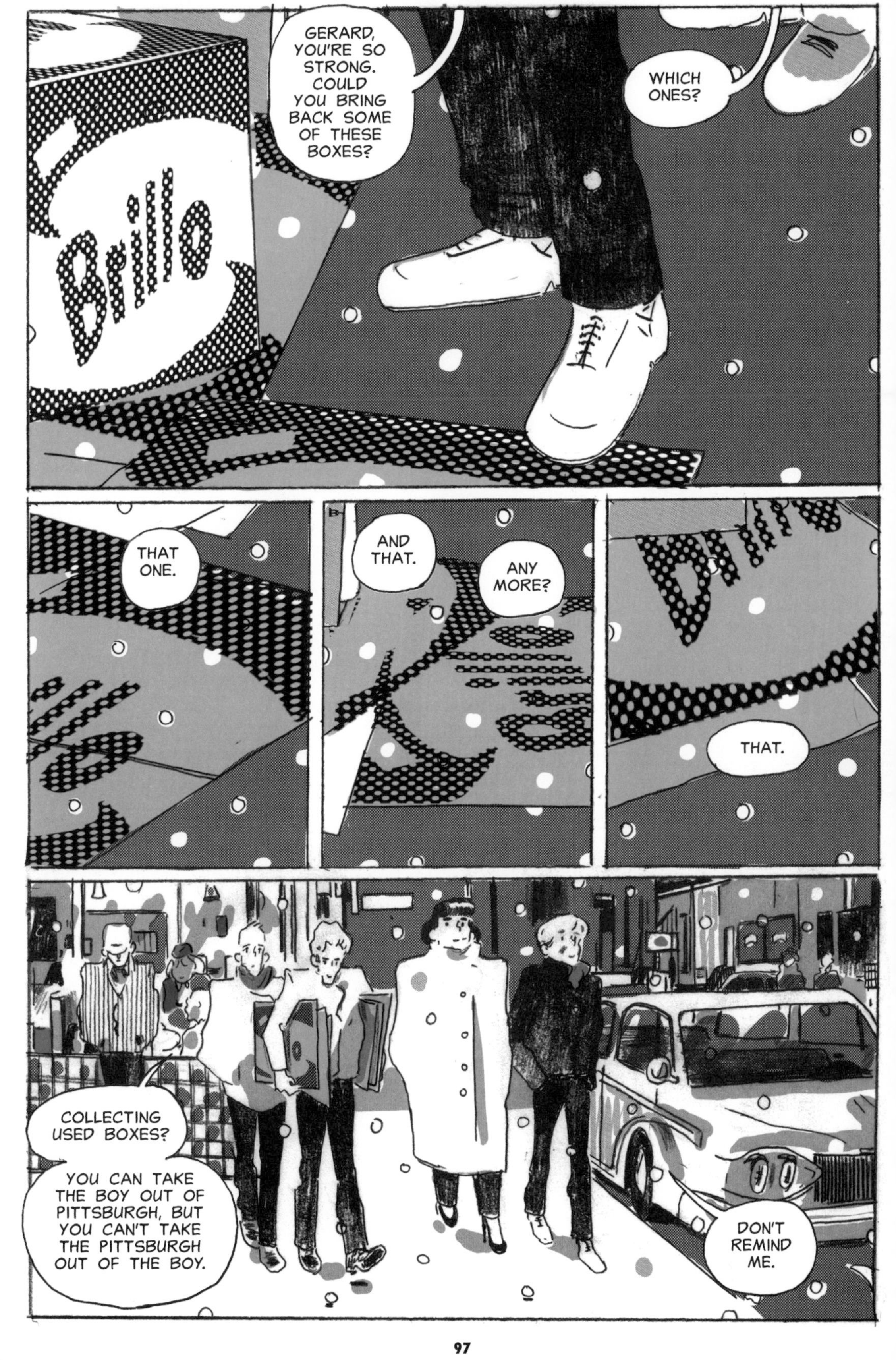
GERARD, YOU'RE SO STRONG. COULD YOU BRING BACK SOME OF THESE BOXES?
WHICH ONES?
Brillo
THAT ONE.
AND THAT.
ANY MORE?
THAT.
COLLECTING USED BOXES?
YOU CAN TAKE THE BOY OUT OF PITTSBURGH, BUT YOU CAN'T TAKE THE PITTSBURGH OUT OF THE BOY.
DON'T REMIND ME.

CHAPTER THIRTEEN

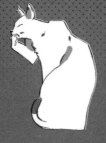

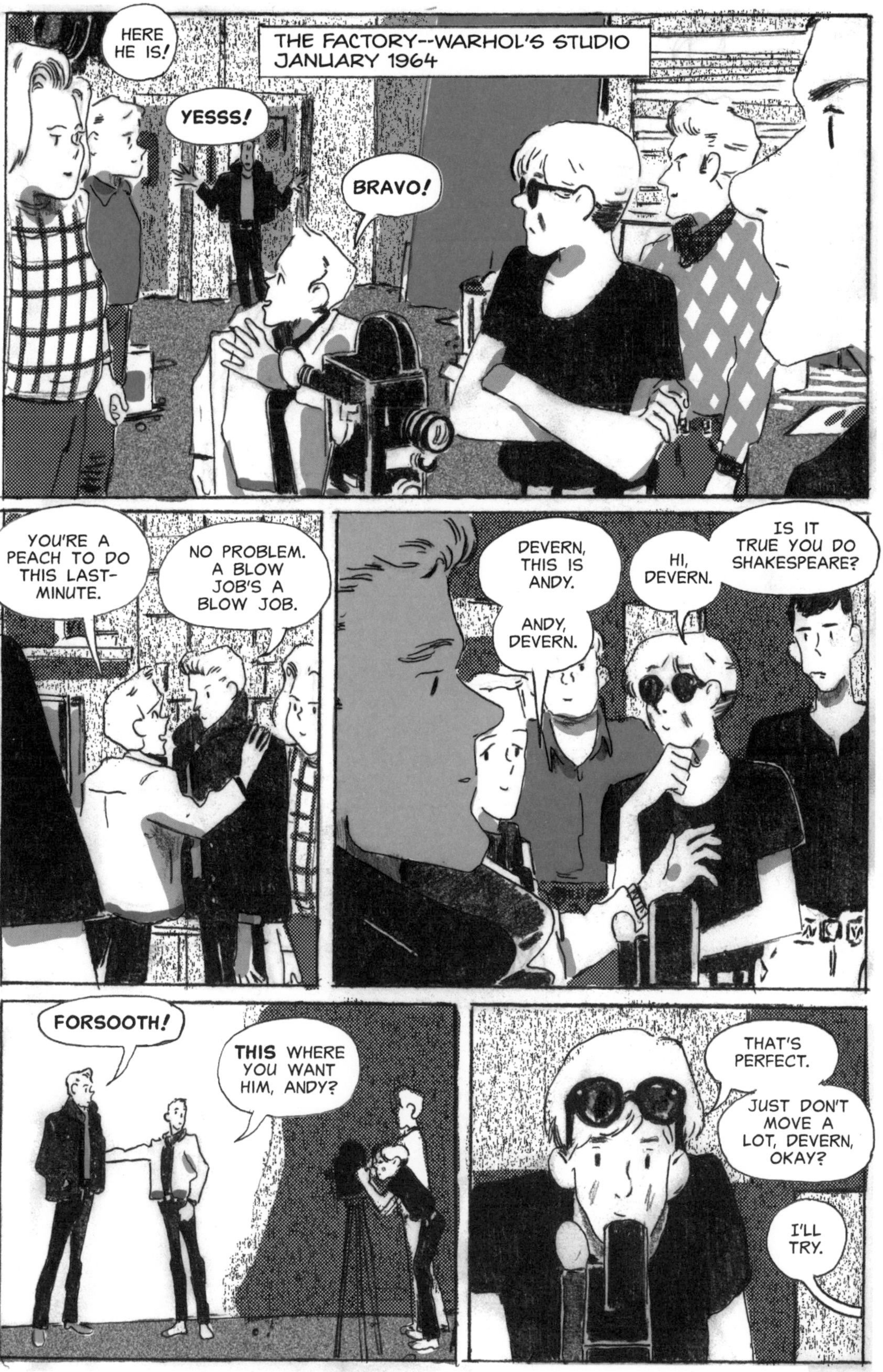
HERE HE IS!
THE FACTORY--WARHOL'S STUDIO JANUARY 1964
YESSS!
BRAVO!
YOU'RE A PEACH TO DO THIS LAST-MINUTE.
NO PROBLEM. A BLOW JOB'S A BLOW JOB.
DEVERN, THIS IS ANDY.
ANDY, DEVERN.
HI, DEVERN.
IS IT TRUE YOU DO SHAKESPEARE?
FORSOOTH!
THIS WHERE YOU WANT HIM, ANDY?
THAT'S PERFECT.
JUST DON'T MOVE A LOT, DEVERN, OKAY?
I'LL TRY.

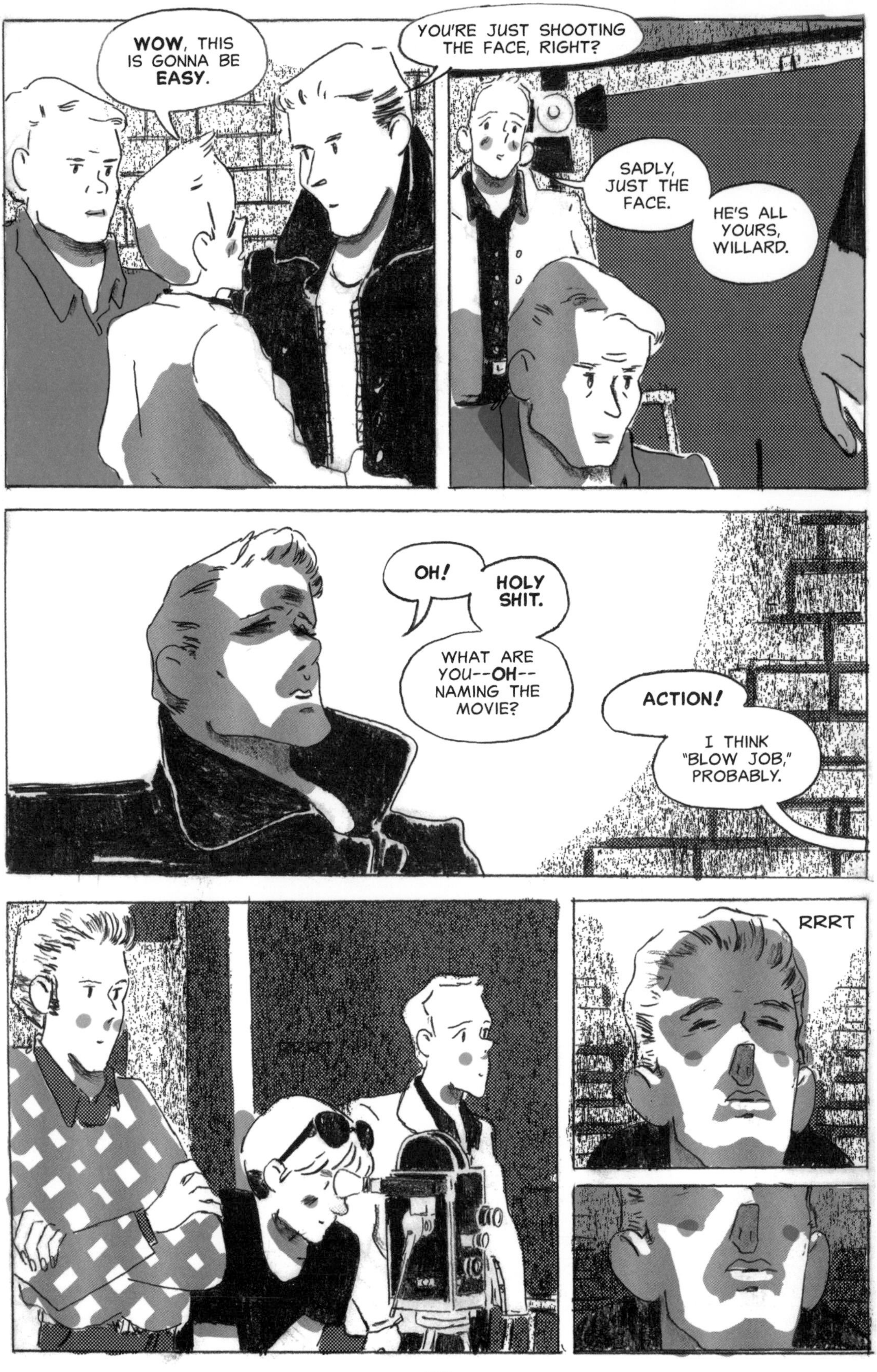
WOW, THIS IS GONNA BE EASY.
YOU'RE JUST SHOOTING THE FACE, RIGHT?
SADLY, JUST THE FACE.
HE'S ALL YOURS, WILLARD.
OH!
HOLY SHIT.
WHAT ARE YOU--OH--NAMING THE MOVIE?
ACTION!
I THINK "BLOW JOB," PROBABLY.
RRRT

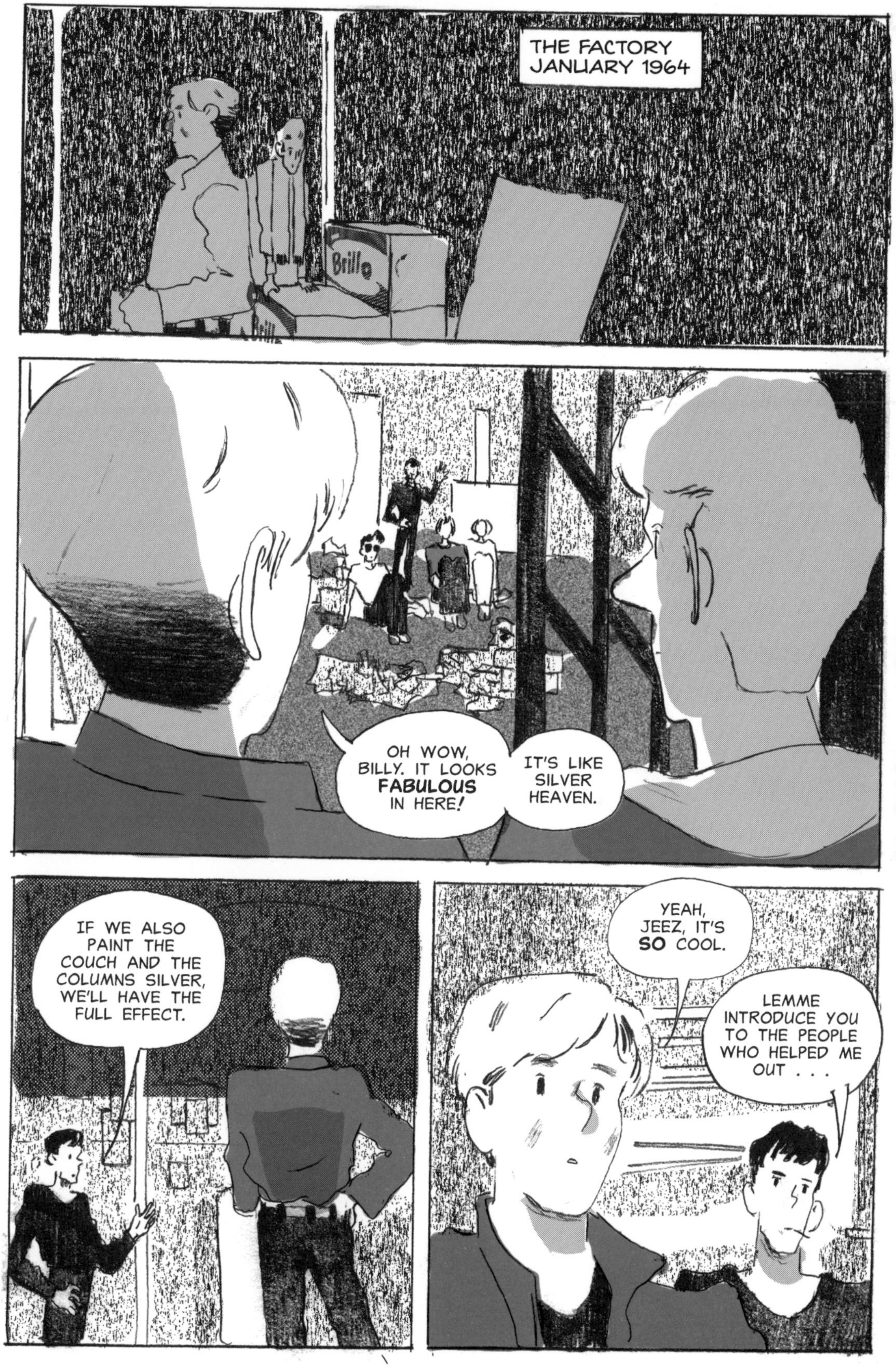
THE FACTORY JANUARY 1964
Brillo
OH WOW, BILLY. IT LOOKS **FABULOUS** IN HERE!
IT'S LIKE SILVER HEAVEN.
IF WE ALSO PAINT THE COUCH AND THE COLUMNS SILVER, WE'LL HAVE THE FULL EFFECT.
YEAH, JEEZ, IT'S **SO** COOL.
LEMME INTRODUCE YOU TO THE PEOPLE WHO HELPED ME OUT . . .

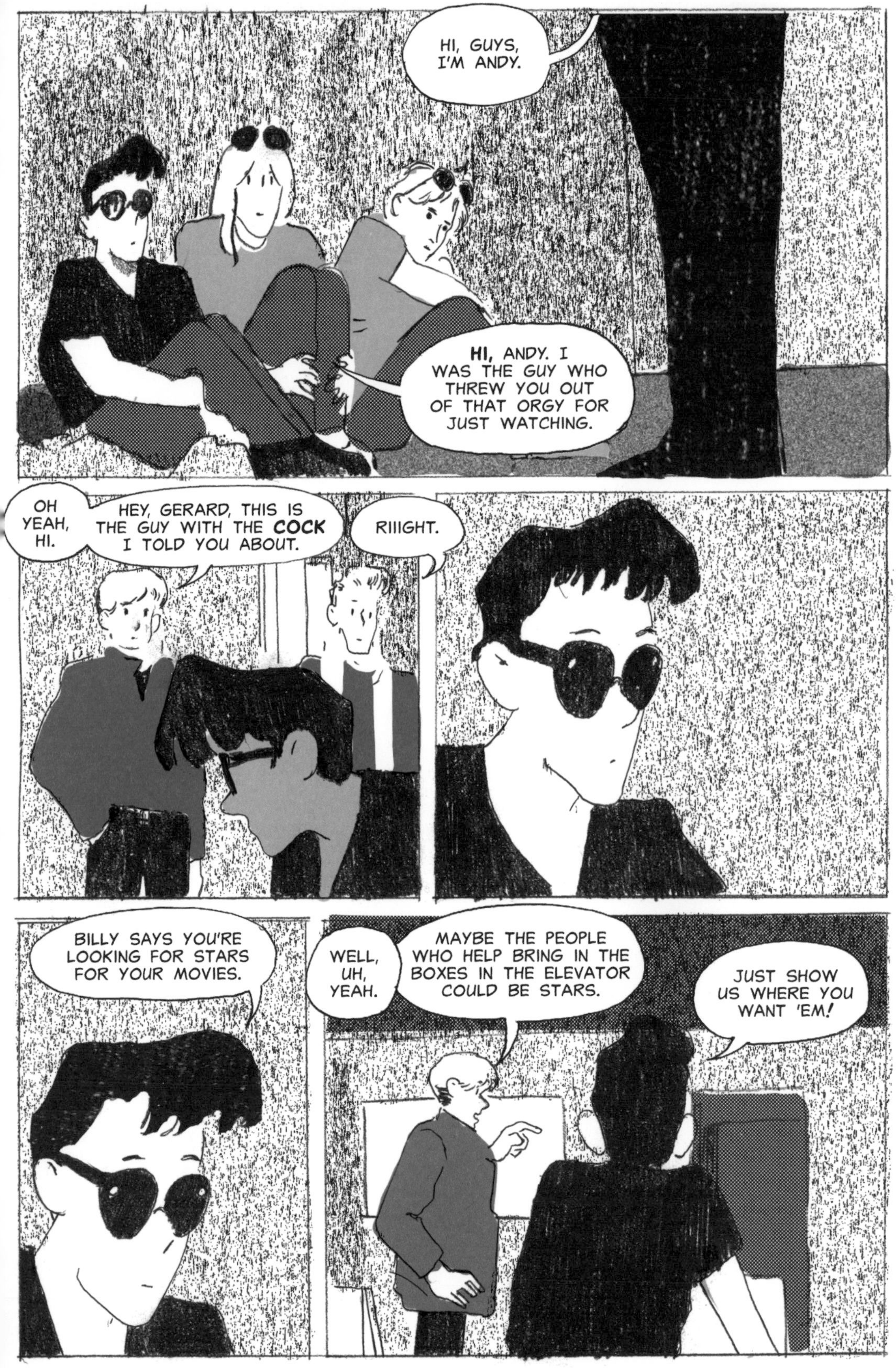
HI, GUYS, I'M ANDY.
HI, ANDY. I WAS THE GUY WHO THREW YOU OUT OF THAT ORGY FOR JUST WATCHING.
OH YEAH, HI.
HEY, GERARD, THIS IS THE GUY WITH THE COCK I TOLD YOU ABOUT.
RIIIGHT.
BILLY SAYS YOU'RE LOOKING FOR STARS FOR YOUR MOVIES.
WELL, UH, YEAH.
MAYBE THE PEOPLE WHO HELP BRING IN THE BOXES IN THE ELEVATOR COULD BE STARS.
JUST SHOW US WHERE YOU WANT 'EM!

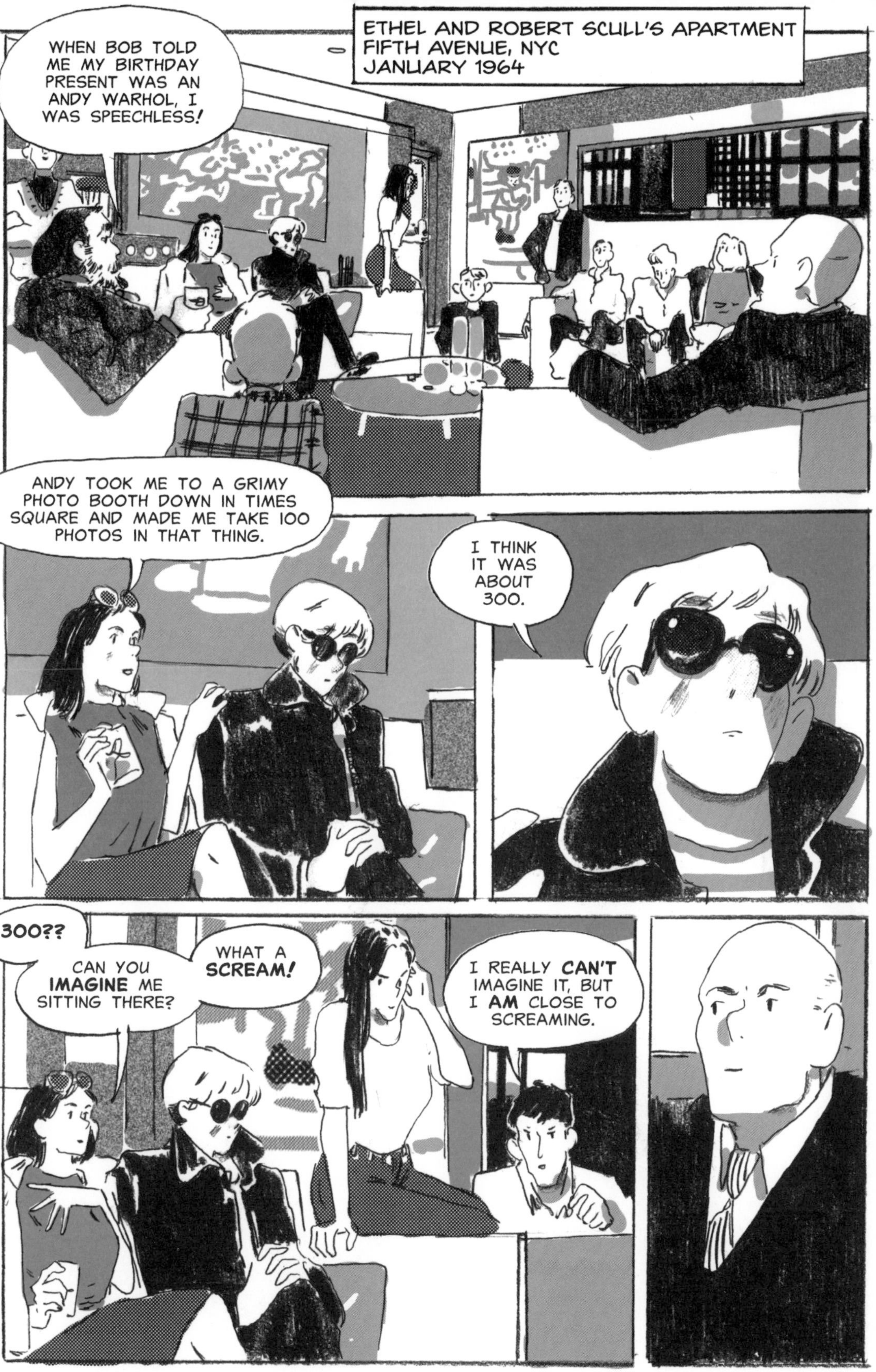
ETHEL AND ROBERT SCULL'S APARTMENT
FIFTH AVENUE, NYC
JANUARY 1964
WHEN BOB TOLD ME MY BIRTHDAY PRESENT WAS AN ANDY WARHOL, I WAS SPEECHLESS!
ANDY TOOK ME TO A GRIMY PHOTO BOOTH DOWN IN TIMES SQUARE AND MADE ME TAKE 100 PHOTOS IN THAT THING.
I THINK IT WAS ABOUT 300.
300??
CAN YOU IMAGINE ME SITTING THERE?
WHAT A SCREAM!
I REALLY CAN'T IMAGINE IT, BUT I AM CLOSE TO SCREAMING.

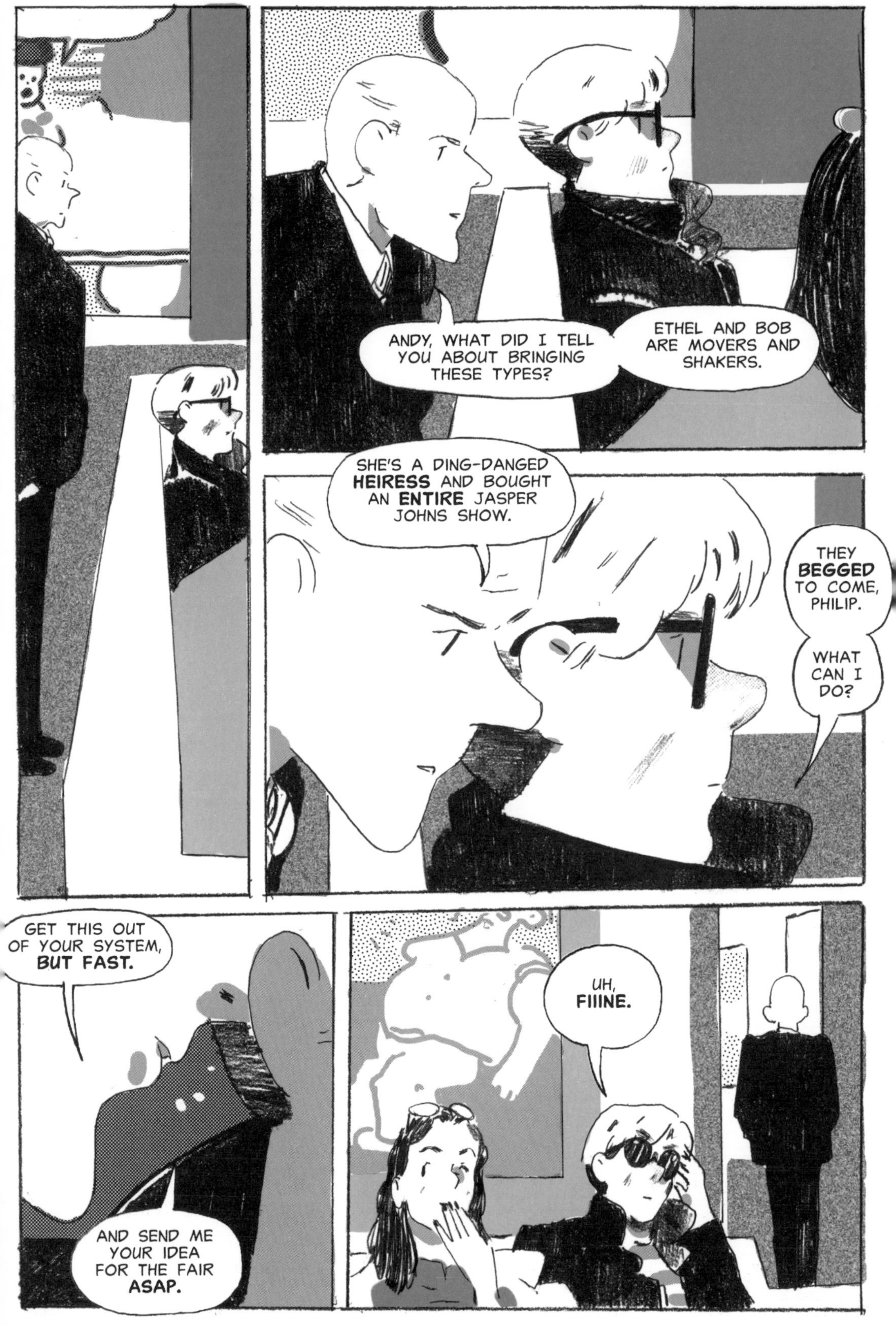
ANDY, WHAT DID I TELL YOU ABOUT BRINGING THESE TYPES?
ETHEL AND BOB ARE MOVERS AND SHAKERS.
SHE'S A DING-DANGED **HEIRESS** AND BOUGHT AN **ENTIRE** JASPER JOHNS SHOW.
THEY **BEGGED** TO COME, PHILIP.
WHAT CAN I DO?
GET THIS OUT OF YOUR SYSTEM, **BUT FAST.**
AND SEND ME YOUR IDEA FOR THE FAIR **ASAP.**
UH, **FIIINE.**

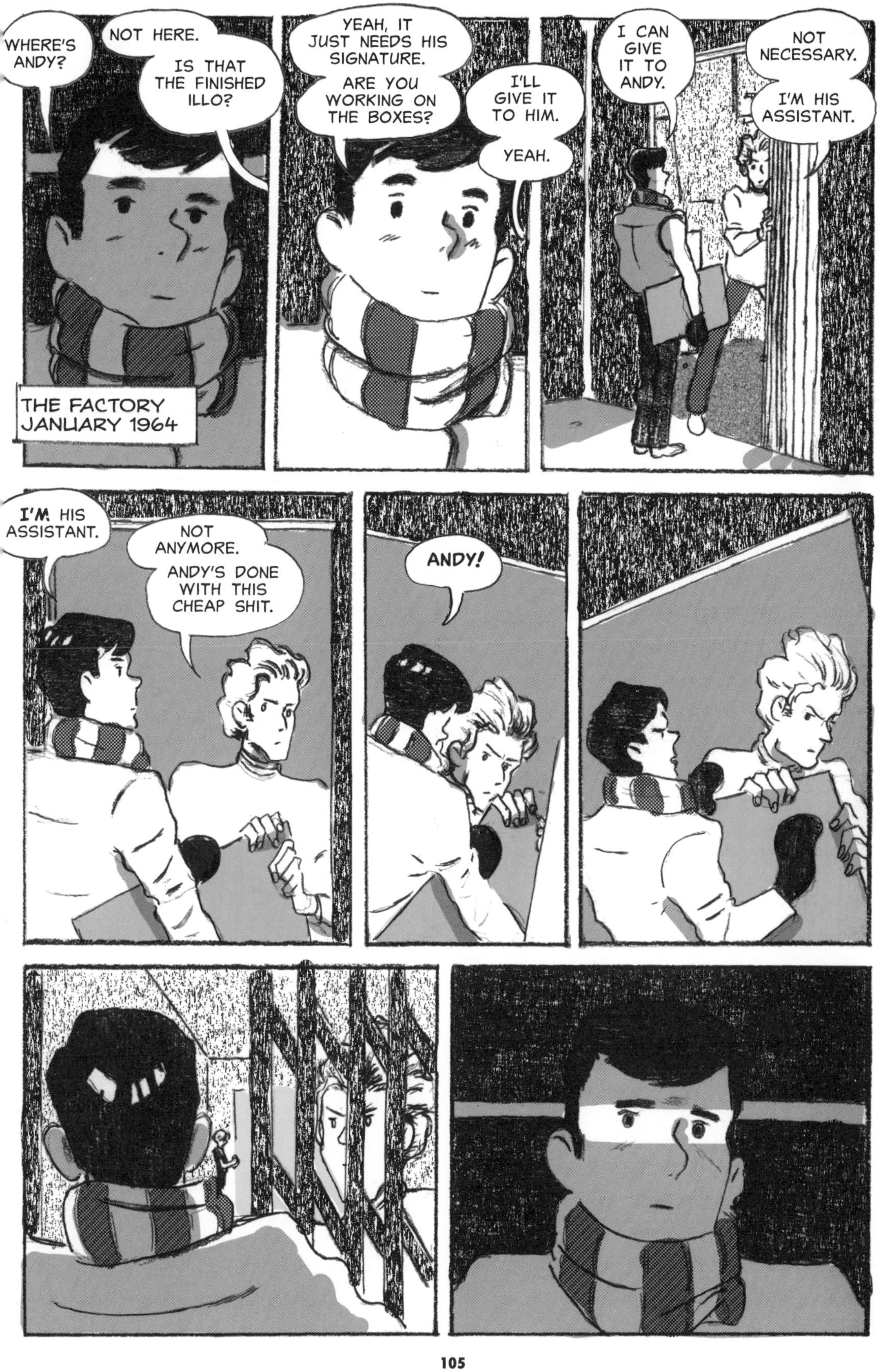
WHERE'S ANDY?
NOT HERE.
IS THAT THE FINISHED ILLO?
THE FACTORY JANUARY 1964
YEAH, IT JUST NEEDS HIS SIGNATURE.
ARE YOU WORKING ON THE BOXES?
I'LL GIVE IT TO HIM.
YEAH.
I CAN GIVE IT TO ANDY.
NOT NECESSARY.
I'M HIS ASSISTANT.
I'M HIS ASSISTANT.
NOT ANYMORE.
ANDY'S DONE WITH THIS CHEAP SHIT.
ANDY!

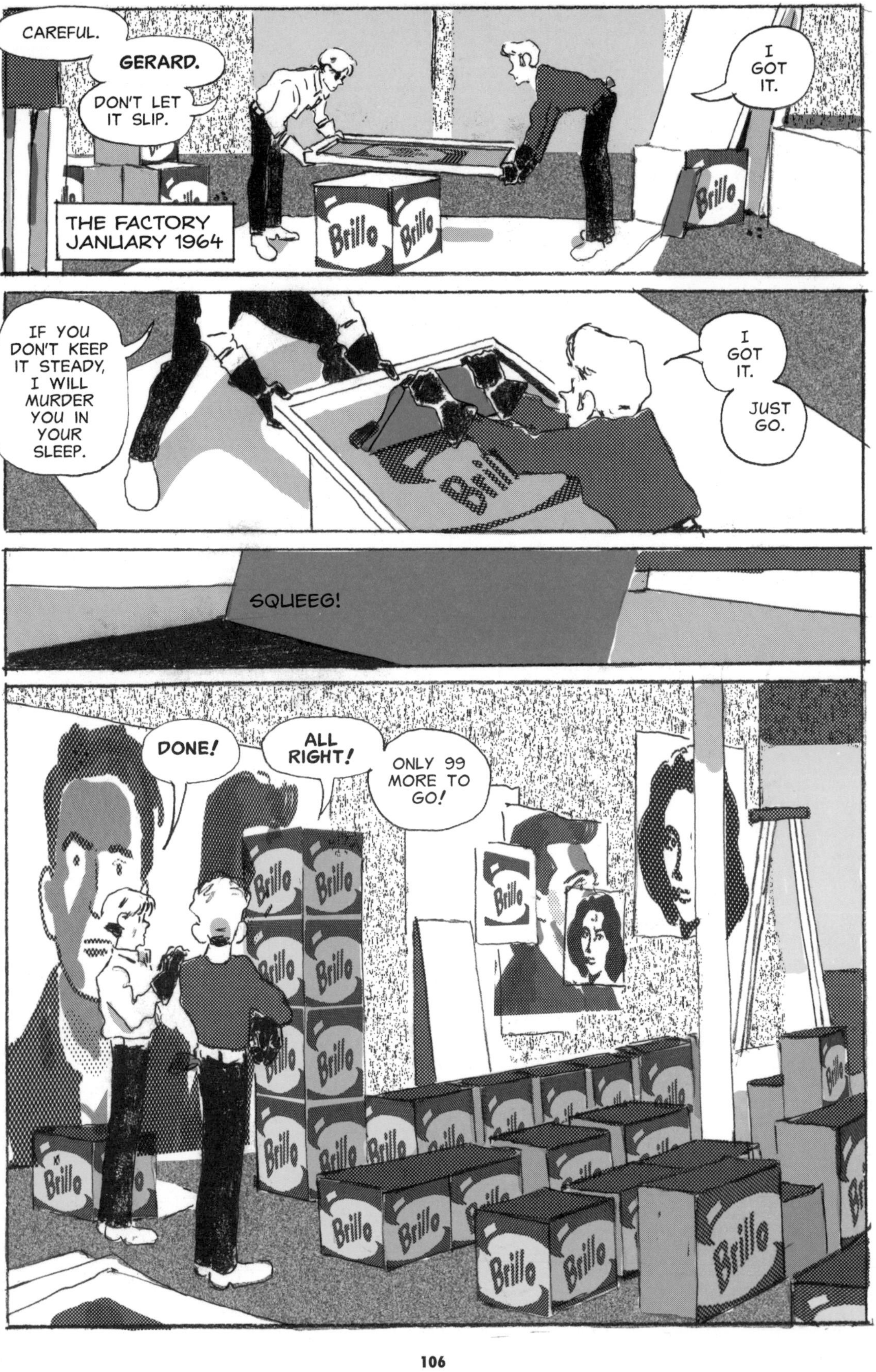
CAREFUL.
GERARD.
DON'T LET IT SLIP.
THE FACTORY JANUARY 1964
I GOT IT.
IF YOU DON'T KEEP IT STEADY, I WILL MURDER YOU IN YOUR SLEEP.
I GOT IT.
JUST GO.
SQUEEG!
DONE!
ALL RIGHT!
ONLY 99 MORE TO GO!

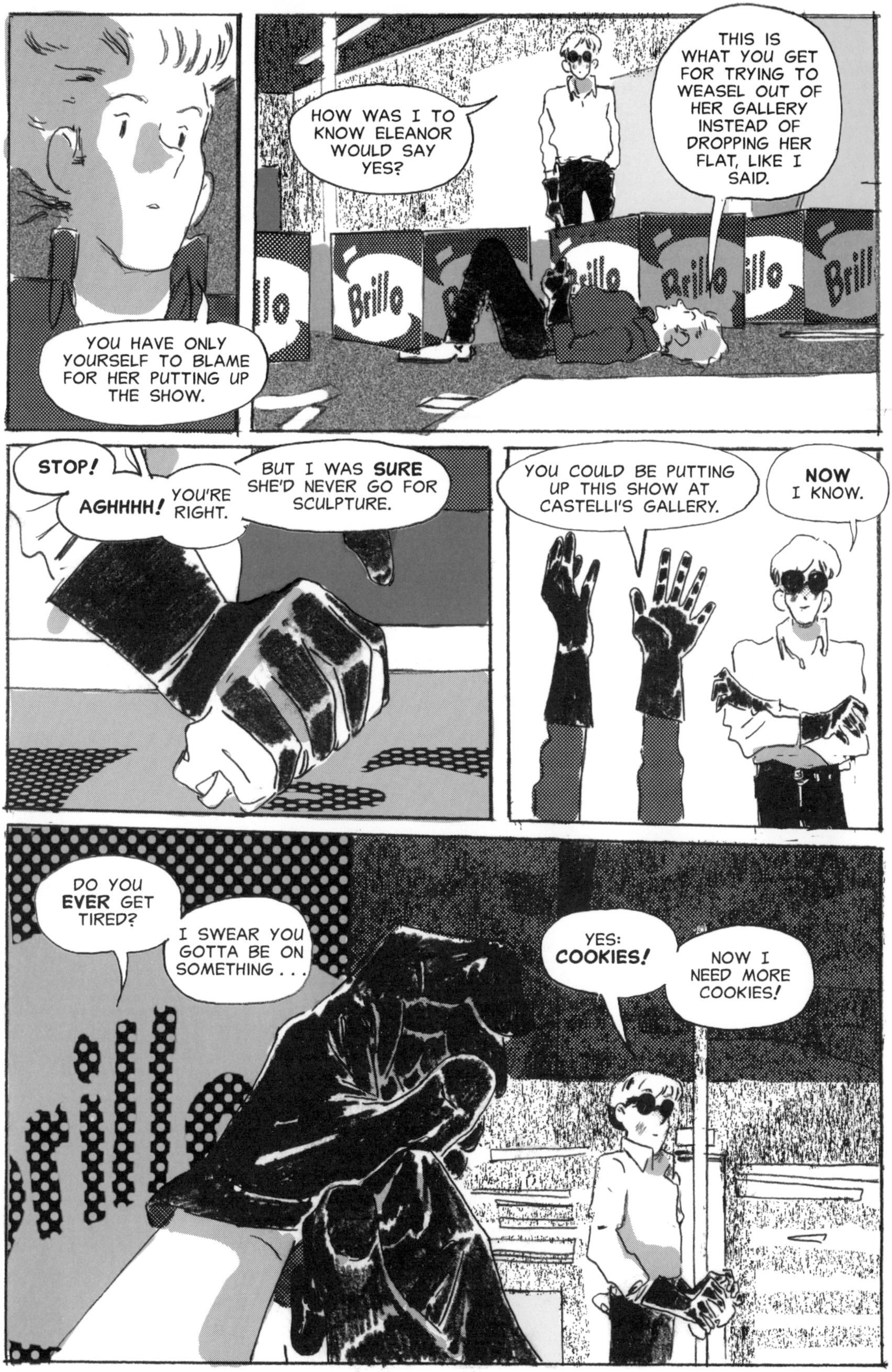

YOU HAVE ONLY YOURSELF TO BLAME FOR HER PUTTING UP THE SHOW.
HOW WAS I TO KNOW ELEANOR WOULD SAY YES?
THIS IS WHAT YOU GET FOR TRYING TO WEASEL OUT OF HER GALLERY INSTEAD OF DROPPING HER FLAT, LIKE I SAID.
Brillo
STOP!
AGHHHH!
YOU'RE RIGHT.
BUT I WAS SURE SHE'D NEVER GO FOR SCULPTURE.
YOU COULD BE PUTTING UP THIS SHOW AT CASTELLI'S GALLERY.
NOW I KNOW.
DO YOU EVER GET TIRED?
I SWEAR YOU GOTTA BE ON SOMETHING . . .
YES: COOKIES!
NOW I NEED MORE COOKIES!

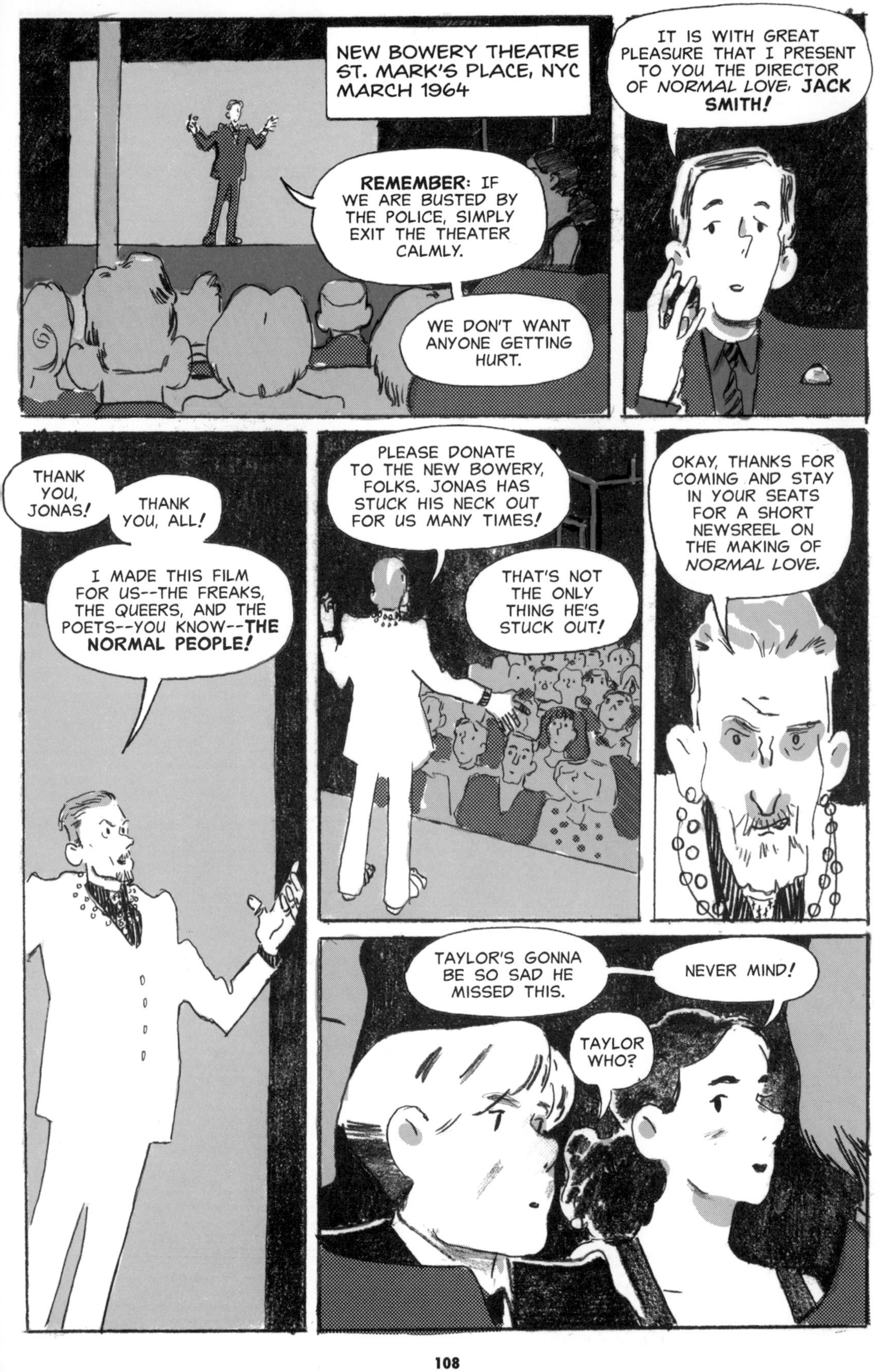

NEW BOWERY THEATRE ST. MARK'S PLACE, NYC MARCH 1964
REMEMBER: IF WE ARE BUSTED BY THE POLICE, SIMPLY EXIT THE THEATER CALMLY.
WE DON'T WANT ANYONE GETTING HURT.
IT IS WITH GREAT PLEASURE THAT I PRESENT TO YOU THE DIRECTOR OF NORMAL LOVE, JACK SMITH!
THANK YOU, JONAS!
THANK YOU, ALL!
I MADE THIS FILM FOR US--THE FREAKS, THE QUEERS, AND THE POETS--YOU KNOW--THE NORMAL PEOPLE!
PLEASE DONATE TO THE NEW BOWERY, FOLKS. JONAS HAS STUCK HIS NECK OUT FOR US MANY TIMES!
THAT'S NOT THE ONLY THING HE'S STUCK OUT!
OKAY, THANKS FOR COMING AND STAY IN YOUR SEATS FOR A SHORT NEWSREEL ON THE MAKING OF NORMAL LOVE.
TAYLOR'S GONNA BE SO SAD HE MISSED THIS.
NEVER MIND!
TAYLOR WHO?

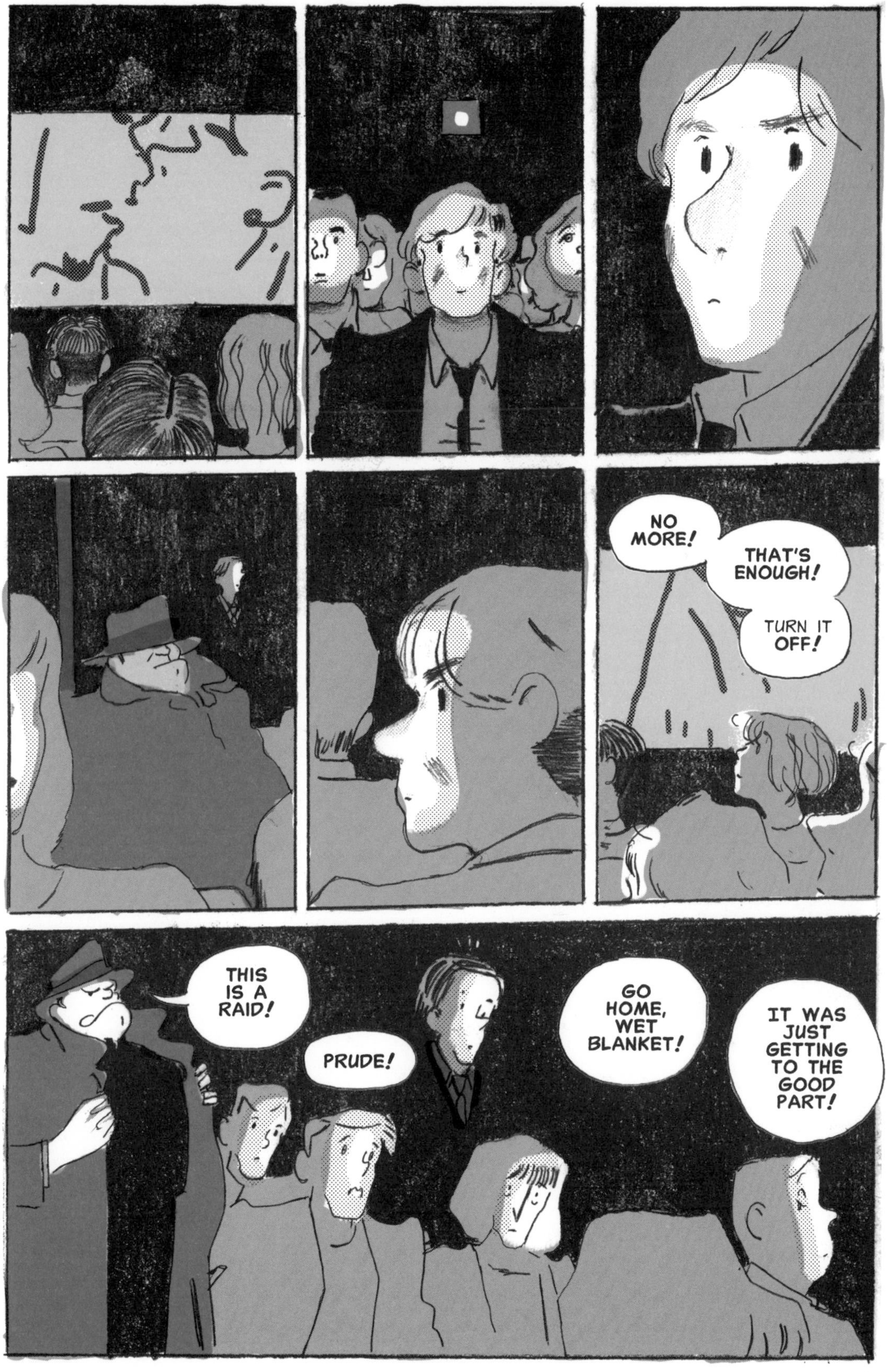
NO MORE!
THAT'S ENOUGH!
TURN IT OFF!
THIS IS A RAID!
PRUDE!
GO HOME, WET BLANKET!
IT WAS JUST GETTING TO THE GOOD PART!

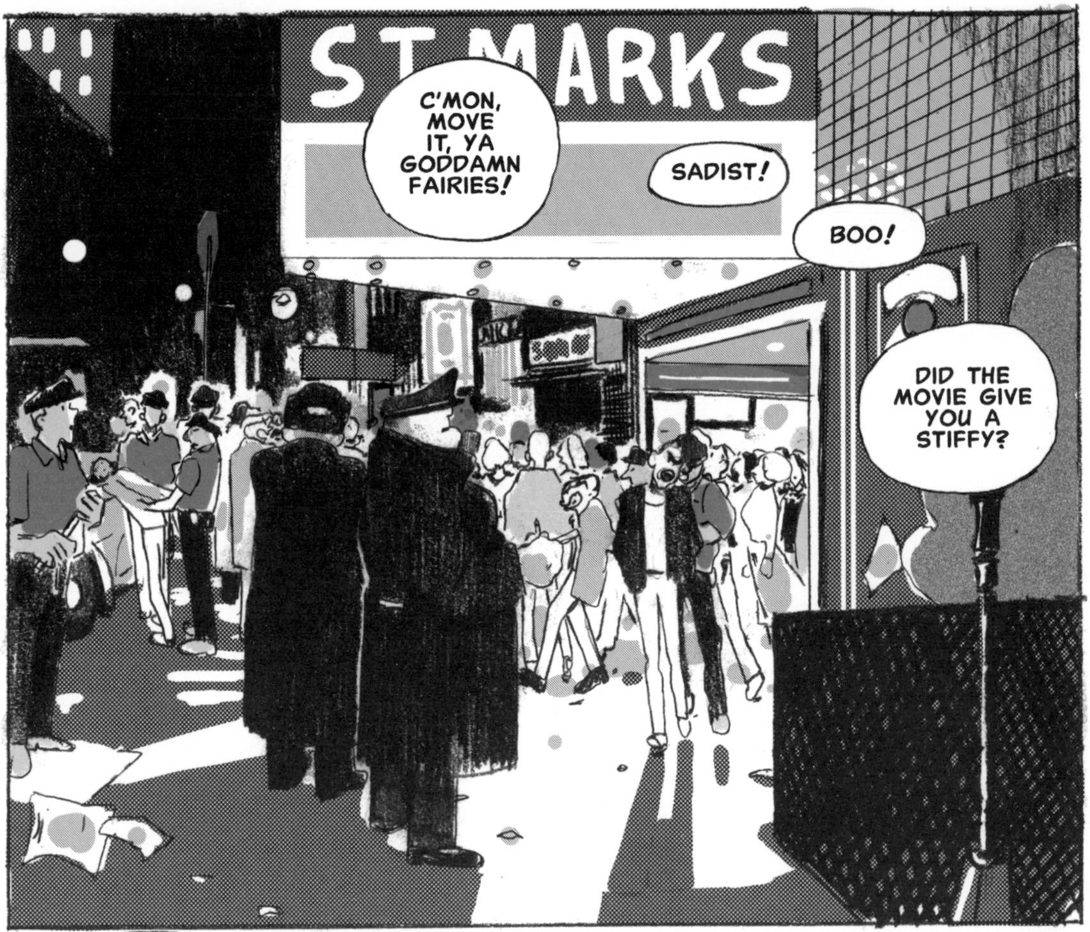
ST MARKS
C'MON, MOVE IT, YA GODDAMN FAIRIES!
SADIST!
BOO!
DID THE MOVIE GIVE YOU A STIFFY?

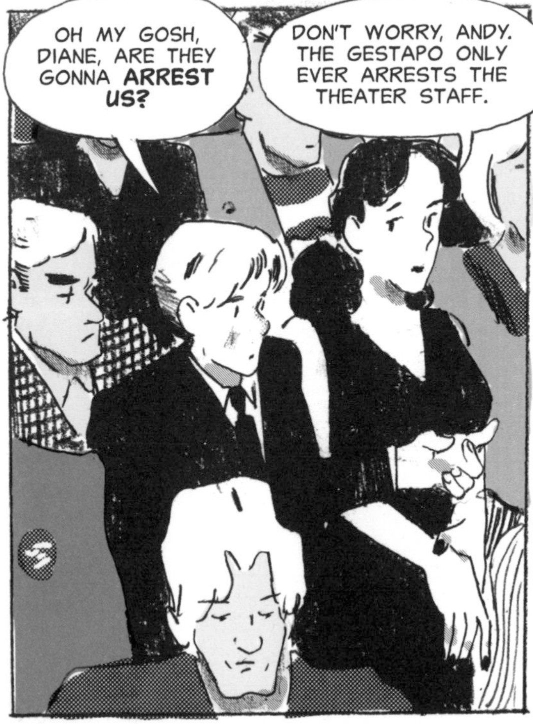
OH MY GOSH, DIANE, ARE THEY GONNA **ARREST US?**
DON'T WORRY, ANDY. THE GESTAPO ONLY EVER ARRESTS THE THEATER STAFF.

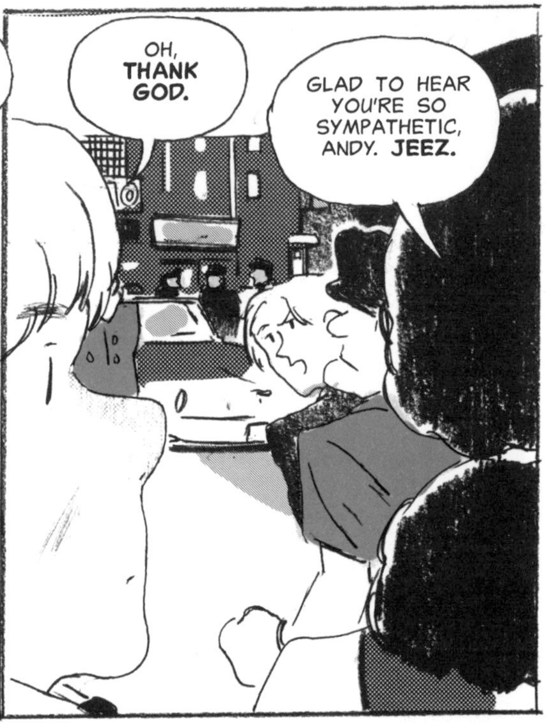
OH, **THANK GOD.**
GLAD TO HEAR YOU'RE SO SYMPATHETIC, ANDY. **JEEZ.**

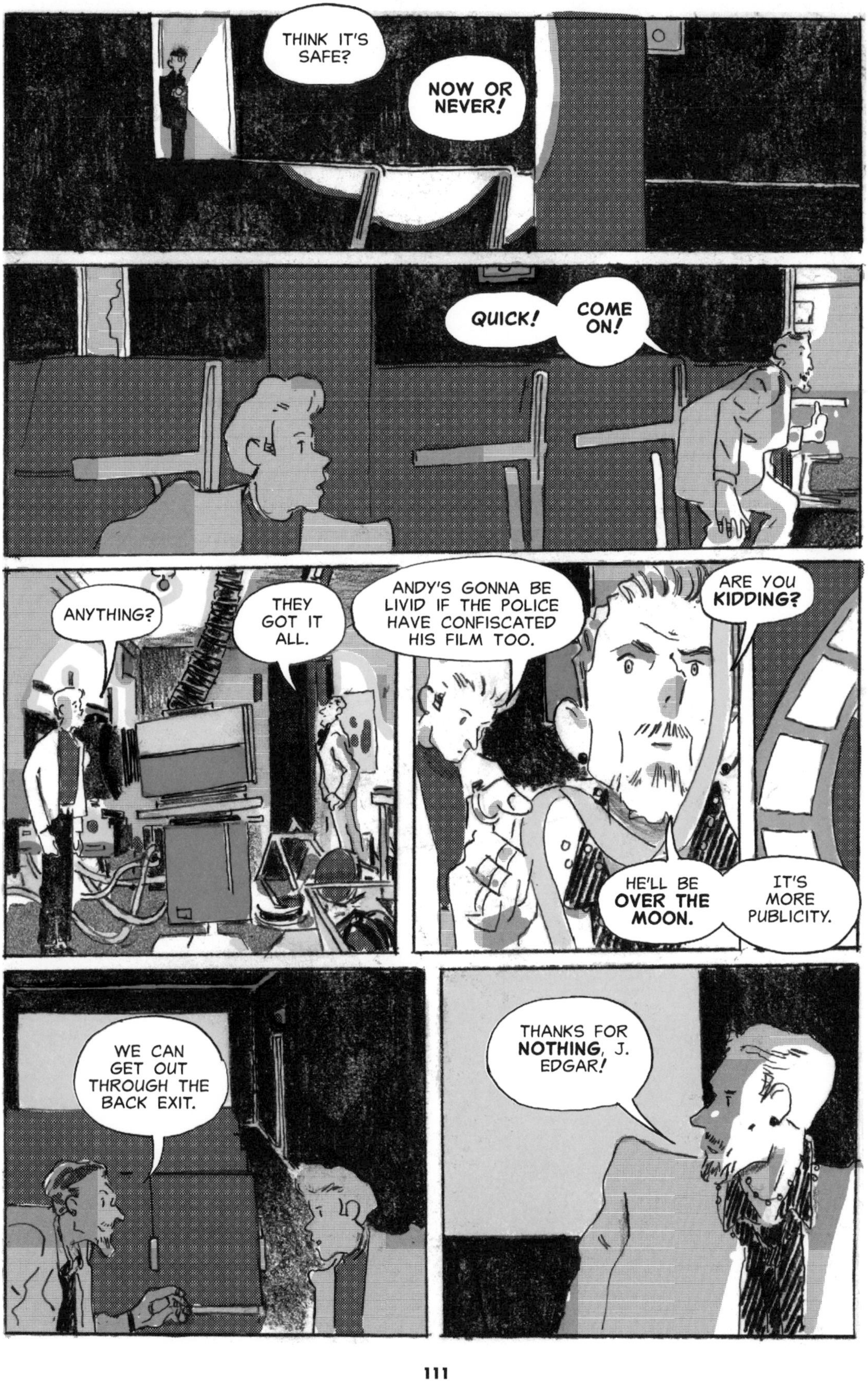
THINK IT'S SAFE?
NOW OR NEVER!
QUICK!
COME ON!
ANYTHING?
THEY GOT IT ALL.
ANDY'S GONNA BE LIVID IF THE POLICE HAVE CONFISCATED HIS FILM TOO.
ARE YOU KIDDING?
HE'LL BE OVER THE MOON.
IT'S MORE PUBLICITY.
WE CAN GET OUT THROUGH THE BACK EXIT.
THANKS FOR NOTHING, J. EDGAR!

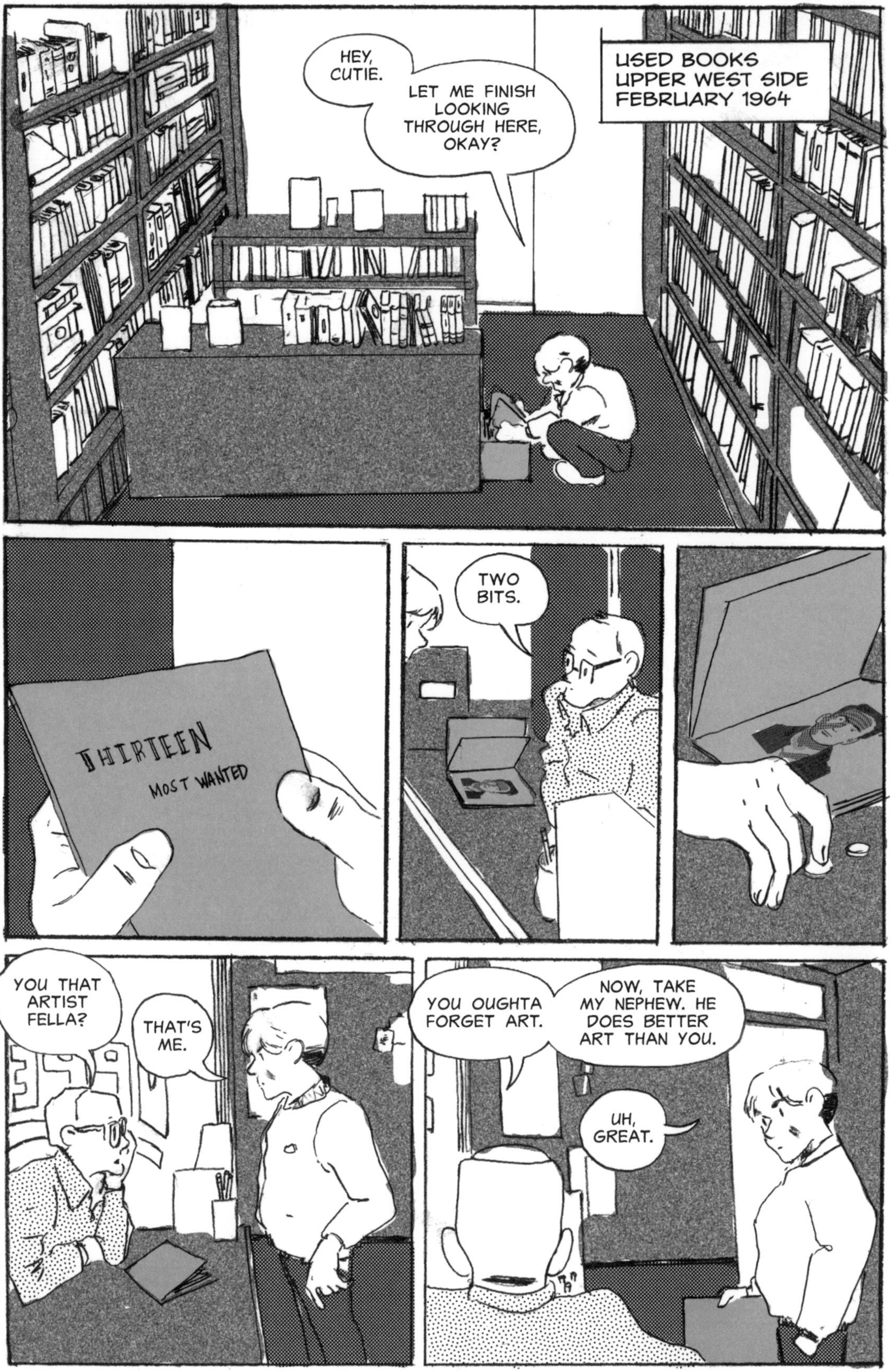
HEY, CUTIE.
LET ME FINISH LOOKING THROUGH HERE, OKAY?
USED BOOKS UPPER WEST SIDE FEBRUARY 1964
THIRTEEN MOST WANTED
TWO BITS.
YOU THAT ARTIST FELLA?
THAT'S ME.
YOU OUGHTA FORGET ART.
NOW, TAKE MY NEPHEW. HE DOES BETTER ART THAN YOU.
UH, GREAT.

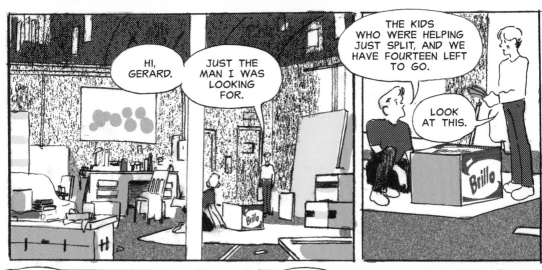

HI, GERARD.

JUST THE MAN I WAS LOOKING FOR.

THE KIDS WHO WERE HELPING JUST SPLIT, AND WE HAVE FOURTEEN LEFT TO GO.

LOOK AT THIS.

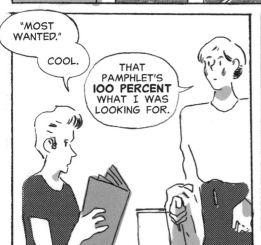

"MOST WANTED."

COOL.

THAT PAMPHLET'S **100 PERCENT** WHAT I WAS LOOKING FOR.

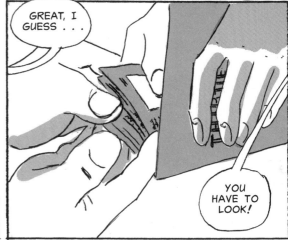

GREAT, I GUESS . . .

YOU HAVE TO LOOK!

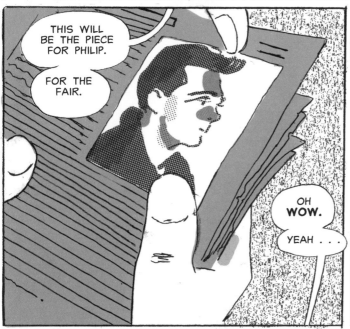

THIS WILL BE THE PIECE FOR PHILIP.

FOR THE FAIR.

OH **WOW.**

YEAH . . .

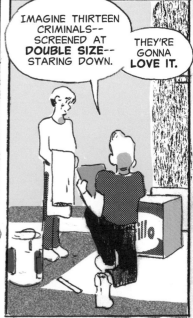

IMAGINE THIRTEEN CRIMINALS-- SCREENED AT **DOUBLE SIZE--** STARING DOWN.

THEY'RE GONNA **LOVE IT.**

CHAPTER FOURTEEN

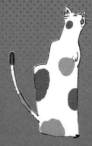

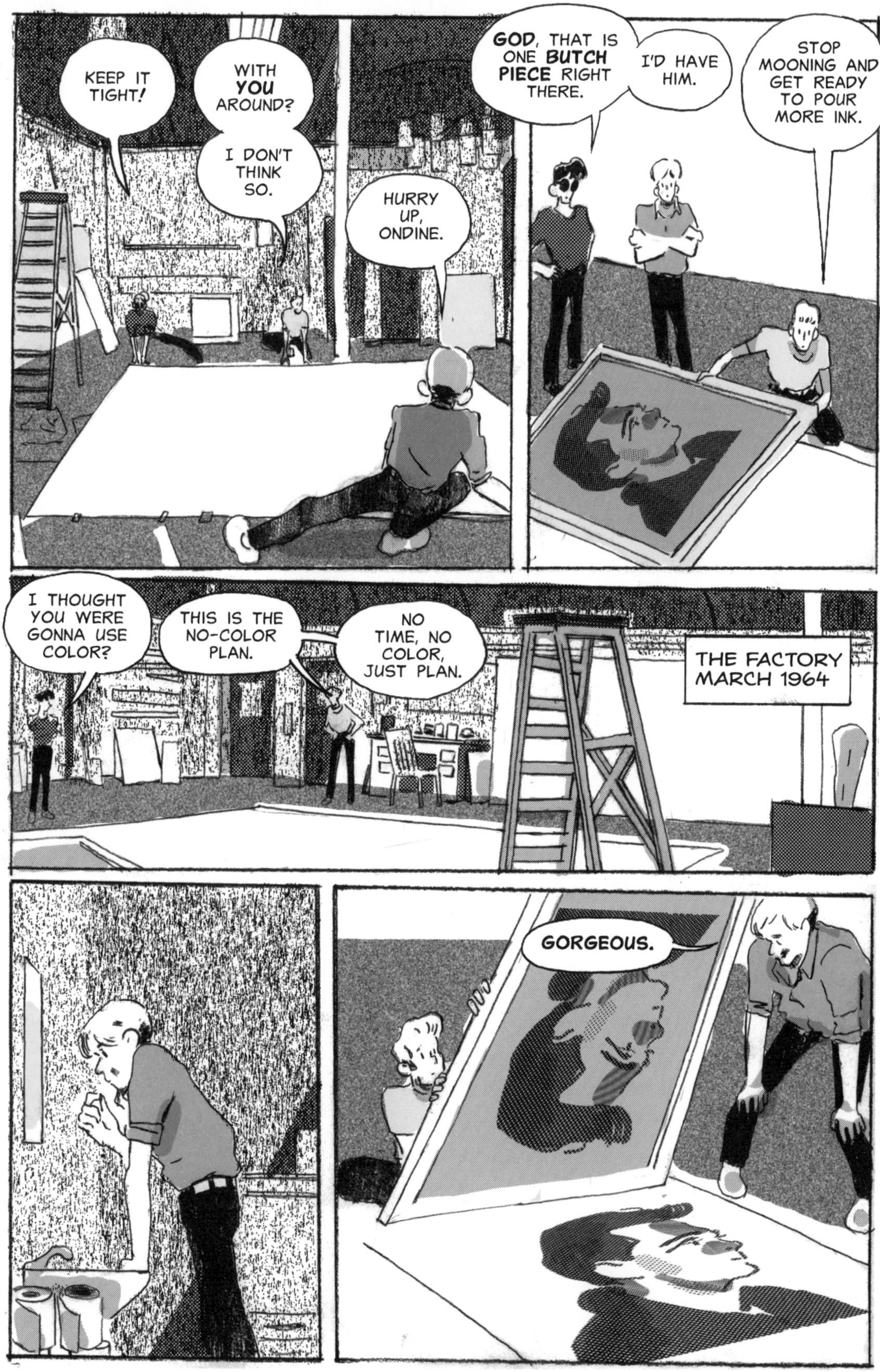
KEEP IT TIGHT!
WITH YOU AROUND?
I DON'T THINK SO.
HURRY UP, ONDINE.
GOD, THAT IS ONE BUTCH PIECE RIGHT THERE.
I'D HAVE HIM.
STOP MOONING AND GET READY TO POUR MORE INK.
THE FACTORY MARCH 1964
I THOUGHT YOU WERE GONNA USE COLOR?
THIS IS THE NO-COLOR PLAN.
NO TIME, NO COLOR, JUST PLAN.
GORGEOUS.

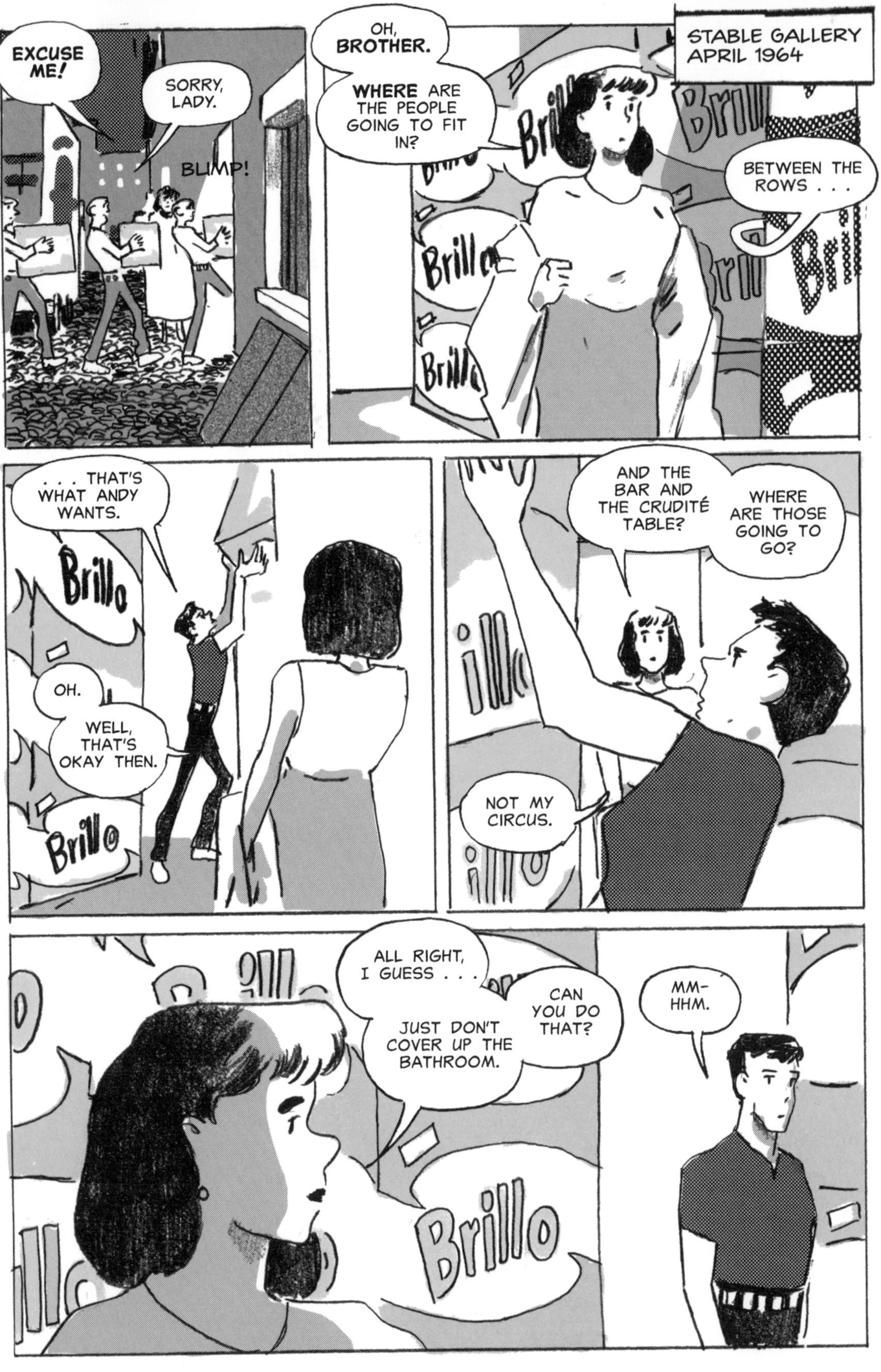
STABLE GALLERY
APRIL 1964
EXCUSE ME!
SORRY, LADY.
BLUMP!
OH, BROTHER.
WHERE ARE THE PEOPLE GOING TO FIT IN?
BETWEEN THE ROWS . . .
. . . THAT'S WHAT ANDY WANTS.
OH.
WELL, THAT'S OKAY THEN.
AND THE BAR AND THE CRUDITÉ TABLE?
WHERE ARE THOSE GOING TO GO?
NOT MY CIRCUS.
ALL RIGHT, I GUESS . . .
JUST DON'T COVER UP THE BATHROOM.
CAN YOU DO THAT?
MM-HHM.

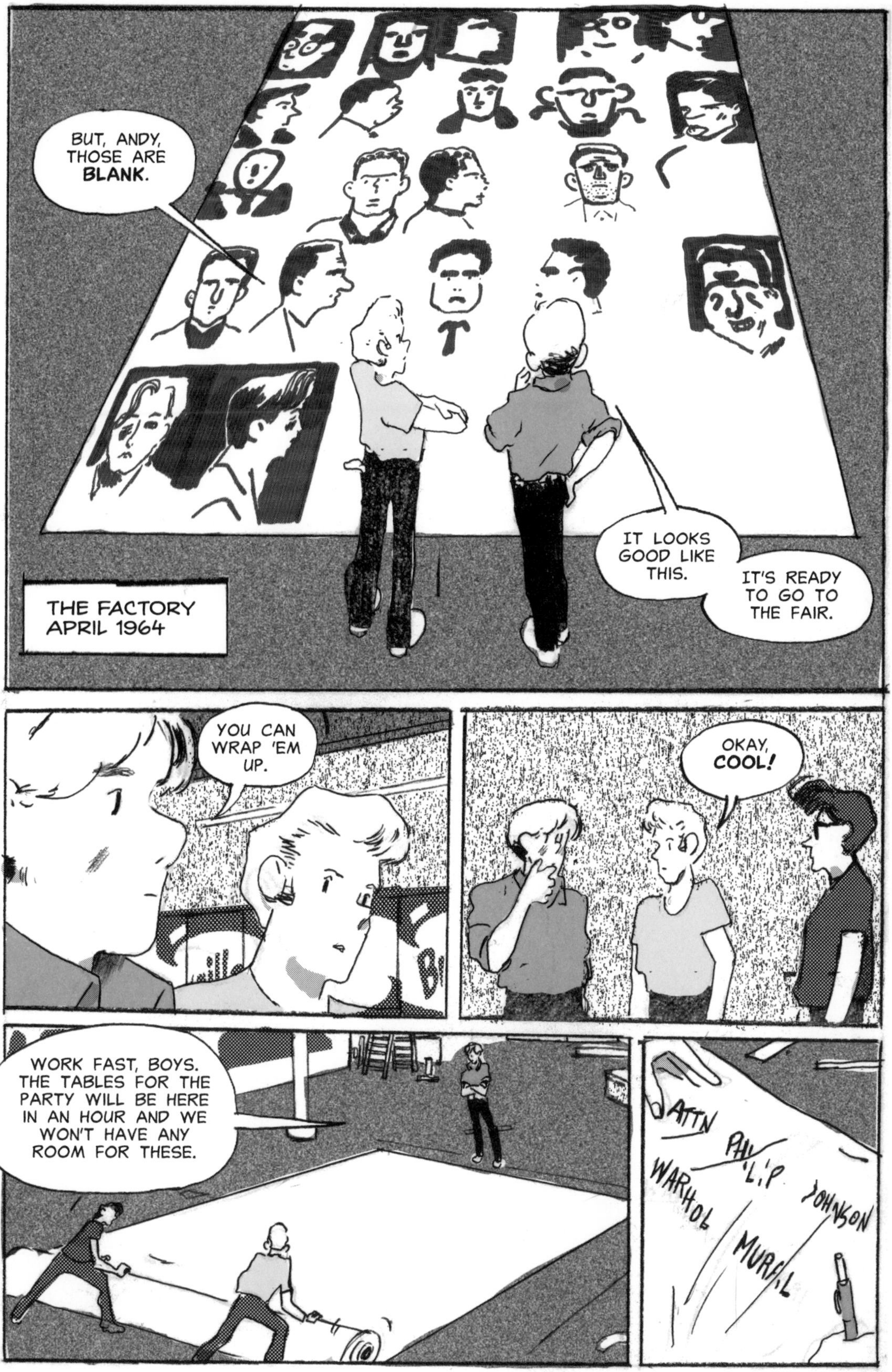
BUT, ANDY, THOSE ARE **BLANK**.
IT LOOKS GOOD LIKE THIS.
IT'S READY TO GO TO THE FAIR.
THE FACTORY APRIL 1964
YOU CAN WRAP 'EM UP.
OKAY, **COOL!**
WORK FAST, BOYS. THE TABLES FOR THE PARTY WILL BE HERE IN AN HOUR AND WE WON'T HAVE ANY ROOM FOR THESE.
ATTN PHILIP JOHNSON
WARHOL MURAL

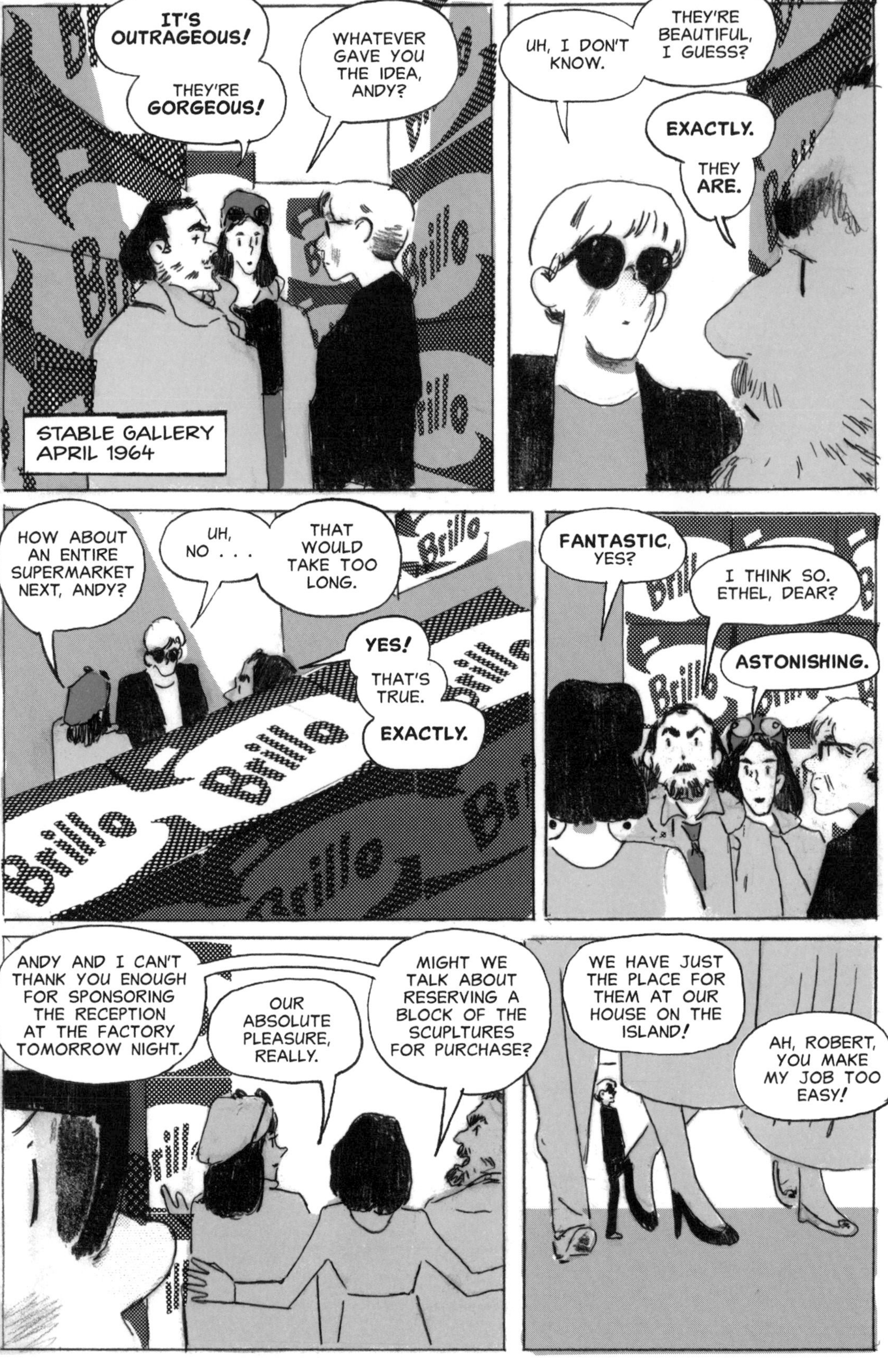
IT'S OUTRAGEOUS!
THEY'RE GORGEOUS!
WHATEVER GAVE YOU THE IDEA, ANDY?
STABLE GALLERY APRIL 1964
UH, I DON'T KNOW.
THEY'RE BEAUTIFUL, I GUESS?
EXACTLY.
THEY ARE.
HOW ABOUT AN ENTIRE SUPERMARKET NEXT, ANDY?
UH, NO . . .
THAT WOULD TAKE TOO LONG.
YES!
THAT'S TRUE.
EXACTLY.
FANTASTIC, YES?
I THINK SO. ETHEL, DEAR?
ASTONISHING.
ANDY AND I CAN'T THANK YOU ENOUGH FOR SPONSORING THE RECEPTION AT THE FACTORY TOMORROW NIGHT.
OUR ABSOLUTE PLEASURE, REALLY.
MIGHT WE TALK ABOUT RESERVING A BLOCK OF THE SCUPLTURES FOR PURCHASE?
WE HAVE JUST THE PLACE FOR THEM AT OUR HOUSE ON THE ISLAND!
AH, ROBERT, YOU MAKE MY JOB TOO EASY!

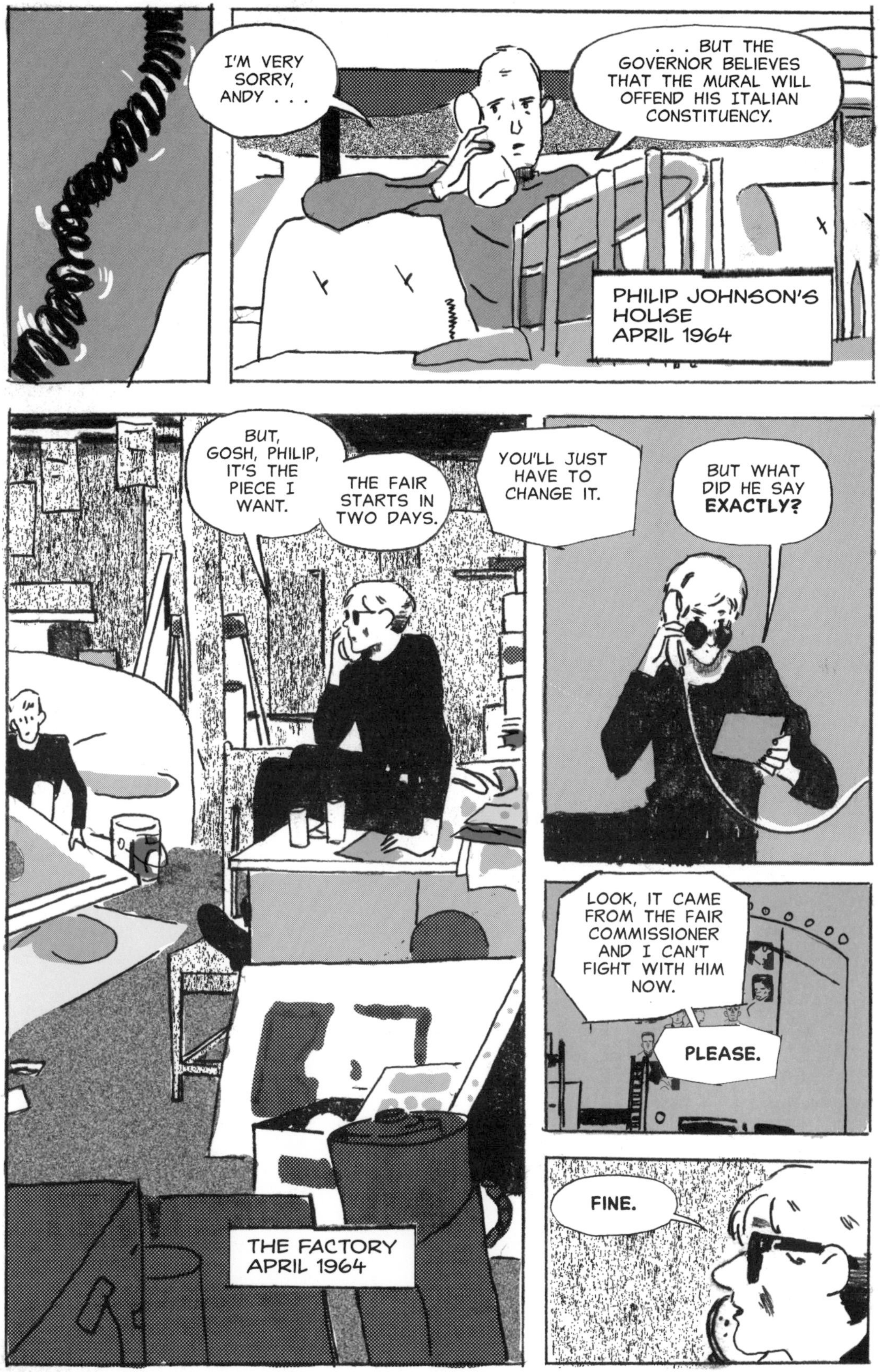
I'M VERY SORRY, ANDY . . .
. . . BUT THE GOVERNOR BELIEVES THAT THE MURAL WILL OFFEND HIS ITALIAN CONSTITUENCY.
PHILIP JOHNSON'S HOUSE APRIL 1964
BUT, GOSH, PHILIP, IT'S THE PIECE I WANT.
THE FAIR STARTS IN TWO DAYS.
YOU'LL JUST HAVE TO CHANGE IT.
THE FACTORY APRIL 1964
BUT WHAT DID HE SAY **EXACTLY?**
LOOK, IT CAME FROM THE FAIR COMMISSIONER AND I CAN'T FIGHT WITH HIM NOW.
PLEASE.
FINE.

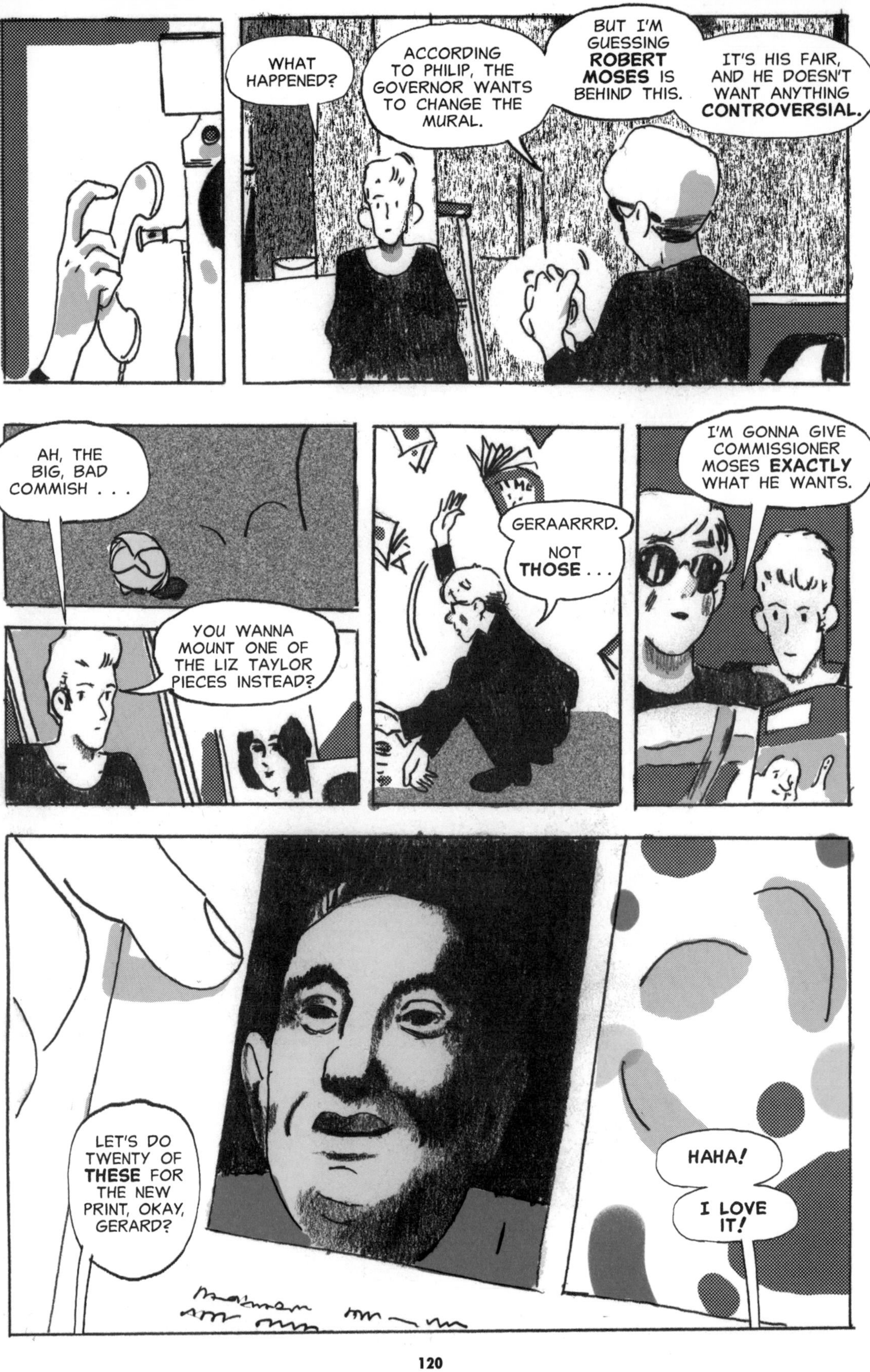
WHAT HAPPENED?
ACCORDING TO PHILIP, THE GOVERNOR WANTS TO CHANGE THE MURAL.
BUT I'M GUESSING **ROBERT MOSES** IS BEHIND THIS.
IT'S HIS FAIR, AND HE DOESN'T WANT ANYTHING **CONTROVERSIAL.**
AH, THE BIG, BAD COMMISH . . .
YOU WANNA MOUNT ONE OF THE LIZ TAYLOR PIECES INSTEAD?
GERAARRRD.
NOT **THOSE** . . .
I'M GONNA GIVE COMMISSIONER MOSES **EXACTLY** WHAT HE WANTS.
LET'S DO TWENTY OF **THESE** FOR THE NEW PRINT, OKAY, GERARD?
HAHA!
I LOVE IT!

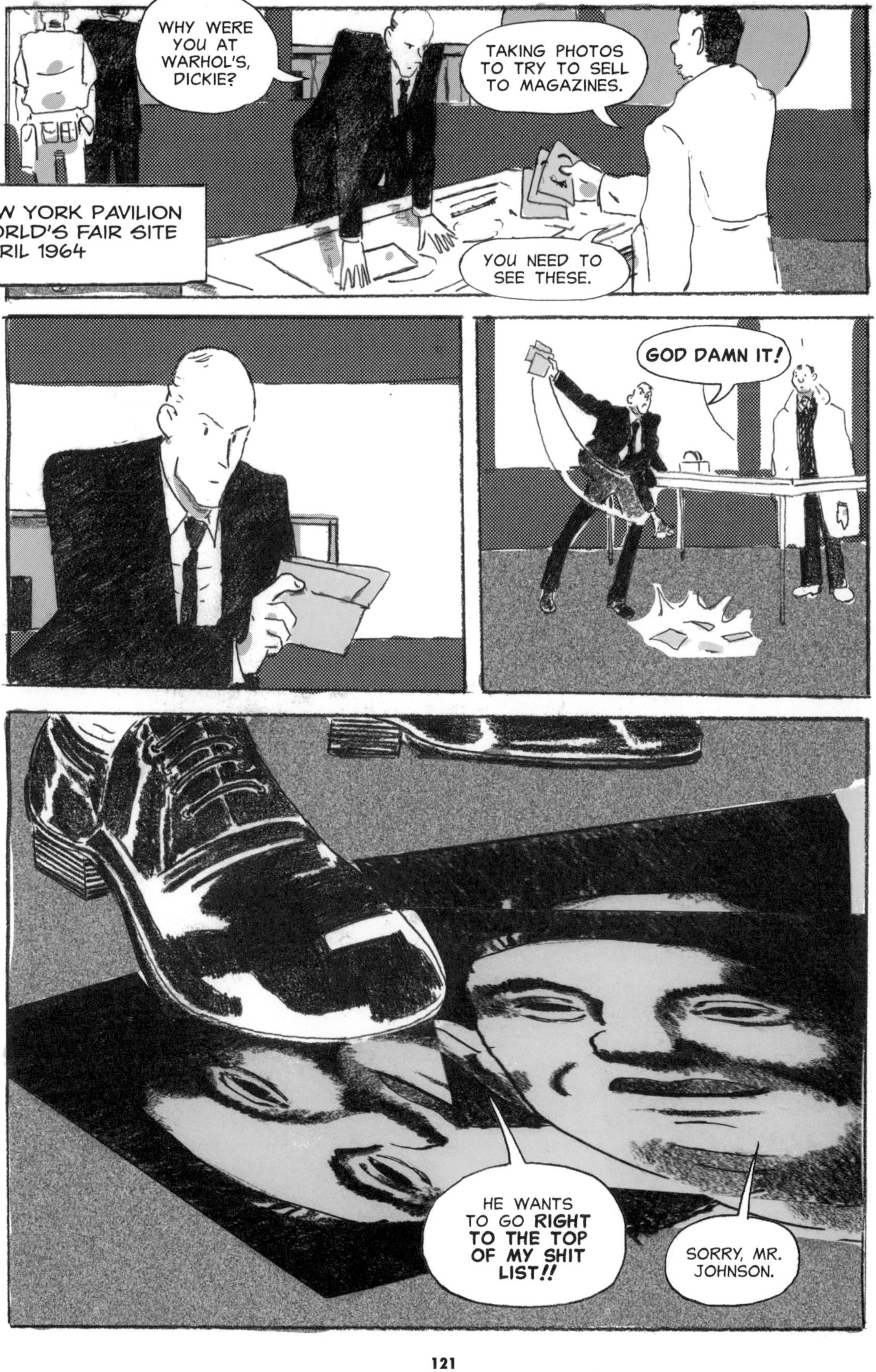
WHY WERE YOU AT WARHOL'S, DICKIE?
TAKING PHOTOS TO TRY TO SELL TO MAGAZINES.
EW YORK PAVILION
ORLD'S FAIR SITE
PRIL 1964
YOU NEED TO SEE THESE.
GOD DAMN IT!
HE WANTS TO GO RIGHT TO THE TOP OF MY SHIT LIST!!
SORRY, MR. JOHNSON.

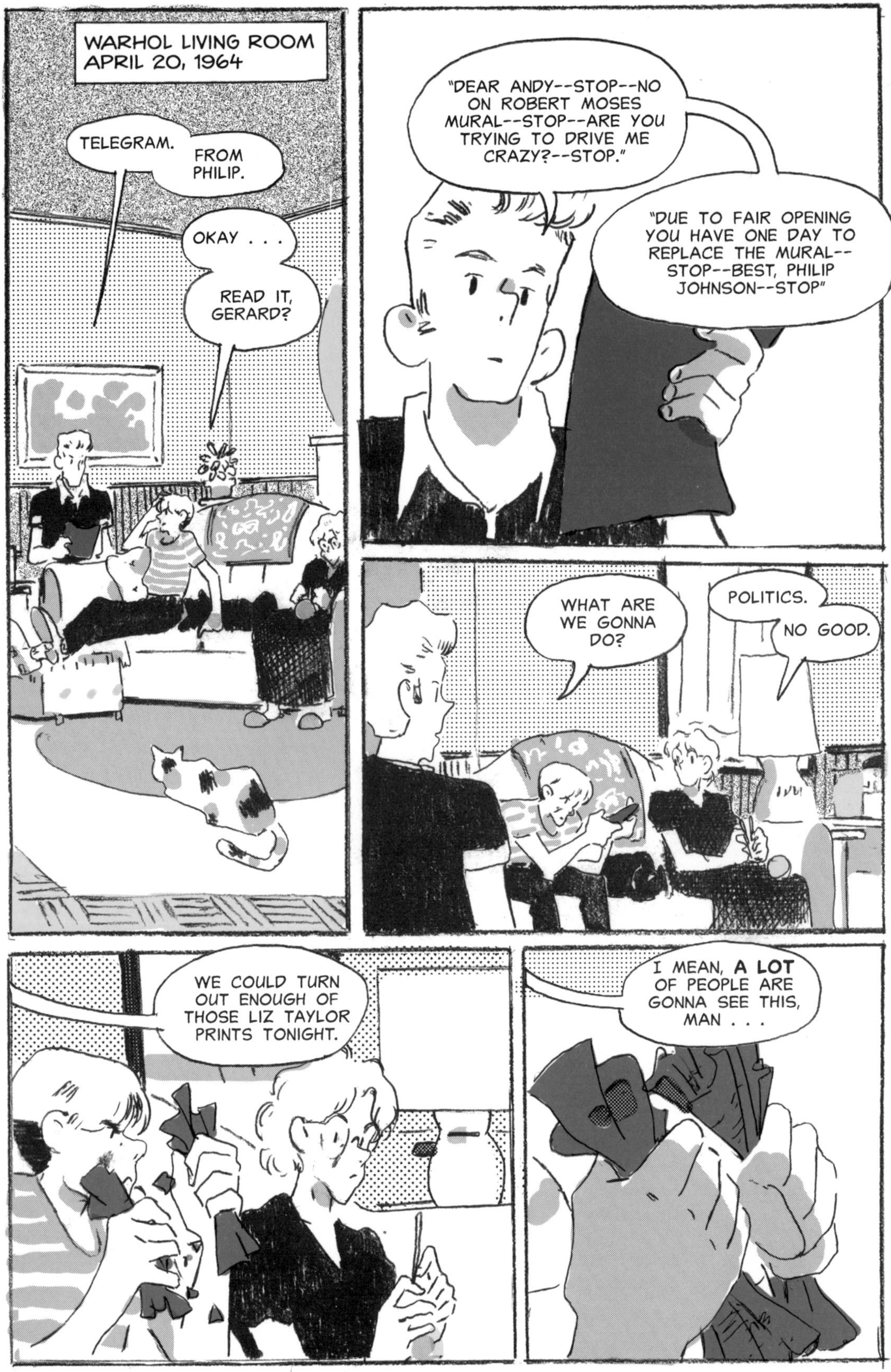
WARHOL LIVING ROOM
APRIL 20, 1964
TELEGRAM. FROM PHILIP.
OKAY . . .
READ IT, GERARD?
"DEAR ANDY--STOP--NO ON ROBERT MOSES MURAL--STOP--ARE YOU TRYING TO DRIVE ME CRAZY?--STOP."
"DUE TO FAIR OPENING YOU HAVE ONE DAY TO REPLACE THE MURAL--STOP--BEST, PHILIP JOHNSON--STOP"
WHAT ARE WE GONNA DO?
POLITICS.
NO GOOD.
WE COULD TURN OUT ENOUGH OF THOSE LIZ TAYLOR PRINTS TONIGHT.
I MEAN, A LOT OF PEOPLE ARE GONNA SEE THIS, MAN . . .

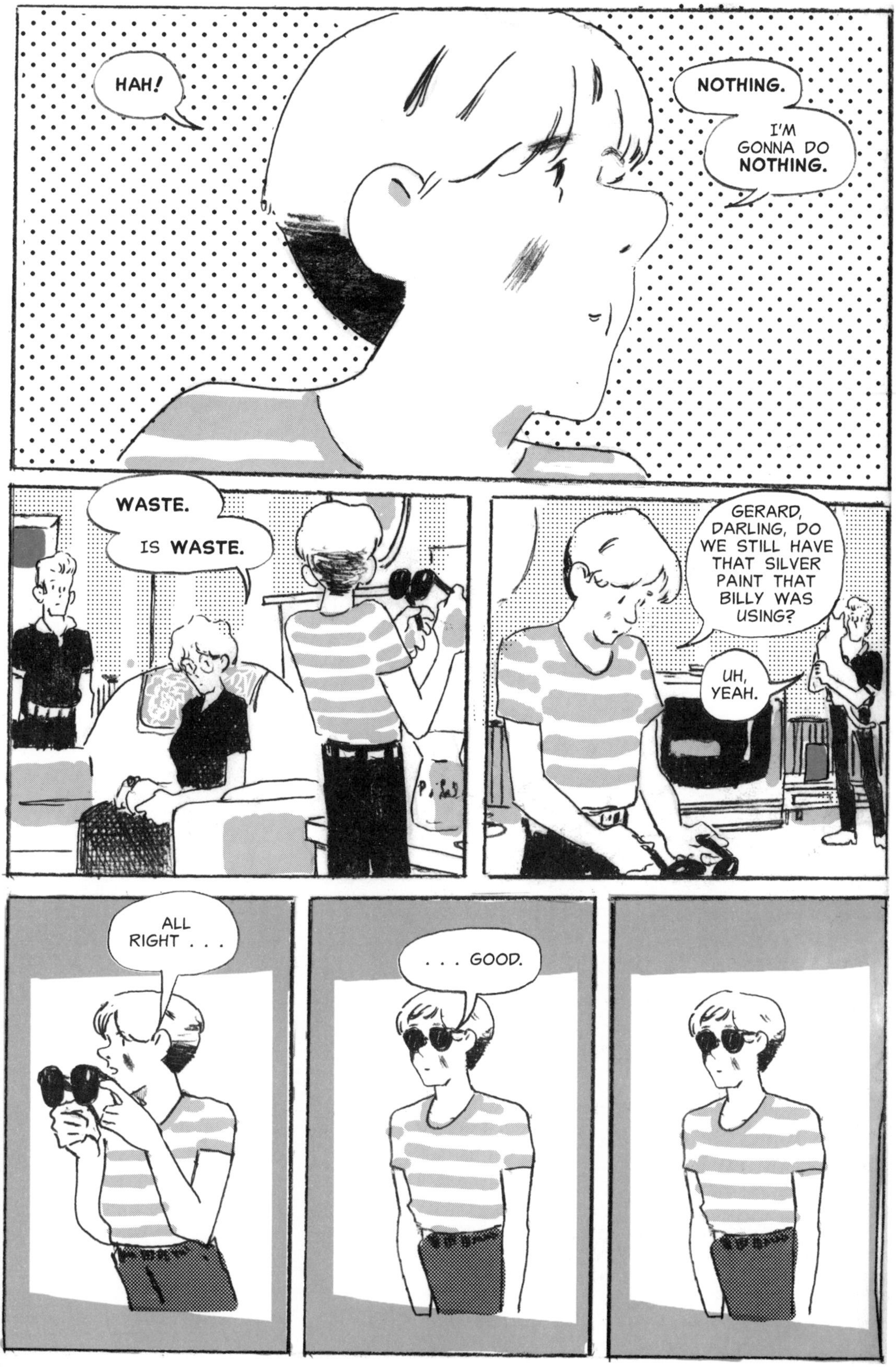
HAH!
NOTHING.
I'M GONNA DO NOTHING.
WASTE.
IS WASTE.
GERARD, DARLING, DO WE STILL HAVE THAT SILVER PAINT THAT BILLY WAS USING?
UH, YEAH.
ALL RIGHT . . .
. . . GOOD.

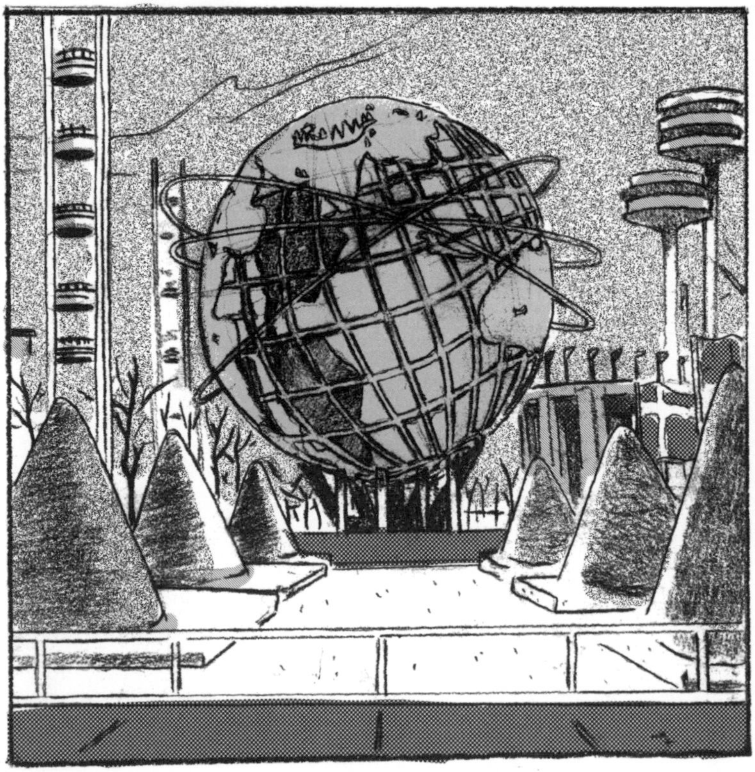

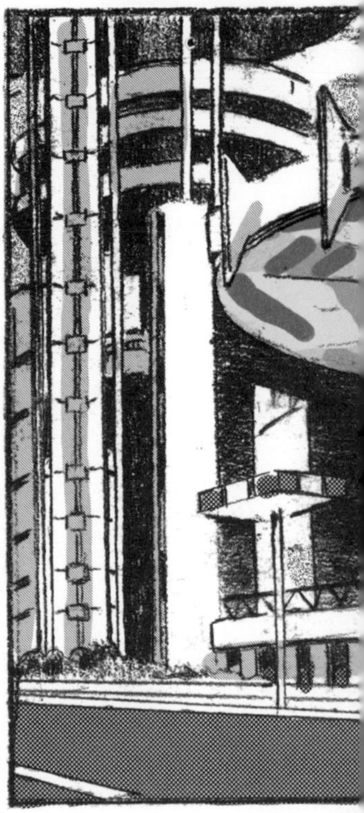

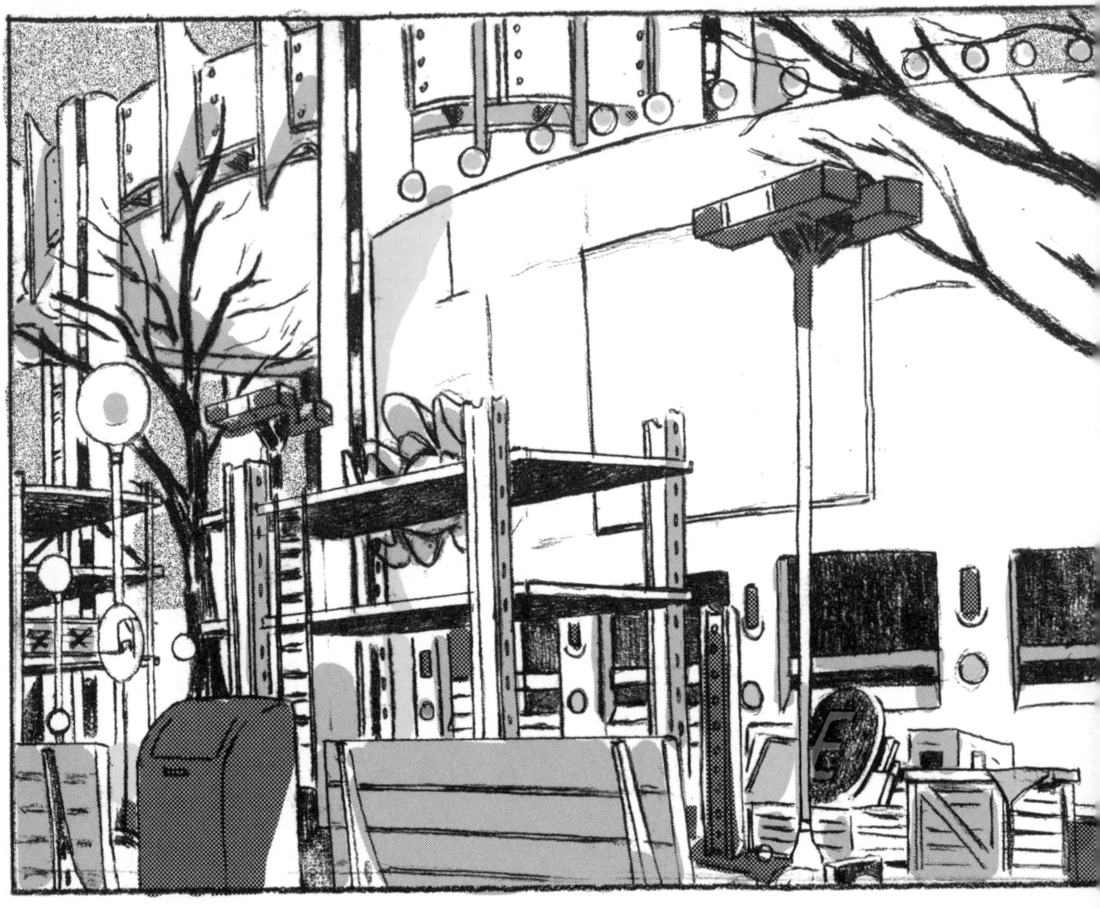

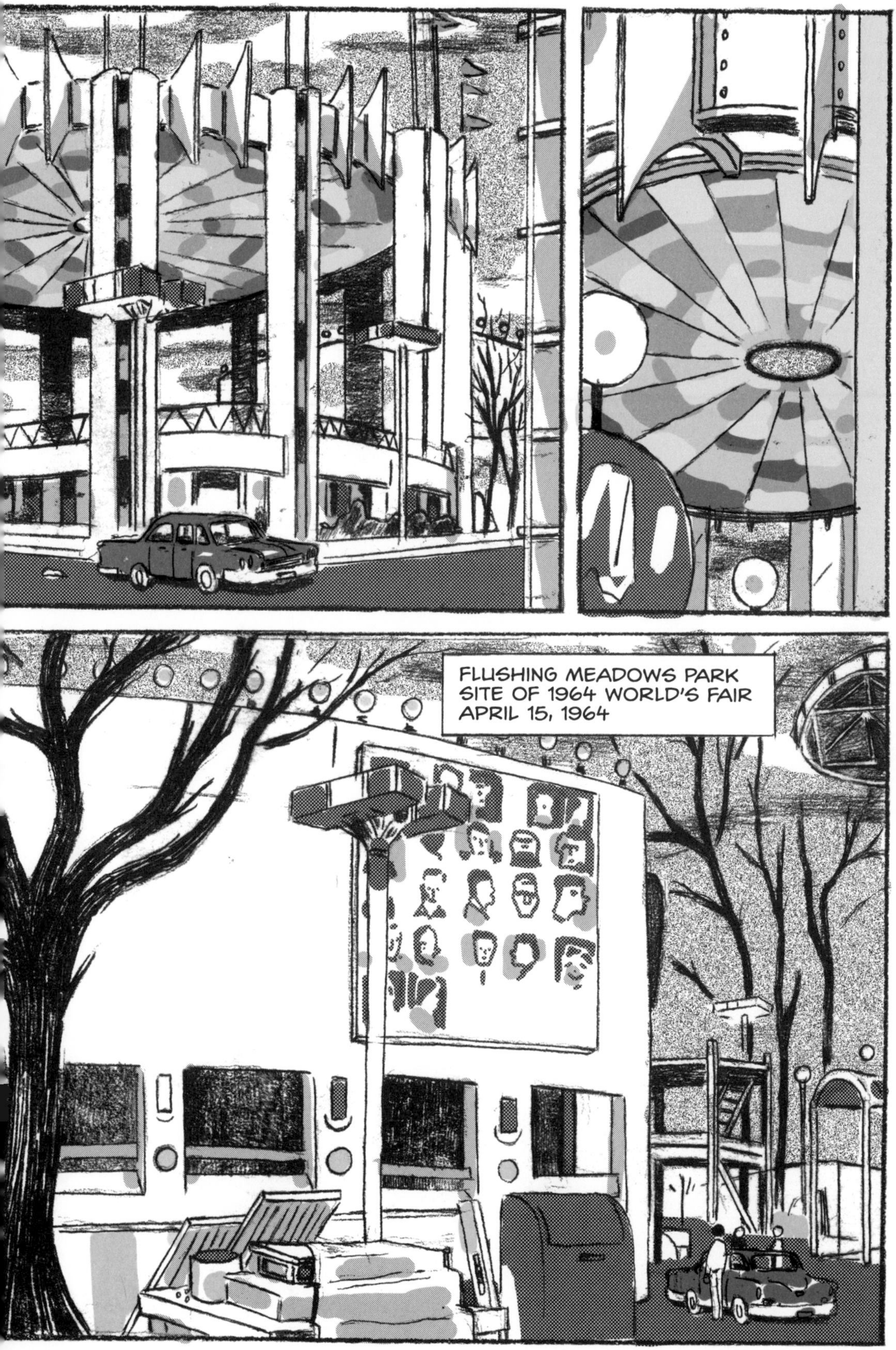
FLUSHING MEADOWS PARK
SITE OF 1964 WORLD'S FAIR
APRIL 15, 1964

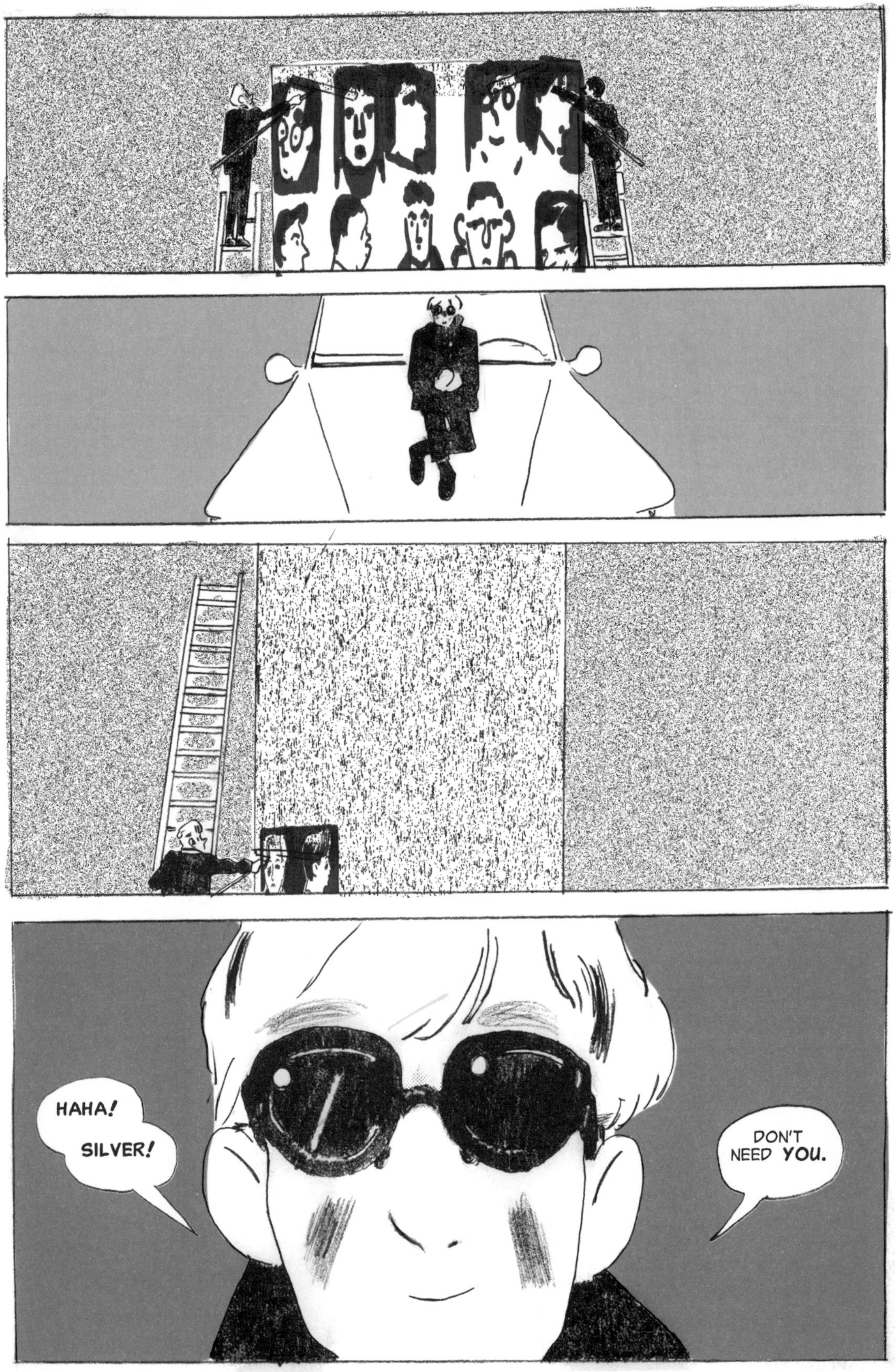
HAHA! SILVER!
DON'T NEED YOU.

CHAPTER FIFTEEN

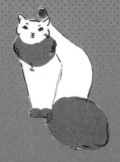

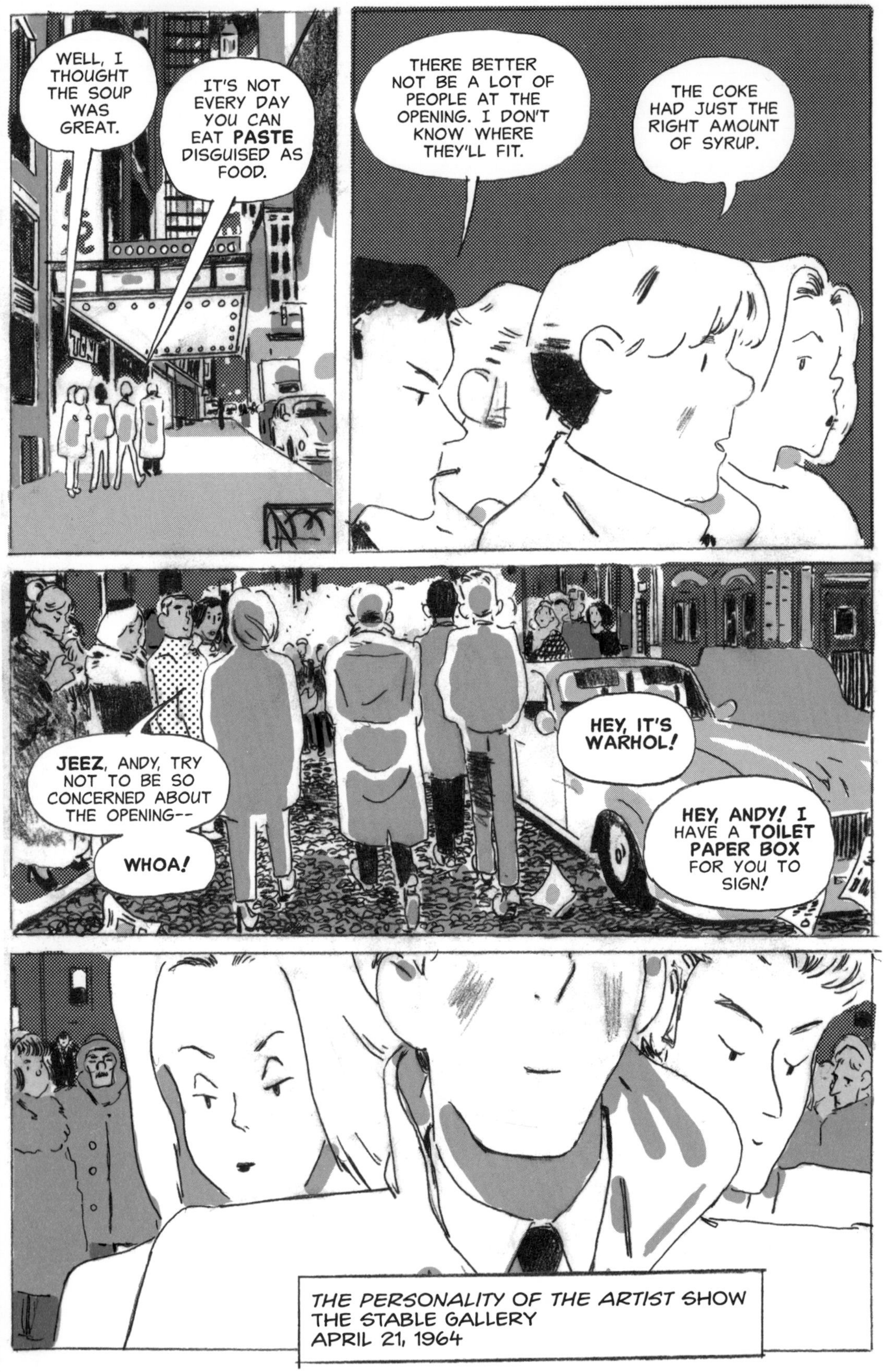
WELL, I THOUGHT THE SOUP WAS GREAT.
IT'S NOT EVERY DAY YOU CAN EAT **PASTE** DISGUISED AS FOOD.
THERE BETTER NOT BE A LOT OF PEOPLE AT THE OPENING. I DON'T KNOW WHERE THEY'LL FIT.
THE COKE HAD JUST THE RIGHT AMOUNT OF SYRUP.
JEEZ, ANDY, TRY NOT TO BE SO CONCERNED ABOUT THE OPENING--
WHOA!
HEY, IT'S WARHOL!
HEY, ANDY! I HAVE A **TOILET PAPER BOX** FOR YOU TO SIGN!
THE PERSONALITY OF THE ARTIST SHOW
THE STABLE GALLERY
APRIL 21, 1964

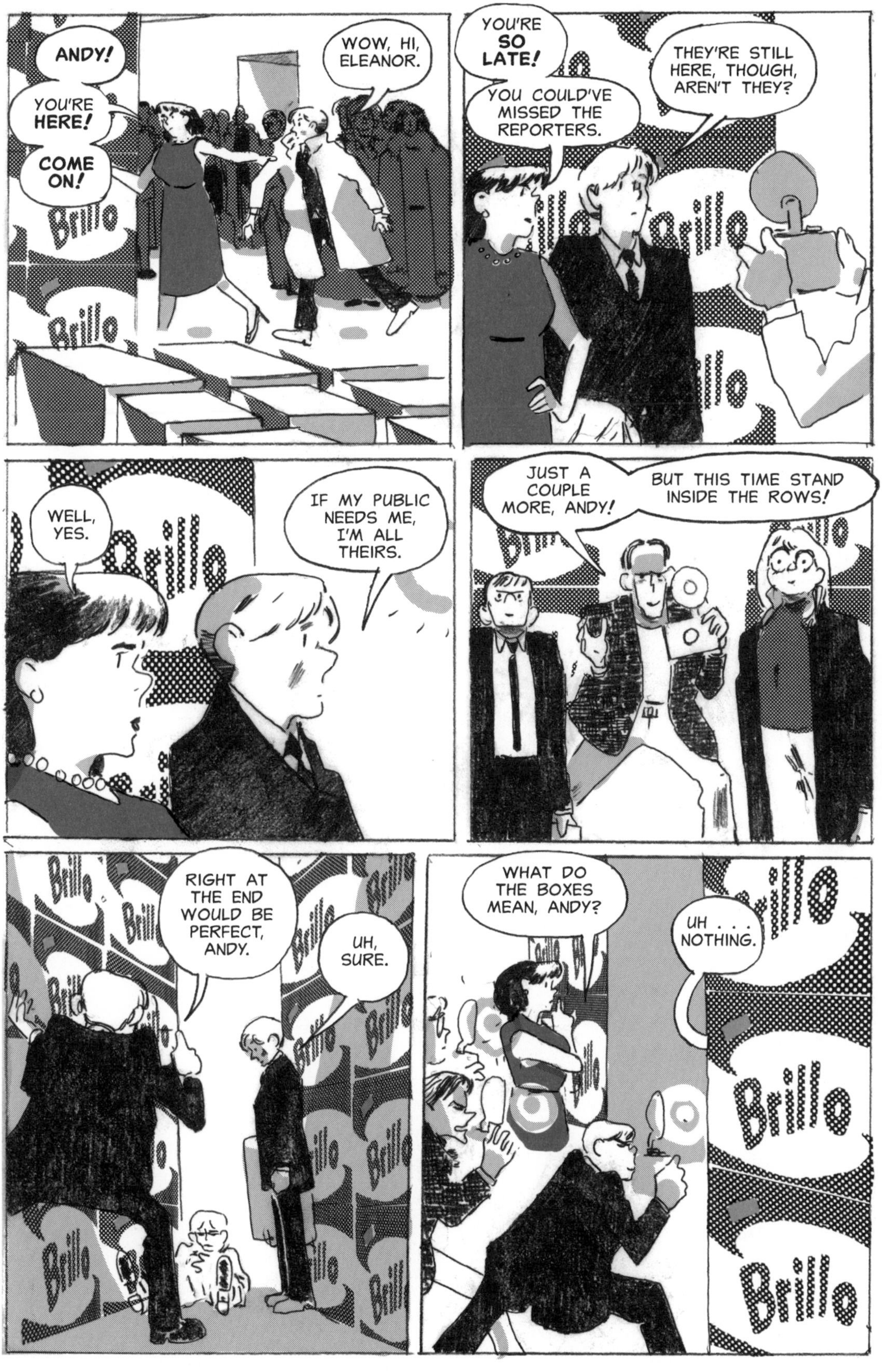
ANDY!
YOU'RE HERE!
COME ON!
WOW, HI, ELEANOR.
Brillo
YOU'RE SO LATE!
YOU COULD'VE MISSED THE REPORTERS.
THEY'RE STILL HERE, THOUGH, AREN'T THEY?
WELL, YES.
IF MY PUBLIC NEEDS ME, I'M ALL THEIRS.
JUST A COUPLE MORE, ANDY!
BUT THIS TIME STAND INSIDE THE ROWS!
RIGHT AT THE END WOULD BE PERFECT, ANDY.
UH, SURE.
WHAT DO THE BOXES MEAN, ANDY?
UH . . . NOTHING.

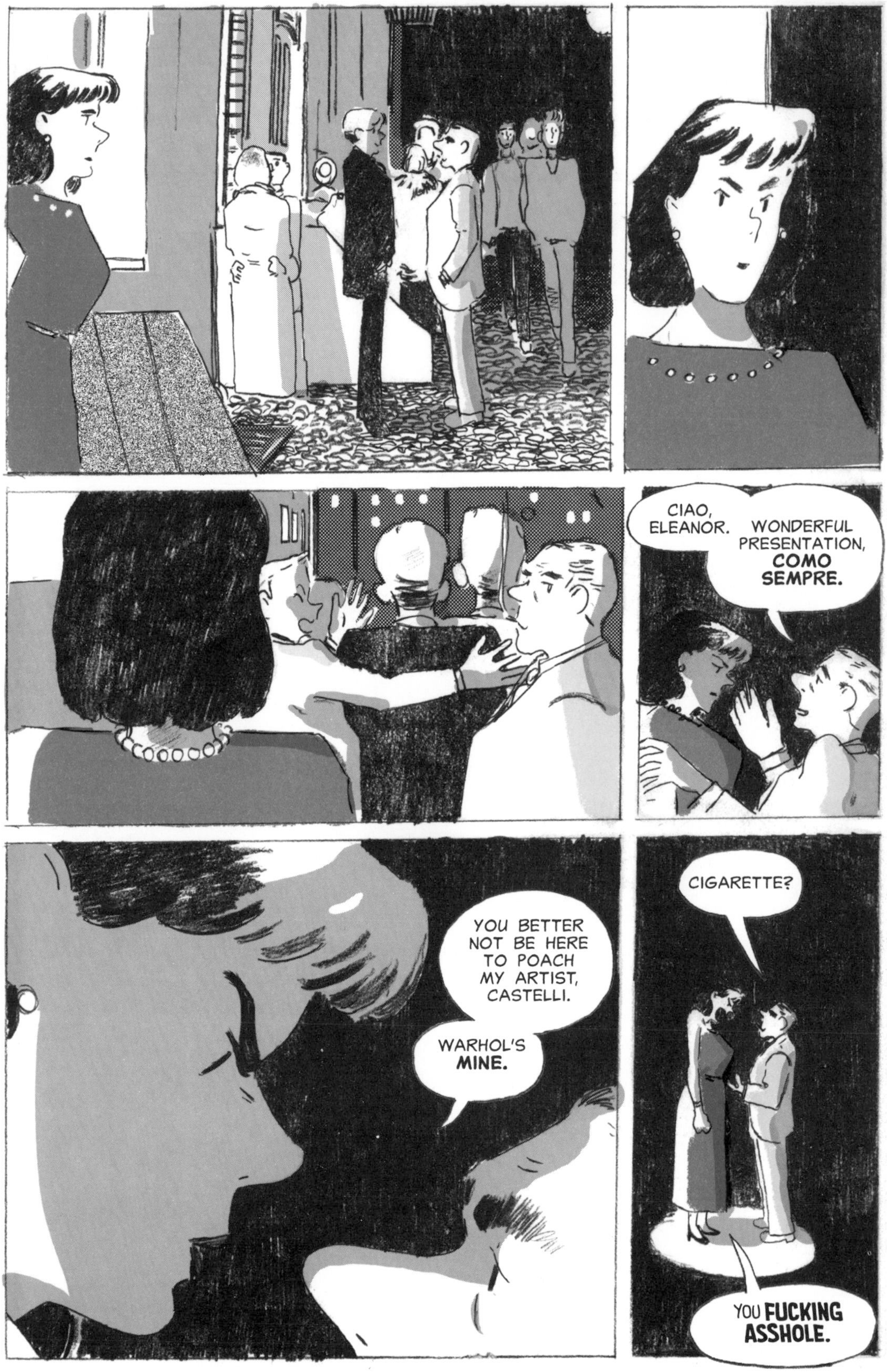
CIAO, ELEANOR. WONDERFUL PRESENTATION, COMO SEMPRE.
YOU BETTER NOT BE HERE TO POACH MY ARTIST, CASTELLI.
WARHOL'S MINE.
CIGARETTE?
YOU FUCKING ASSHOLE.

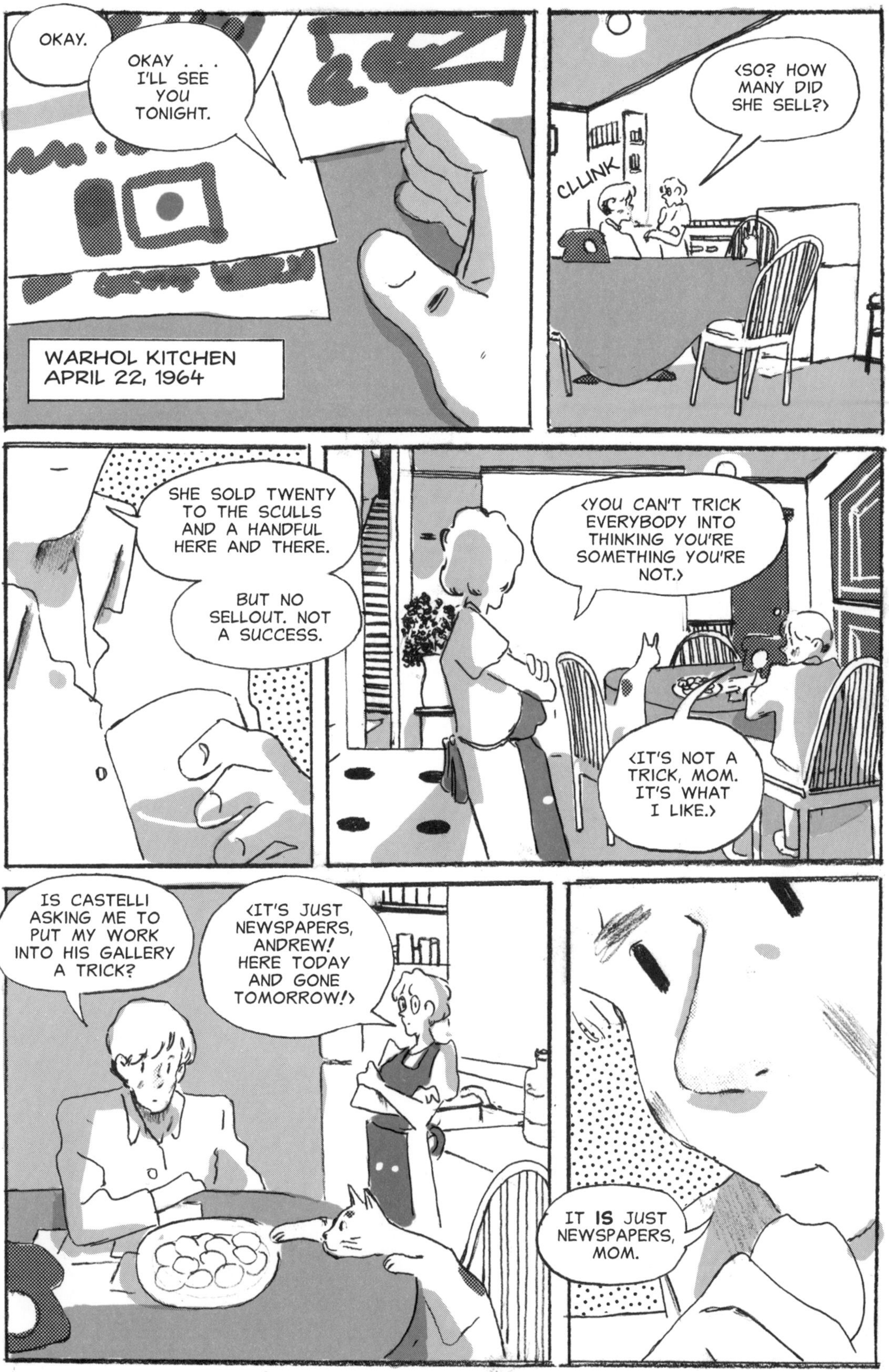
OKAY.
OKAY . . . I'LL SEE YOU TONIGHT.
WARHOL KITCHEN APRIL 22, 1964
CLLINK
<SO? HOW MANY DID SHE SELL?>
SHE SOLD TWENTY TO THE SCULLS AND A HANDFUL HERE AND THERE.
BUT NO SELLOUT. NOT A SUCCESS.
<YOU CAN'T TRICK EVERYBODY INTO THINKING YOU'RE SOMETHING YOU'RE NOT.>
<IT'S NOT A TRICK, MOM. IT'S WHAT I LIKE.>
IS CASTELLI ASKING ME TO PUT MY WORK INTO HIS GALLERY A TRICK?
<IT'S JUST NEWSPAPERS, ANDREW! HERE TODAY AND GONE TOMORROW!>
IT **IS** JUST NEWSPAPERS, MOM.

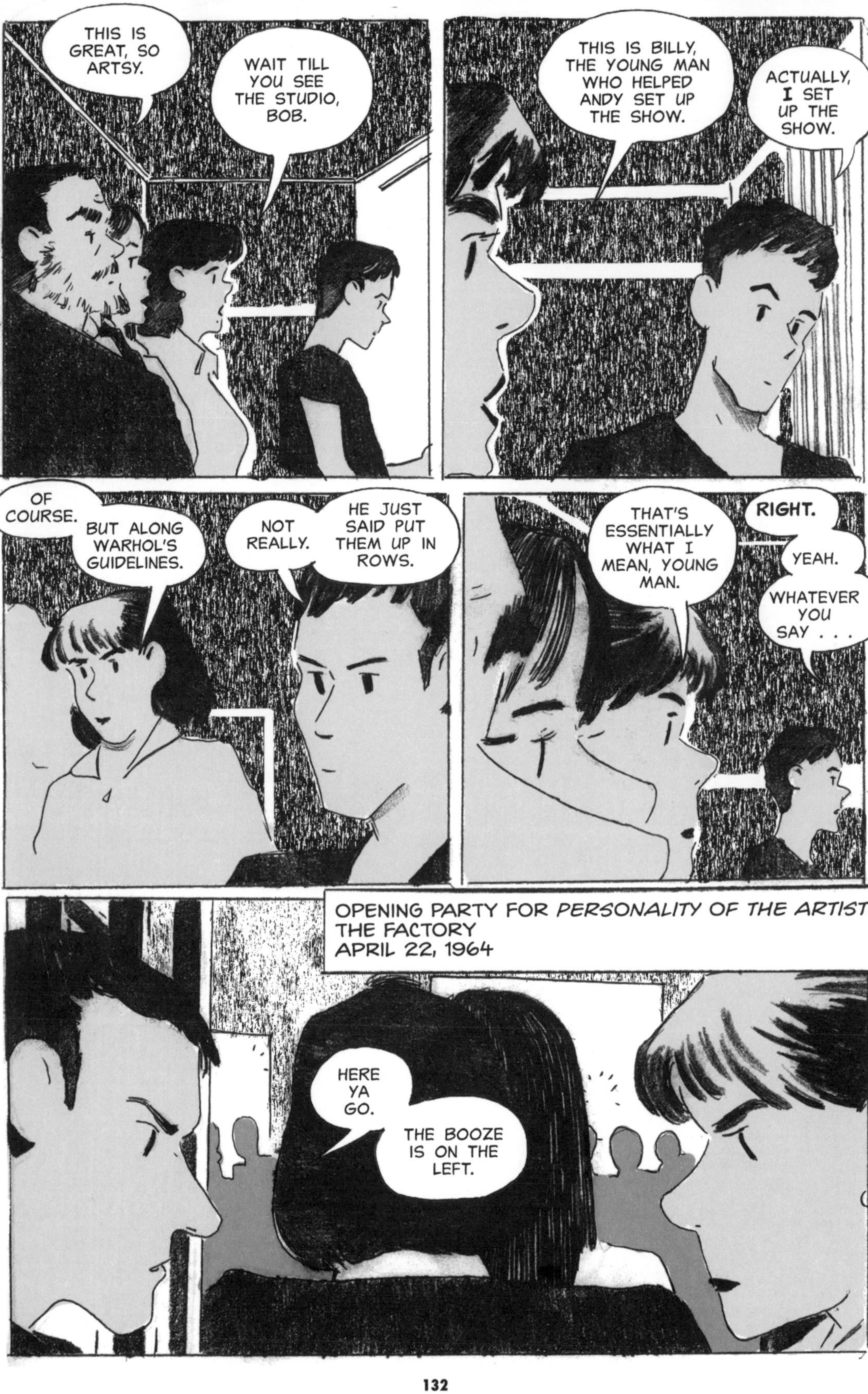
THIS IS GREAT, SO ARTSY.
WAIT TILL YOU SEE THE STUDIO, BOB.
THIS IS BILLY, THE YOUNG MAN WHO HELPED ANDY SET UP THE SHOW.
ACTUALLY, I SET UP THE SHOW.
OF COURSE.
BUT ALONG WARHOL'S GUIDELINES.
NOT REALLY.
HE JUST SAID PUT THEM UP IN ROWS.
THAT'S ESSENTIALLY WHAT I MEAN, YOUNG MAN.
RIGHT.
YEAH.
WHATEVER YOU SAY . . .
OPENING PARTY FOR PERSONALITY OF THE ARTIST
THE FACTORY
APRIL 22, 1964
HERE YA GO.
THE BOOZE IS ON THE LEFT.

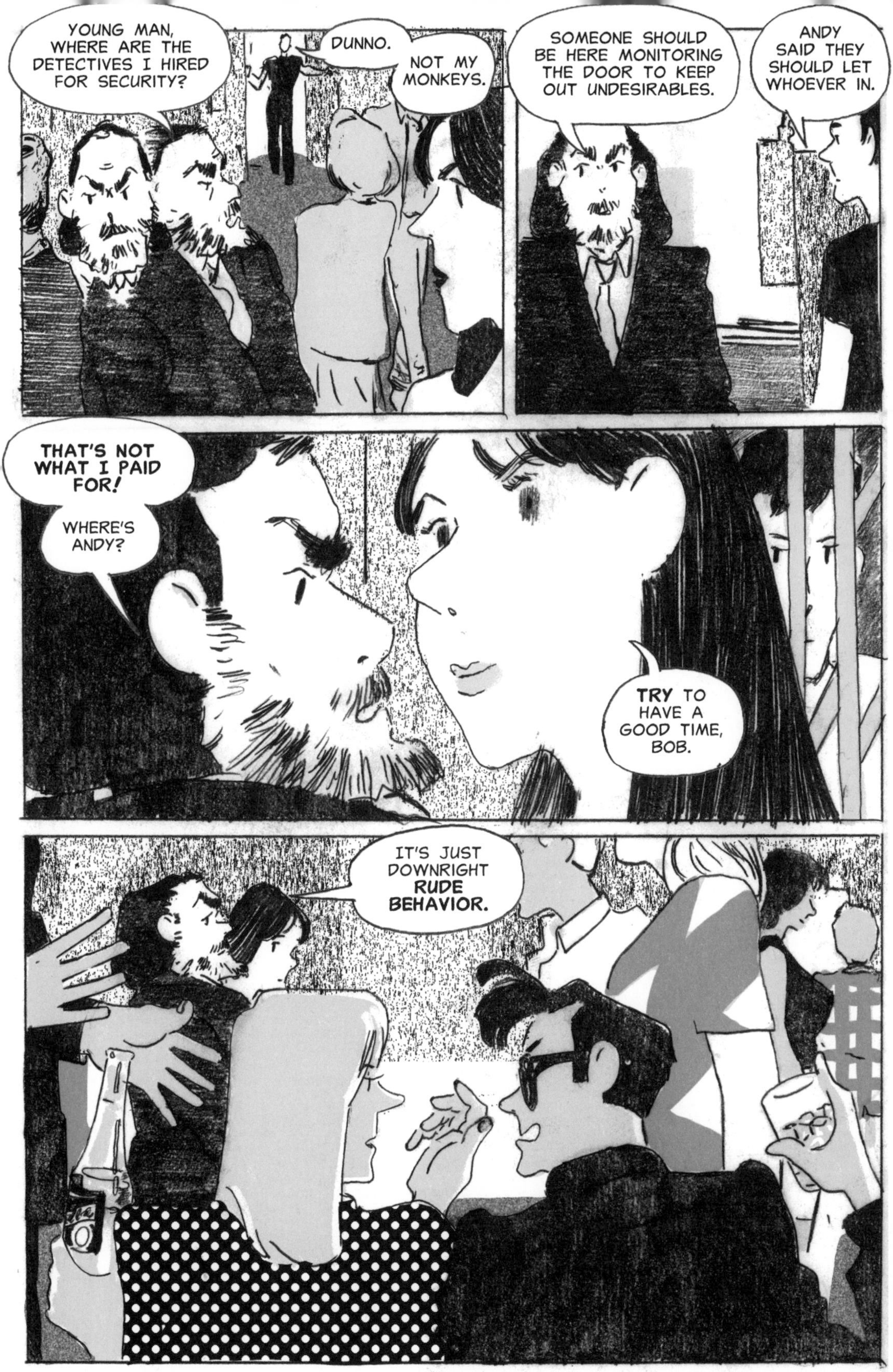
YOUNG MAN, WHERE ARE THE DETECTIVES I HIRED FOR SECURITY?
DUNNO.
NOT MY MONKEYS.
SOMEONE SHOULD BE HERE MONITORING THE DOOR TO KEEP OUT UNDESIRABLES.
ANDY SAID THEY SHOULD LET WHOEVER IN.
THAT'S NOT WHAT I PAID FOR!
WHERE'S ANDY?
TRY TO HAVE A GOOD TIME, BOB.
IT'S JUST DOWNRIGHT RUDE BEHAVIOR.

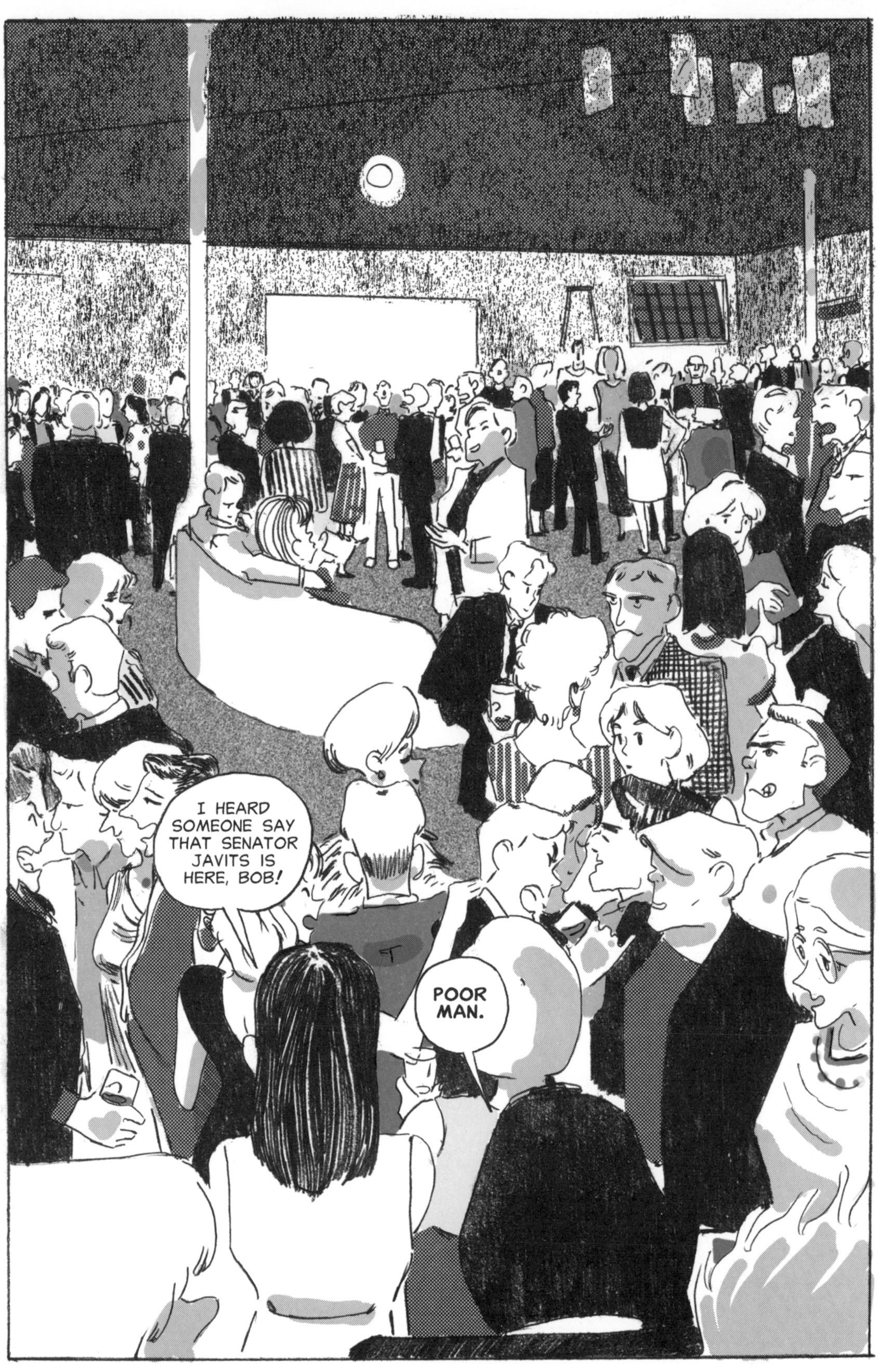
I HEARD SOMEONE SAY THAT SENATOR JAVITS IS HERE, BOB!
POOR MAN.

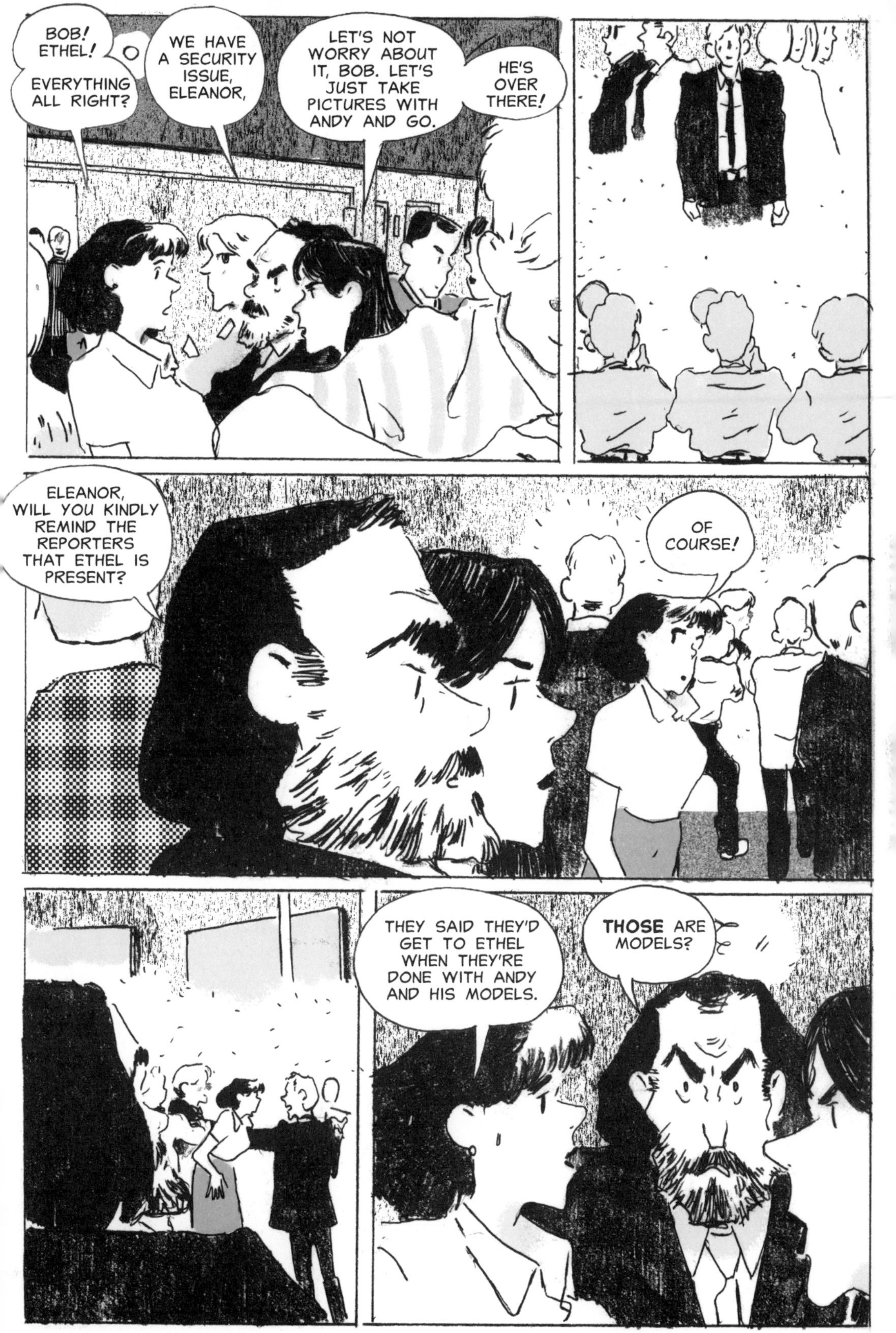
BOB! ETHEL!
EVERYTHING ALL RIGHT?
WE HAVE A SECURITY ISSUE, ELEANOR,
LET'S NOT WORRY ABOUT IT, BOB. LET'S JUST TAKE PICTURES WITH ANDY AND GO.
HE'S OVER THERE!
ELEANOR, WILL YOU KINDLY REMIND THE REPORTERS THAT ETHEL IS PRESENT?
OF COURSE!
THEY SAID THEY'D GET TO ETHEL WHEN THEY'RE DONE WITH ANDY AND HIS MODELS.
THOSE ARE MODELS?

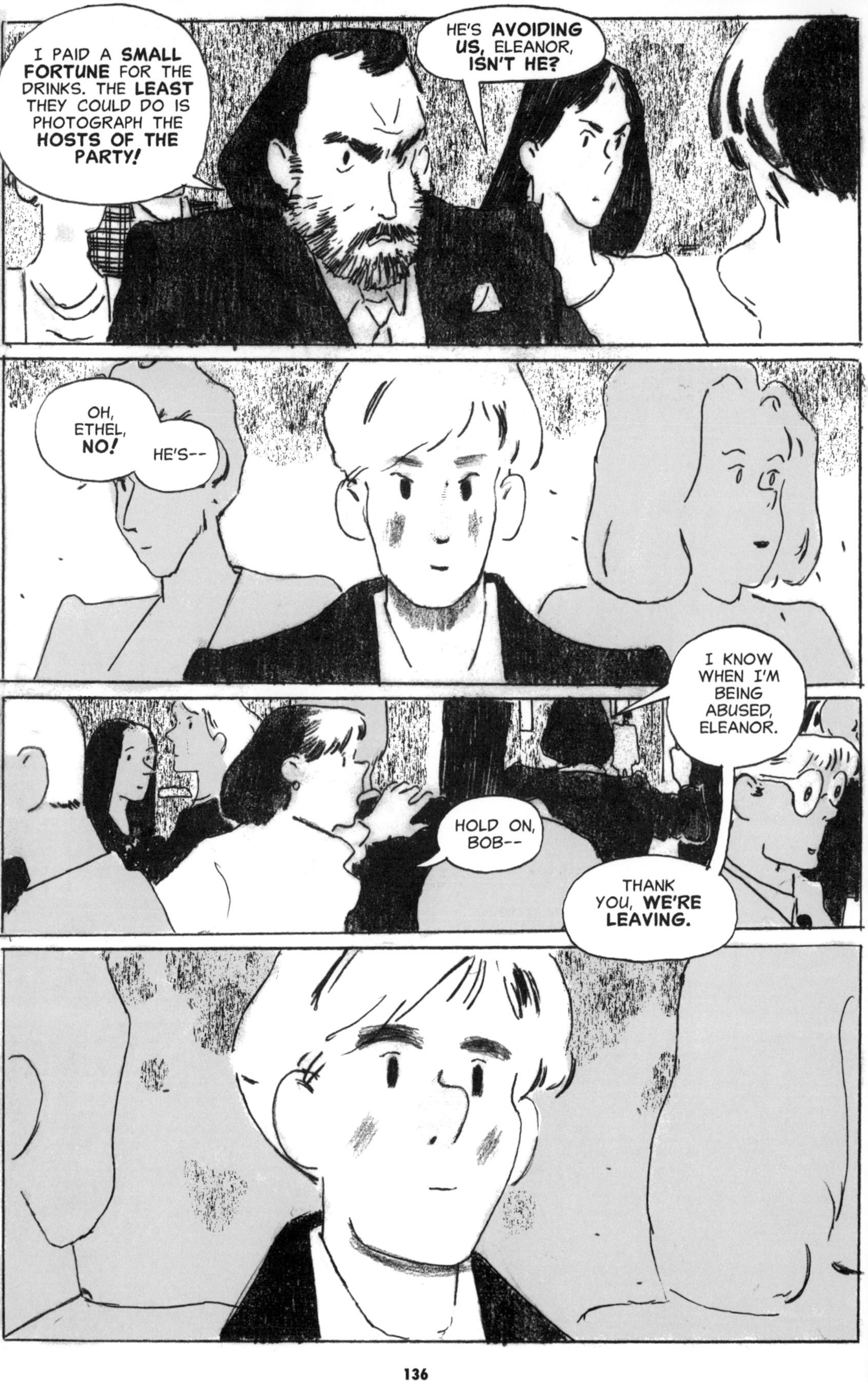
I PAID A SMALL FORTUNE FOR THE DRINKS. THE LEAST THEY COULD DO IS PHOTOGRAPH THE HOSTS OF THE PARTY!
HE'S AVOIDING US, ELEANOR, ISN'T HE?
OH, ETHEL, NO!
HE'S--
I KNOW WHEN I'M BEING ABUSED, ELEANOR.
HOLD ON, BOB--
THANK YOU, WE'RE LEAVING.

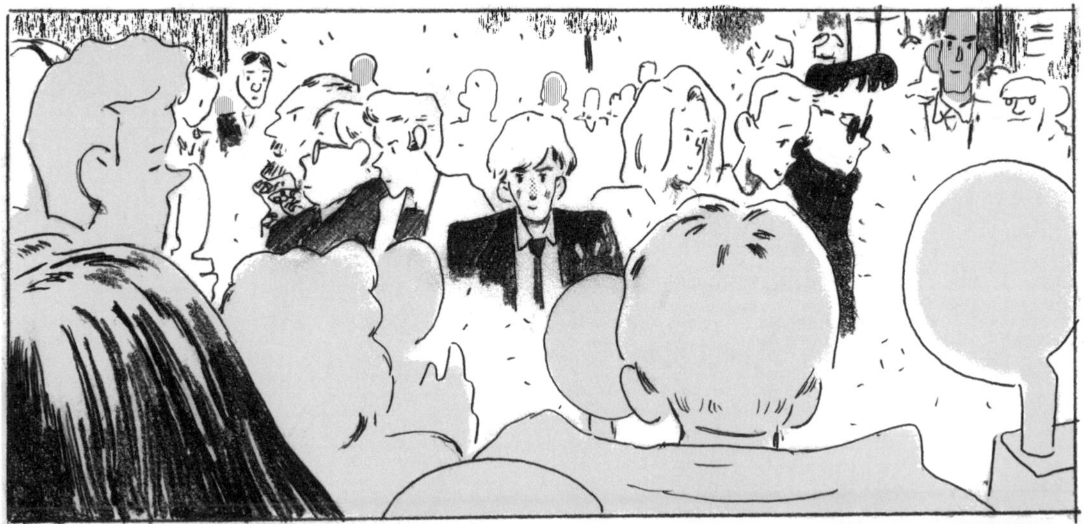

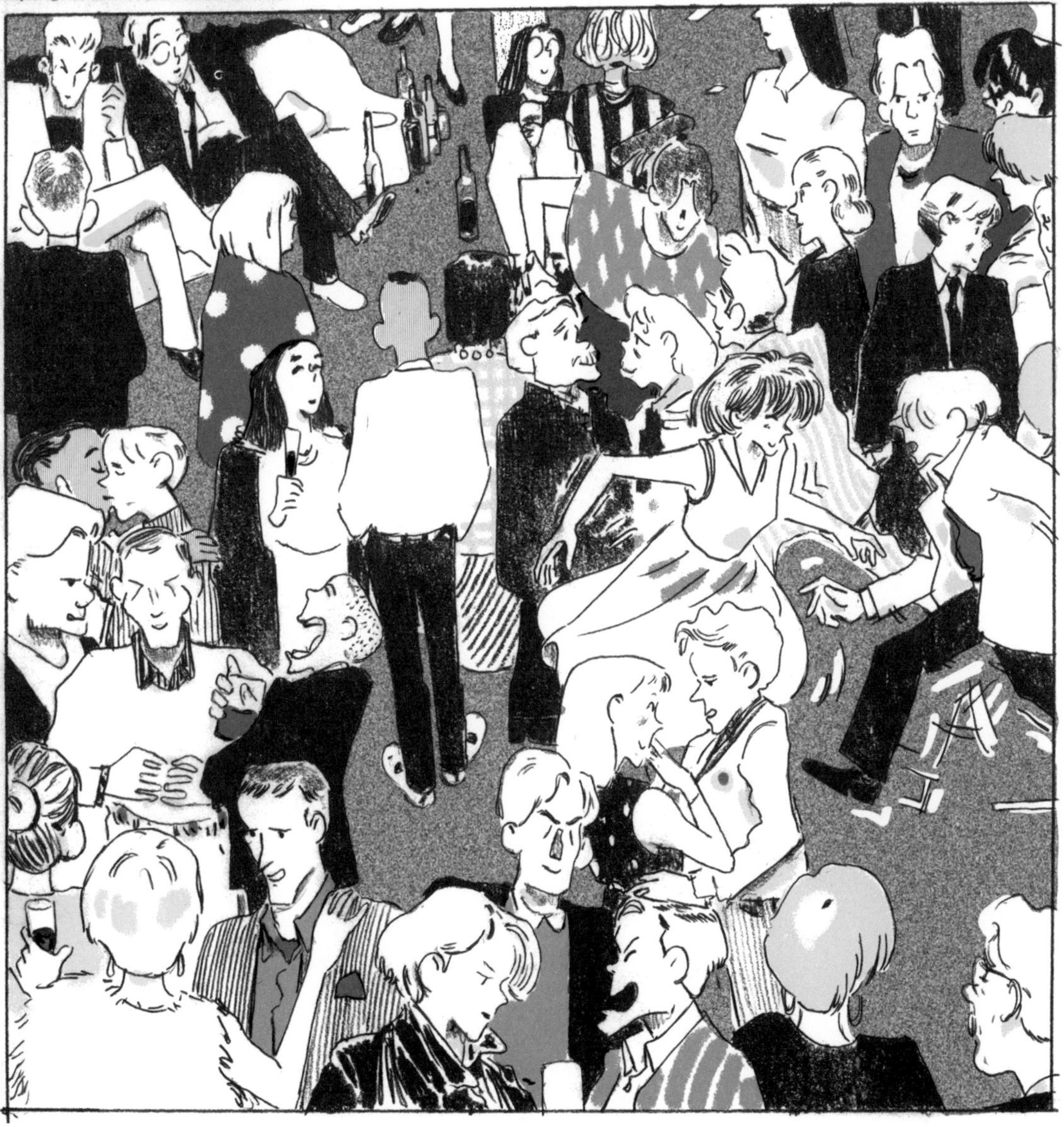

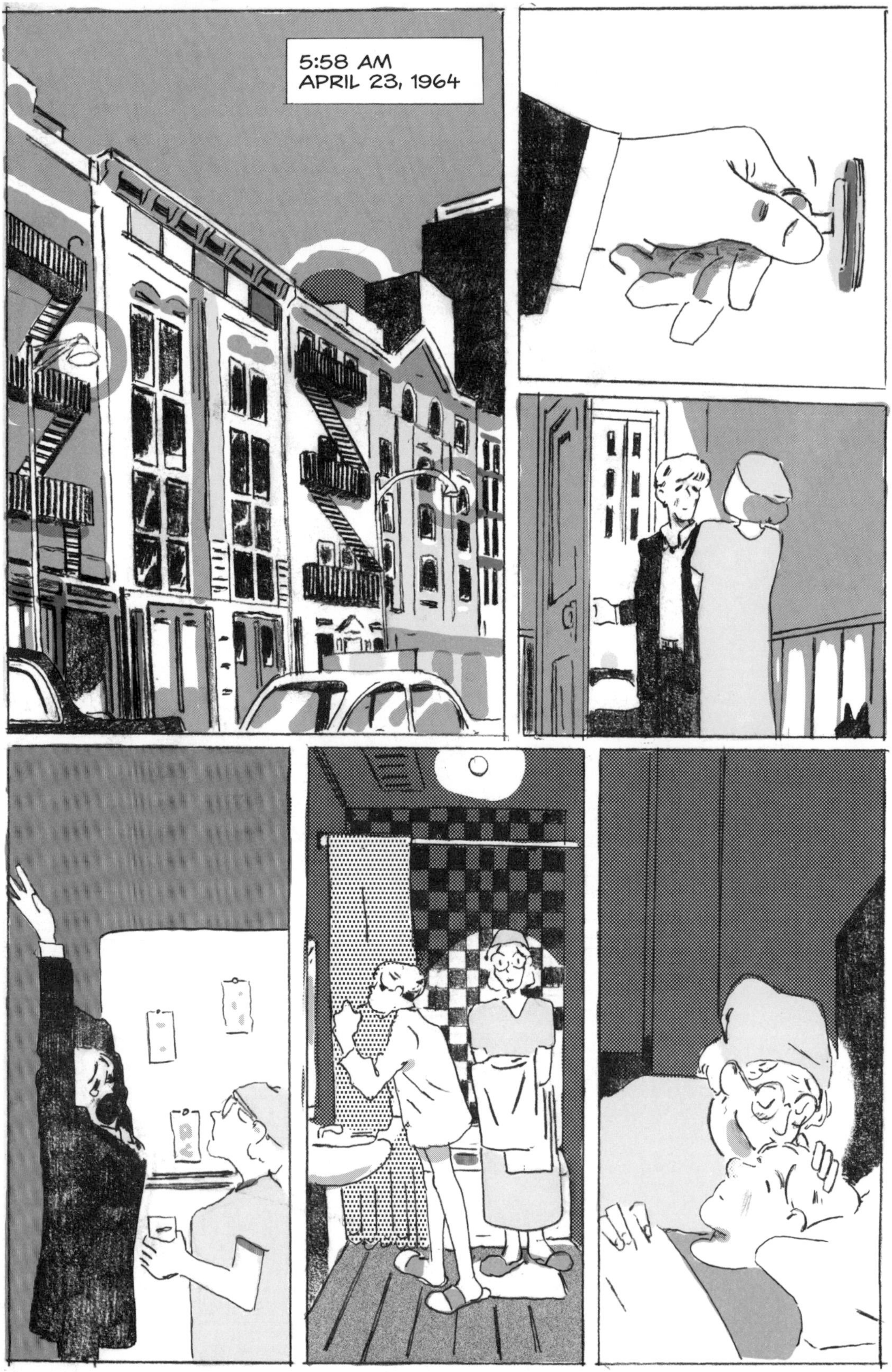
5:58 AM
APRIL 23, 1964

CHAPTER SIXTEEN

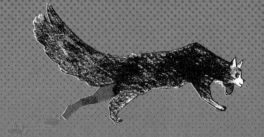

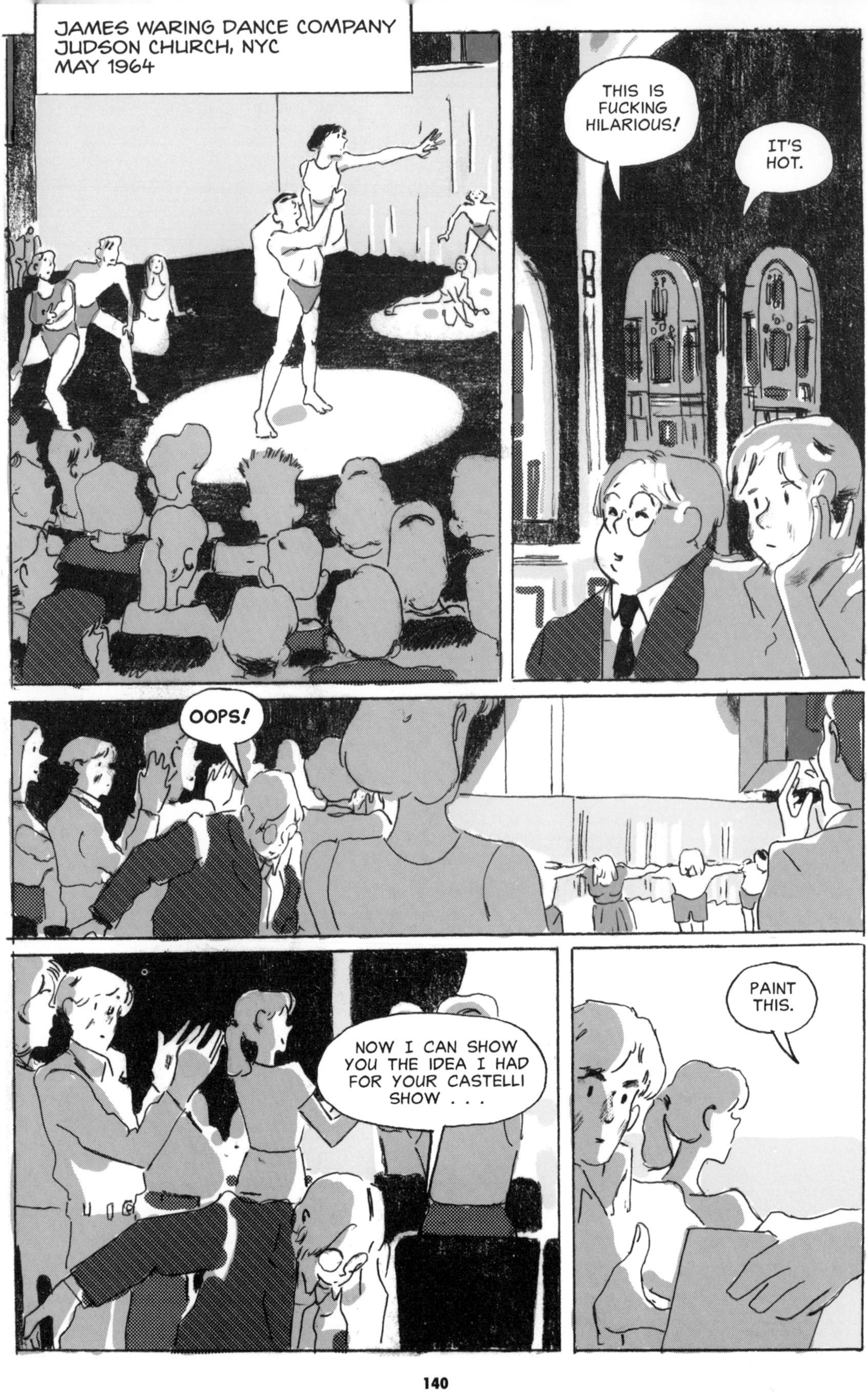
JAMES WARING DANCE COMPANY
JUDSON CHURCH, NYC
MAY 1964
THIS IS FUCKING HILARIOUS!
IT'S HOT.
OOPS!
NOW I CAN SHOW YOU THE IDEA I HAD FOR YOUR CASTELLI SHOW . . .
PAINT THIS.

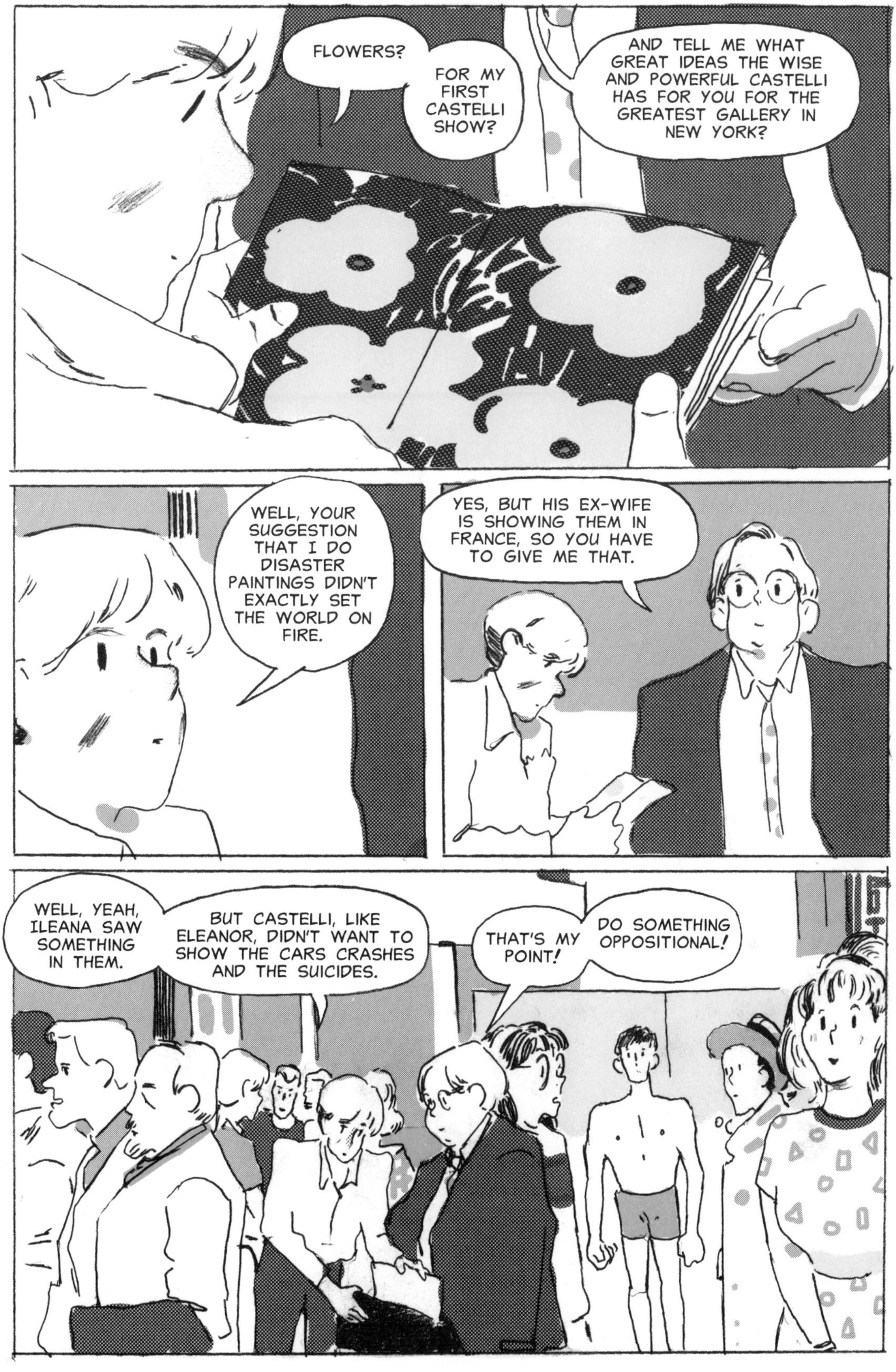
FLOWERS?
FOR MY FIRST CASTELLI SHOW?
AND TELL ME WHAT GREAT IDEAS THE WISE AND POWERFUL CASTELLI HAS FOR YOU FOR THE GREATEST GALLERY IN NEW YORK?
WELL, YOUR SUGGESTION THAT I DO DISASTER PAINTINGS DIDN'T EXACTLY SET THE WORLD ON FIRE.
YES, BUT HIS EX-WIFE IS SHOWING THEM IN FRANCE, SO YOU HAVE TO GIVE ME THAT.
WELL, YEAH, ILEANA SAW SOMETHING IN THEM.
BUT CASTELLI, LIKE ELEANOR, DIDN'T WANT TO SHOW THE CARS CRASHES AND THE SUICIDES.
THAT'S MY POINT!
DO SOMETHING OPPOSITIONAL!

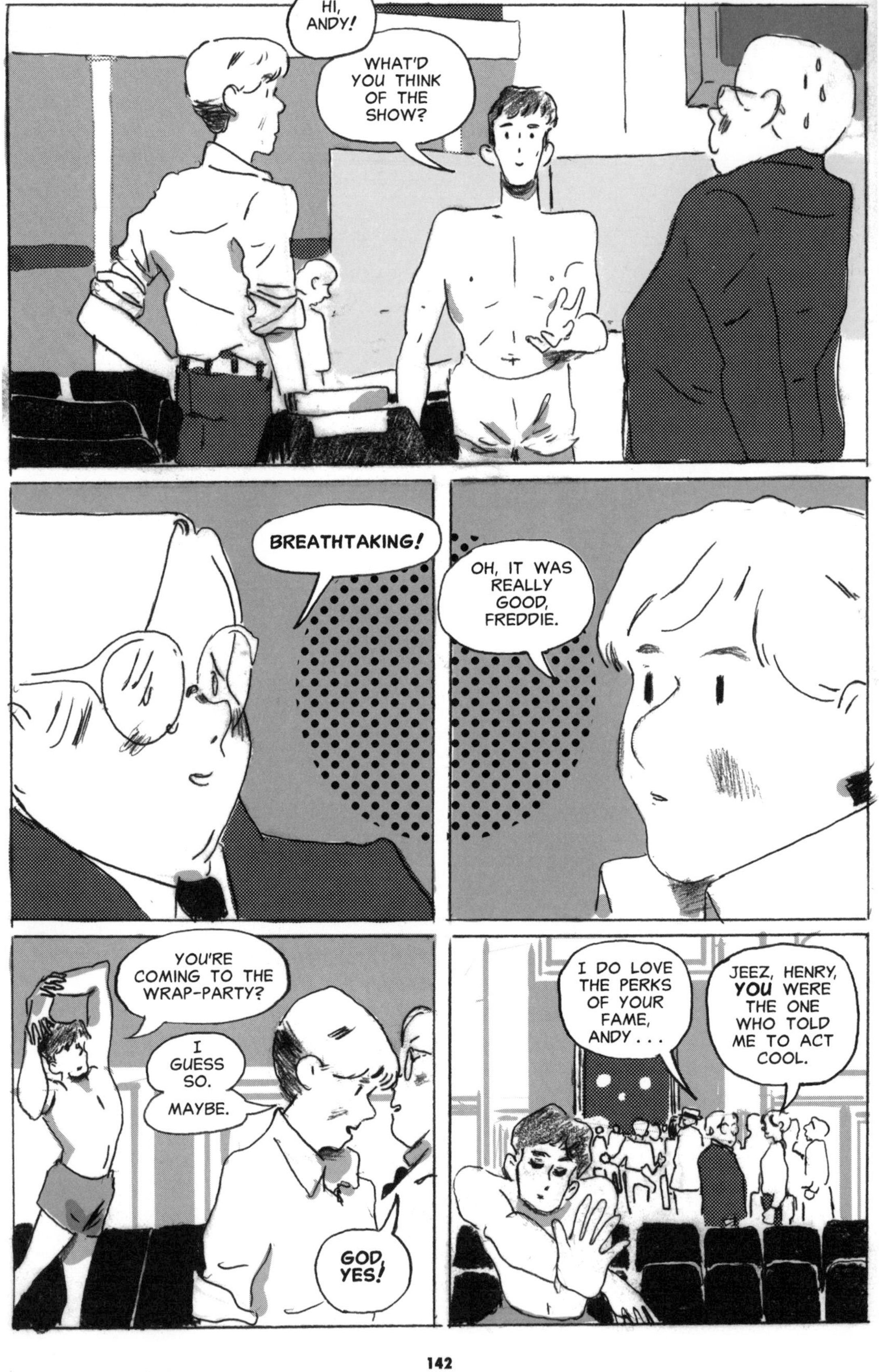
HI, ANDY!
WHAT'D YOU THINK OF THE SHOW?
BREATHTAKING!
OH, IT WAS REALLY GOOD, FREDDIE.
YOU'RE COMING TO THE WRAP-PARTY?
I GUESS SO.
MAYBE.
GOD, YES!
I DO LOVE THE PERKS OF YOUR FAME, ANDY . . .
JEEZ, HENRY, YOU WERE THE ONE WHO TOLD ME TO ACT COOL.

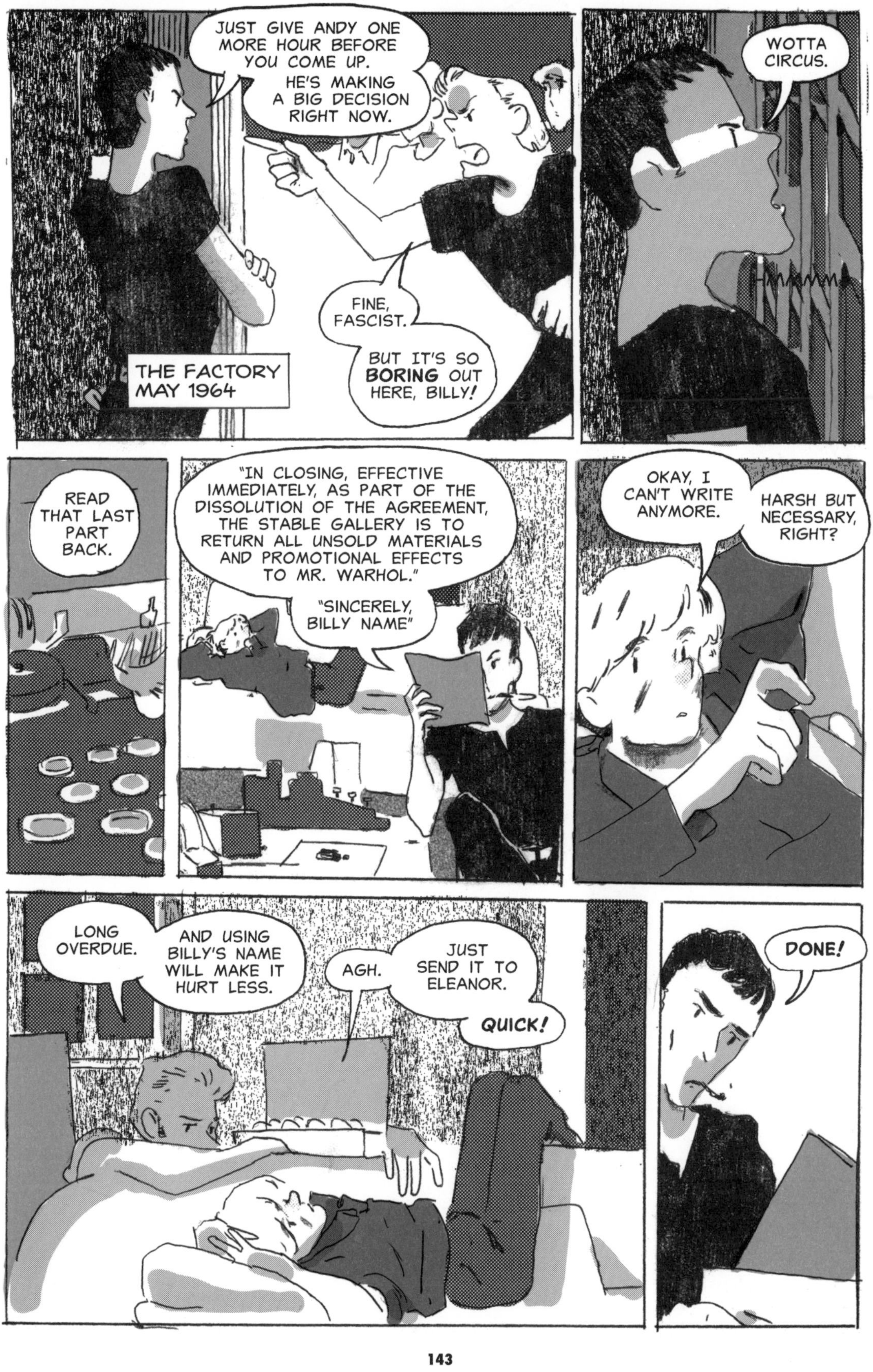

JUST GIVE ANDY ONE MORE HOUR BEFORE YOU COME UP.
HE'S MAKING A BIG DECISION RIGHT NOW.
THE FACTORY MAY 1964
FINE, FASCIST.
BUT IT'S SO **BORING** OUT HERE, BILLY!
WOTTA CIRCUS.
READ THAT LAST PART BACK.
"IN CLOSING, EFFECTIVE IMMEDIATELY, AS PART OF THE DISSOLUTION OF THE AGREEMENT, THE STABLE GALLERY IS TO RETURN ALL UNSOLD MATERIALS AND PROMOTIONAL EFFECTS TO MR. WARHOL."
"SINCERELY, BILLY NAME"
OKAY, I CAN'T WRITE ANYMORE.
HARSH BUT NECESSARY, RIGHT?
LONG OVERDUE.
AND USING BILLY'S NAME WILL MAKE IT HURT LESS.
AGH.
JUST SEND IT TO ELEANOR.
QUICK!
DONE!

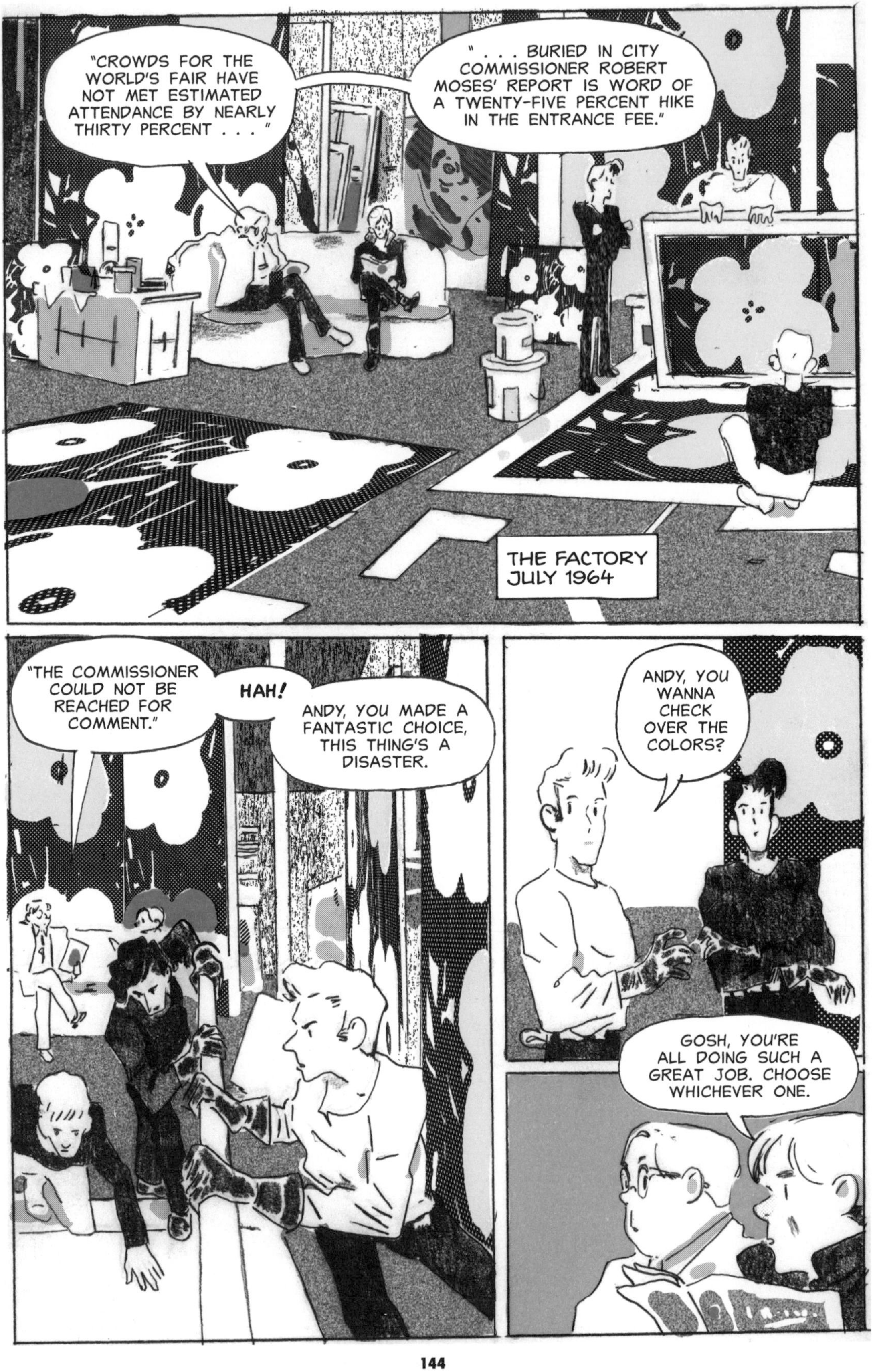
"CROWDS FOR THE WORLD'S FAIR HAVE NOT MET ESTIMATED ATTENDANCE BY NEARLY THIRTY PERCENT . . . "
" . . . BURIED IN CITY COMMISSIONER ROBERT MOSES' REPORT IS WORD OF A TWENTY-FIVE PERCENT HIKE IN THE ENTRANCE FEE."
THE FACTORY JULY 1964
"THE COMMISSIONER COULD NOT BE REACHED FOR COMMENT."
HAH!
ANDY, YOU MADE A FANTASTIC CHOICE, THIS THING'S A DISASTER.
ANDY, YOU WANNA CHECK OVER THE COLORS?
GOSH, YOU'RE ALL DOING SUCH A GREAT JOB. CHOOSE WHICHEVER ONE.

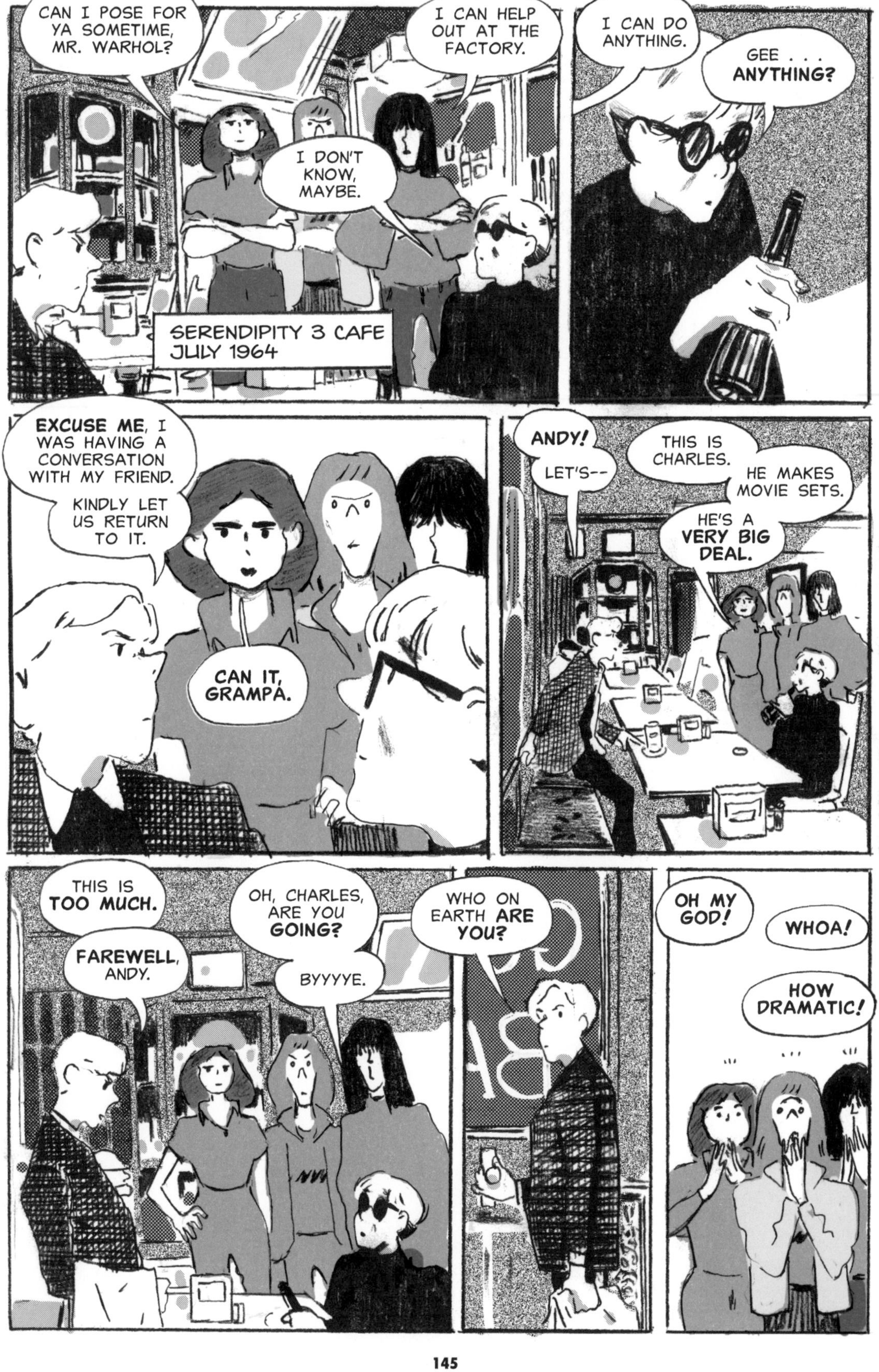
CAN I POSE FOR YA SOMETIME, MR. WARHOL?
I CAN HELP OUT AT THE FACTORY.
I DON'T KNOW, MAYBE.
SERENDIPITY 3 CAFE JULY 1964
I CAN DO ANYTHING.
GEE . . . ANYTHING?
EXCUSE ME, I WAS HAVING A CONVERSATION WITH MY FRIEND.
KINDLY LET US RETURN TO IT.
CAN IT, GRAMPA.
ANDY!
LET'S--
THIS IS CHARLES.
HE MAKES MOVIE SETS.
HE'S A VERY BIG DEAL.
THIS IS TOO MUCH.
FAREWELL, ANDY.
OH, CHARLES, ARE YOU GOING?
BYYYYE.
WHO ON EARTH ARE YOU?
OH MY GOD!
WHOA!
HOW DRAMATIC!

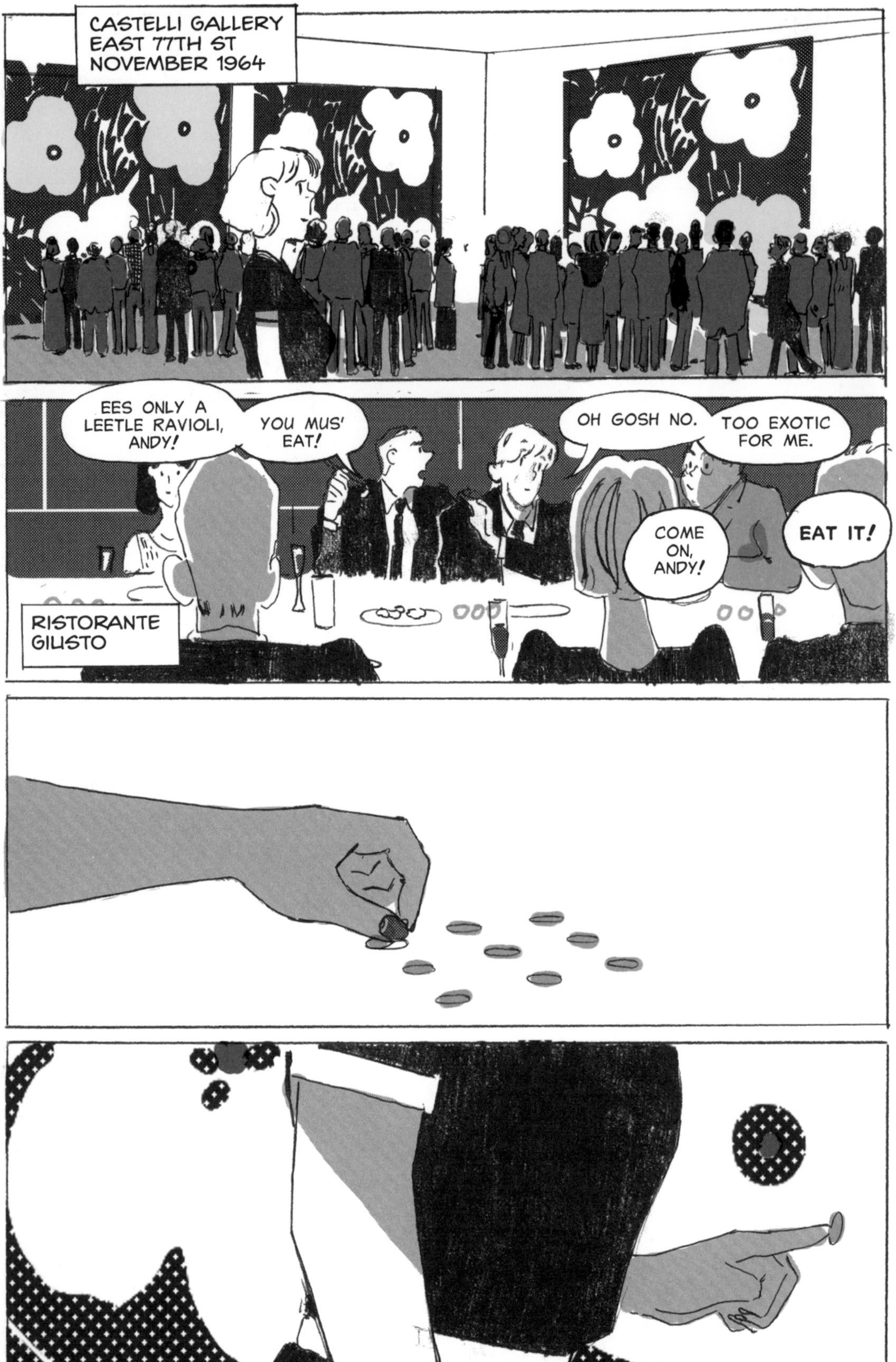
CASTELLI GALLERY
EAST 77TH ST
NOVEMBER 1964
EES ONLY A LEETLE RAVIOLI, ANDY!
YOU MUS' EAT!
OH GOSH NO.
TOO EXOTIC FOR ME.
COME ON, ANDY!
EAT IT!
RISTORANTE GIUSTO

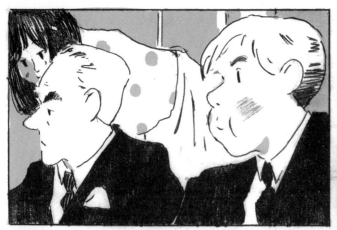

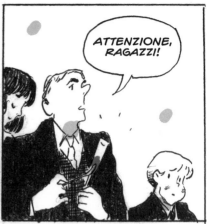

ATTENZIONE, RAGAZZI!

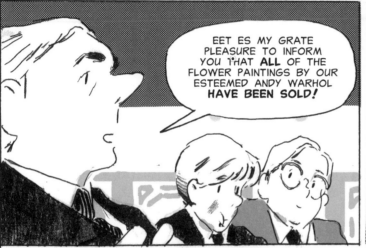

EET ES MY GRATE PLEASURE TO INFORM YOU THAT **ALL** OF THE FLOWER PAINTINGS BY OUR ESTEEMED ANDY WARHOL **HAVE BEEN SOLD!**

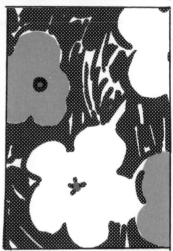

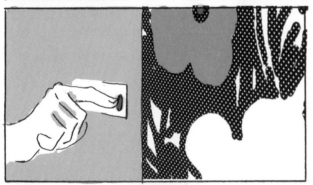

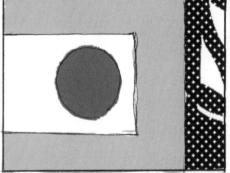

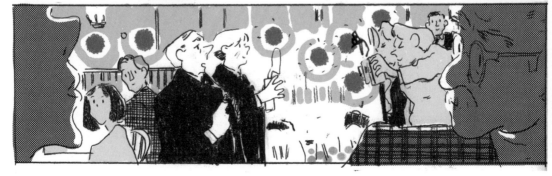

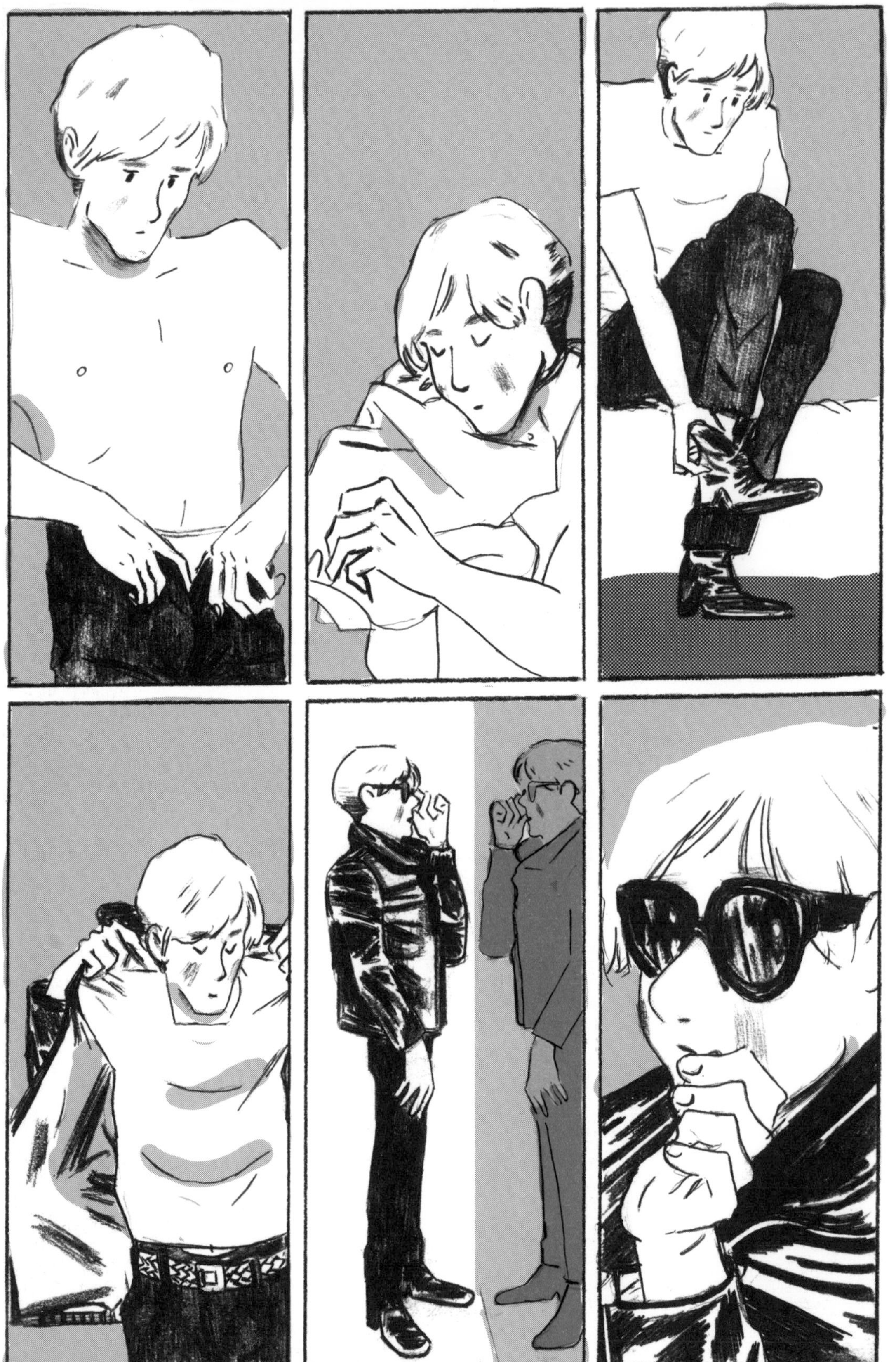

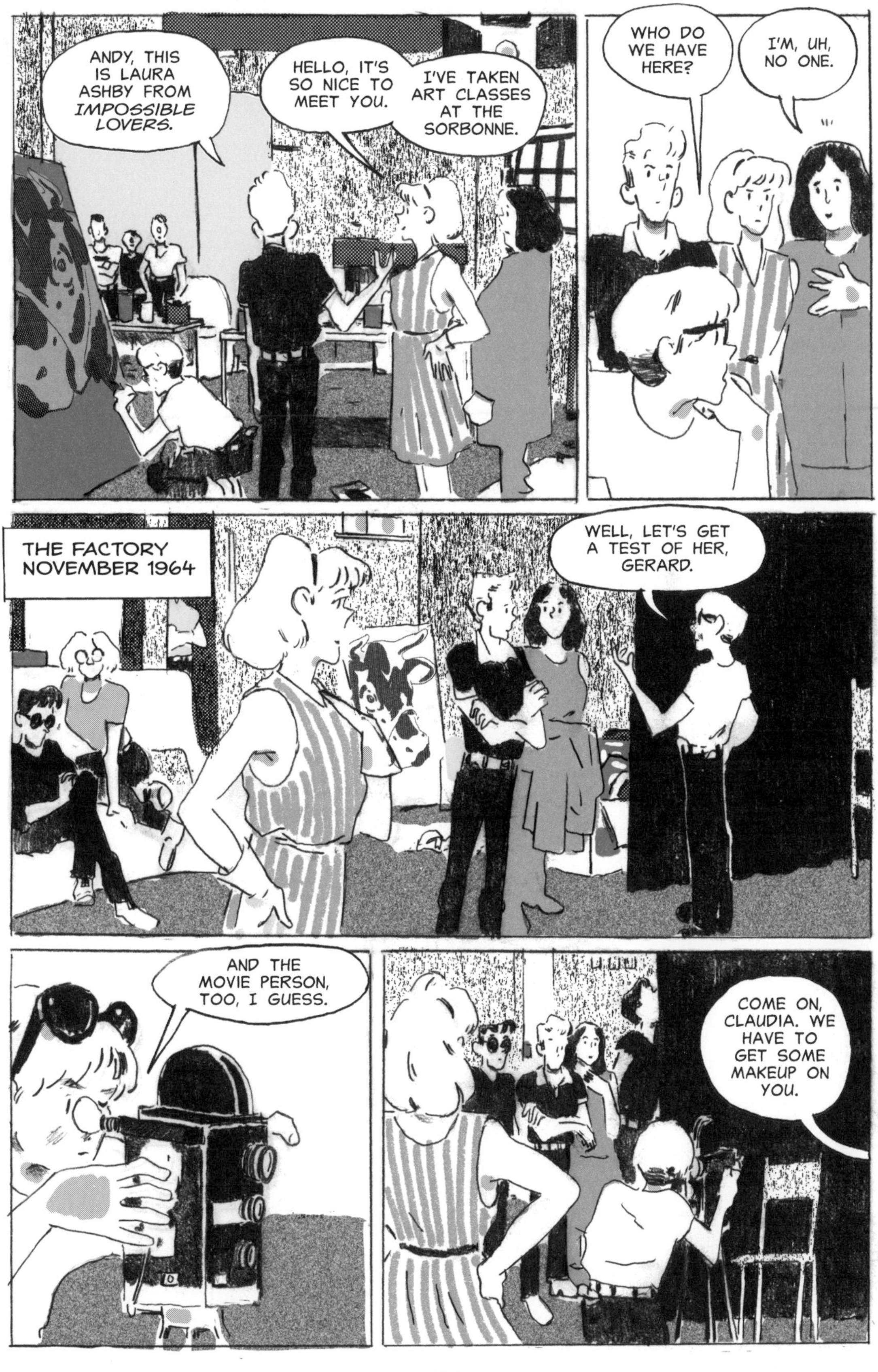
ANDY, THIS IS LAURA ASHBY FROM *IMPOSSIBLE LOVERS.*
HELLO, IT'S SO NICE TO MEET YOU.
I'VE TAKEN ART CLASSES AT THE SORBONNE.
WHO DO WE HAVE HERE?
I'M, UH, NO ONE.
THE FACTORY NOVEMBER 1964
WELL, LET'S GET A TEST OF HER, GERARD.
AND THE MOVIE PERSON, TOO, I GUESS.
COME ON, CLAUDIA. WE HAVE TO GET SOME MAKEUP ON YOU.

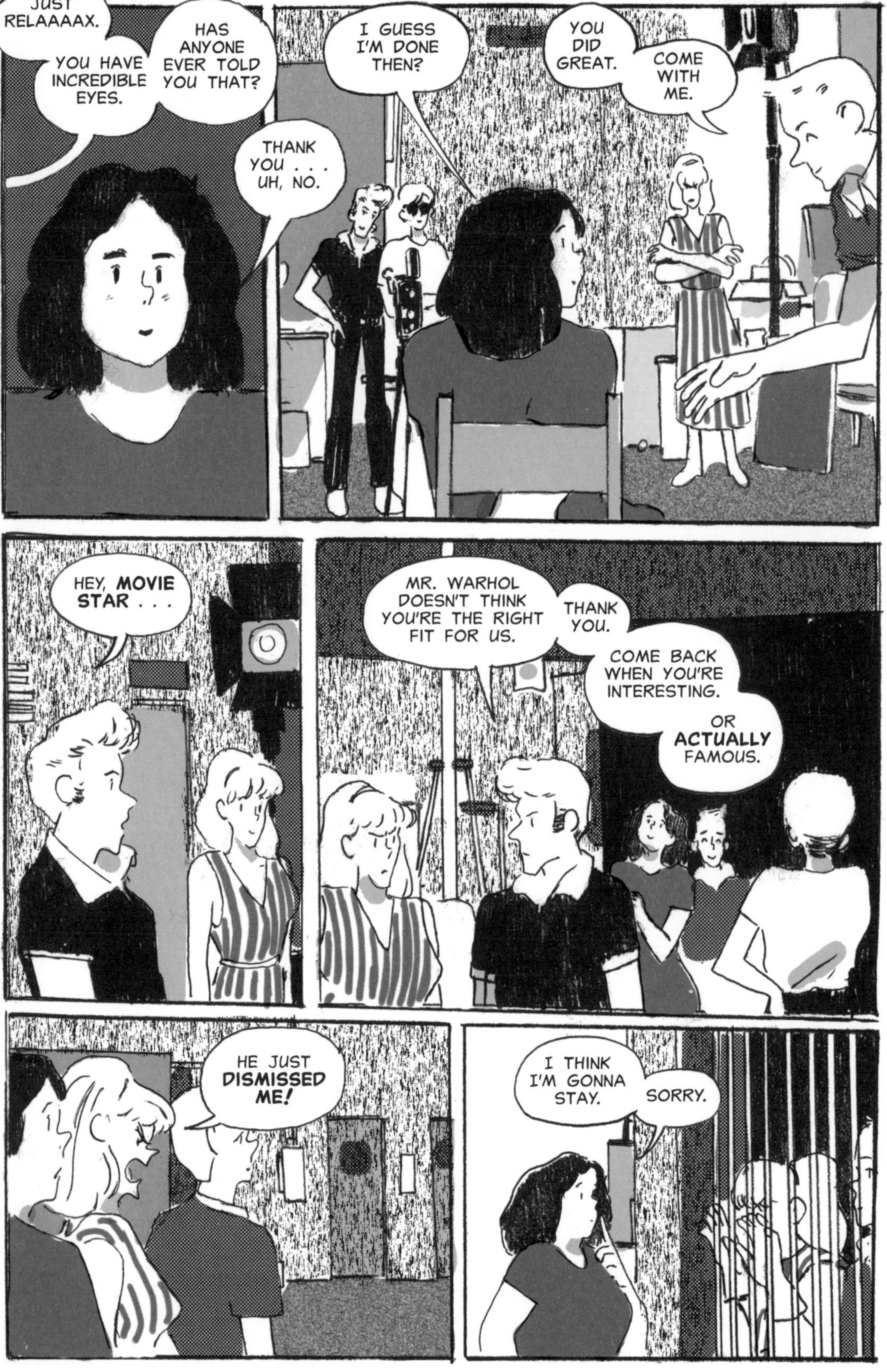
JUST RELAAAAX.
YOU HAVE INCREDIBLE EYES.
HAS ANYONE EVER TOLD YOU THAT?
THANK YOU . . . UH, NO.
I GUESS I'M DONE THEN?
YOU DID GREAT.
COME WITH ME.
HEY, **MOVIE STAR** . . .
MR. WARHOL DOESN'T THINK YOU'RE THE RIGHT FIT FOR US.
THANK YOU.
COME BACK WHEN YOU'RE INTERESTING.
OR **ACTUALLY** FAMOUS.
HE JUST **DISMISSED ME!**
I THINK I'M GONNA STAY.
SORRY.

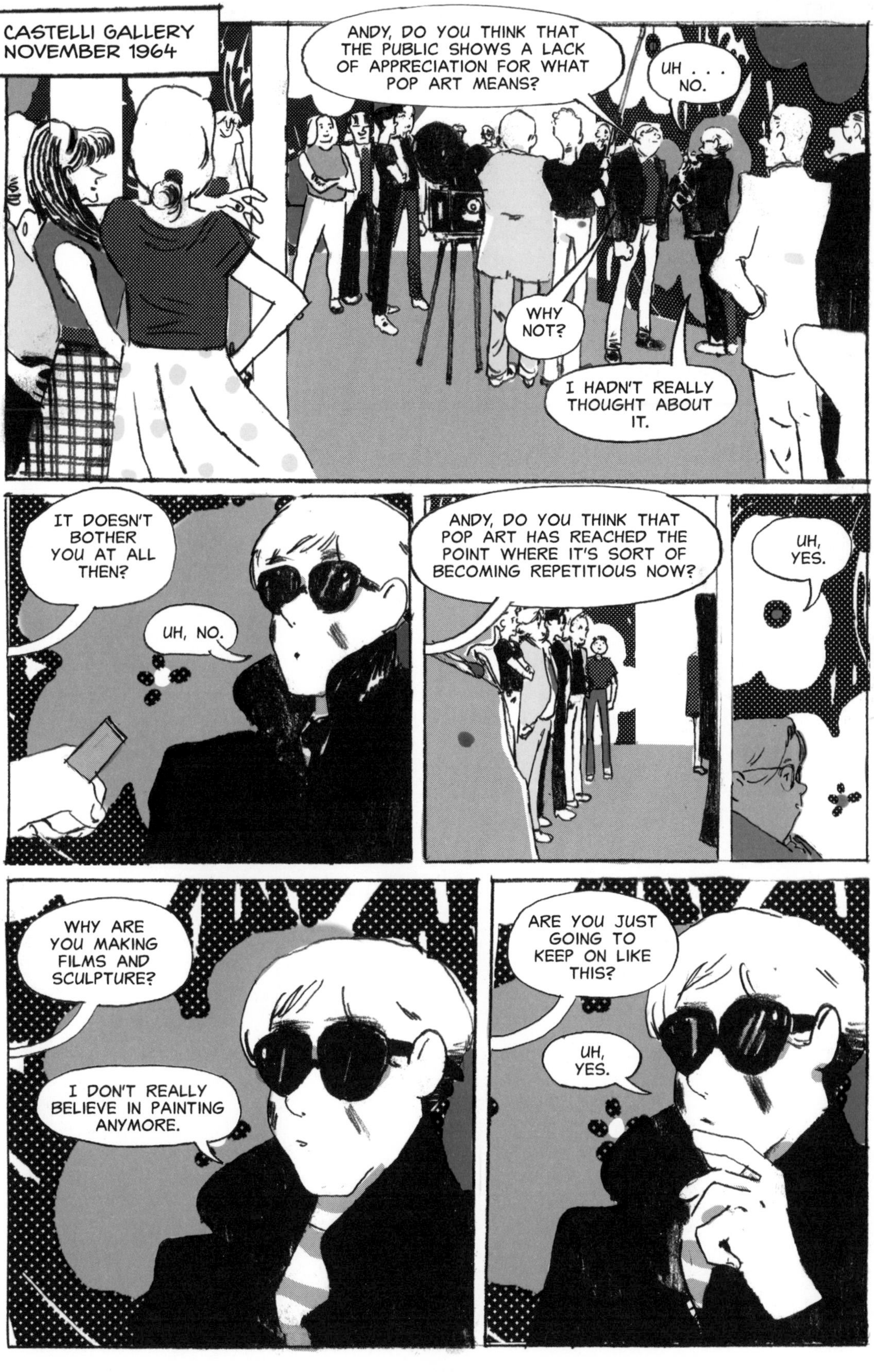
CASTELLI GALLERY
NOVEMBER 1964
ANDY, DO YOU THINK THAT THE PUBLIC SHOWS A LACK OF APPRECIATION FOR WHAT POP ART MEANS?
UH . . . NO.
WHY NOT?
I HADN'T REALLY THOUGHT ABOUT IT.
IT DOESN'T BOTHER YOU AT ALL THEN?
UH, NO.
ANDY, DO YOU THINK THAT POP ART HAS REACHED THE POINT WHERE IT'S SORT OF BECOMING REPETITIOUS NOW?
UH, YES.
WHY ARE YOU MAKING FILMS AND SCULPTURE?
I DON'T REALLY BELIEVE IN PAINTING ANYMORE.
ARE YOU JUST GOING TO KEEP ON LIKE THIS?
UH, YES.

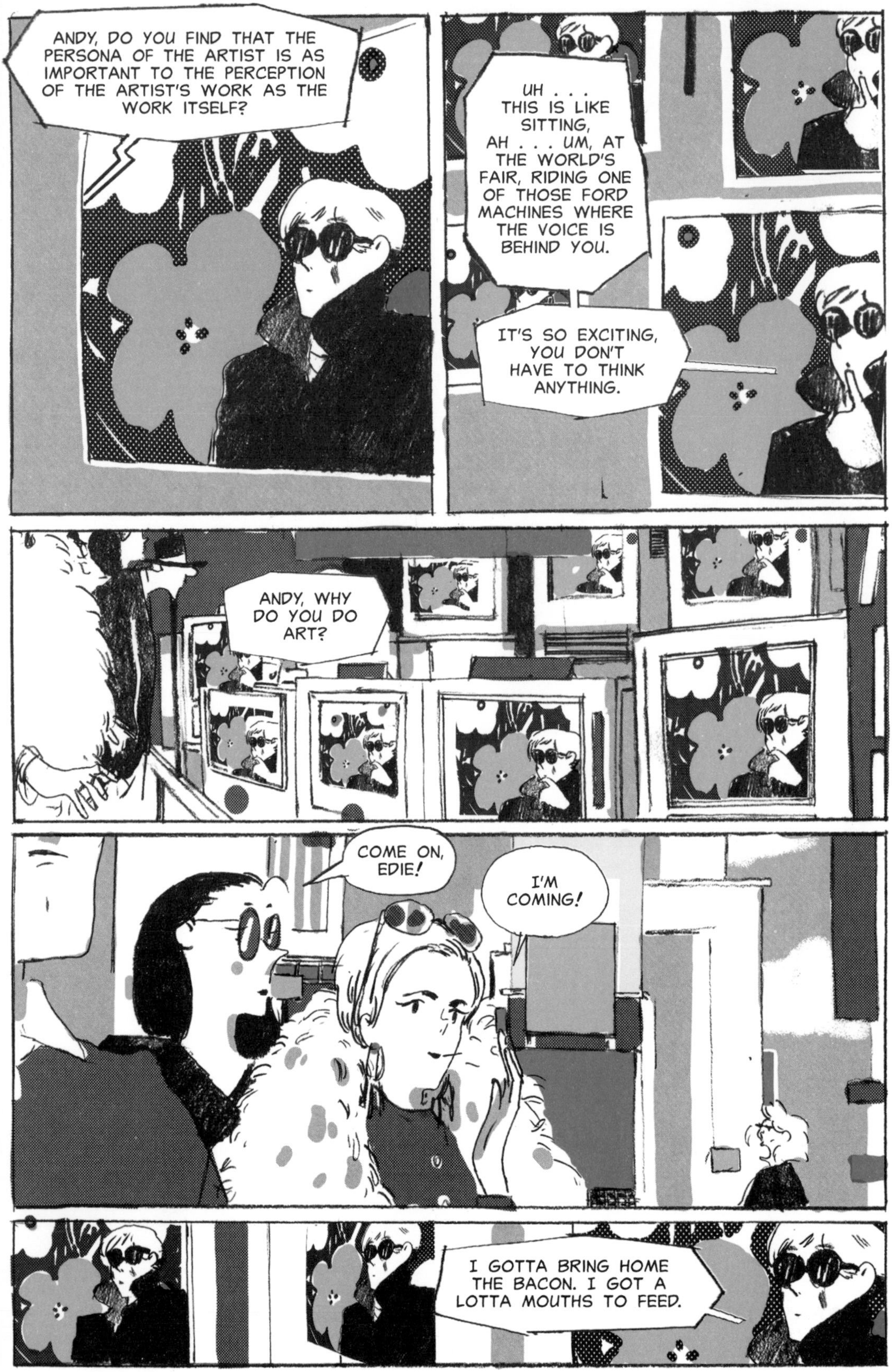
ANDY, DO YOU FIND THAT THE PERSONA OF THE ARTIST IS AS IMPORTANT TO THE PERCEPTION OF THE ARTIST'S WORK AS THE WORK ITSELF?
UH . . . THIS IS LIKE SITTING, AH . . . UM, AT THE WORLD'S FAIR, RIDING ONE OF THOSE FORD MACHINES WHERE THE VOICE IS BEHIND YOU.
IT'S SO EXCITING, YOU DON'T HAVE TO THINK ANYTHING.
ANDY, WHY DO YOU DO ART?
COME ON, EDIE!
I'M COMING!
I GOTTA BRING HOME THE BACON. I GOT A LOTTA MOUTHS TO FEED.

SOURCES

BOOKS

Bockris, Victor. *Warhol: The Biography*. Boston: Da Capo Press, 1997.

Cumming, Alan, and the Andy Warhol Foundation for the Visual Arts. *Andy Warhol: Men*. San Francisco: Chronicle Books, 2004.

Danto, Arthur C. *Andy Warhol*. Icons of America. New Haven, Conn.: Yale University Press, 2010.

Finkelstein, Nat, photographer. Introduction by David Dalton. Designed by Pentagram. *Andy Warhol: The Factory Years, 1964–67*. Edinburgh, U.K.: Canongate, 1999.

Goldsmith, Kenneth, ed. *I'll Be Your Mirror: The Selected Andy Warhol Interviews*. Introduction by Reva Wolf. Preface by Wayne Kostenbaum. Boston: Da Capo Press, 2004.

Koestenbaum, Wayne. *Andy Warhol*. Penguin Lives. New York: Viking, 2001.

Murphy, J. J. *The Black Hole of the Camera: The Films of Andy Warhol*. Berkeley: University of California Press, 2012.

Vartanian, Ivan, ed. *Andy Warhol: Drawings and Illustrations of the 1950s*. New York: D.A.P./Distributed Art Publishers, 2000.

Warhol, Andy. *a, A Novel*. New York: Grove Press, 1968.

———. *The Philosophy of Andy Warhol (From A to B & Back Again)*. New York: Harcourt Brace Jovanovich, 1975.

———. *The Andy Warhol Diaries*. Edited by Pat Hackett. New York: Warner Books, 1989.

———. *Andy Warhol Drawings*. San Francisco: Chronicle Books, 2012.

Warhola, James. *Uncle Andy's*. New York: G. P. Putnam's Sons Books for Young Readers, 2003.

WEBSITES

warhol.org

warhola.com

warholstars.org

ABOUT THE AUTHOR

NICK BERTOZZI has written and drawn numerous comics, including *The Salon*, *Houdini: The Handcuff King*, *Lewis & Clark*, *Jerusalem*, and the *New York Times* bestseller *Shackleton: Antarctic Odyssey*. He lives in New York City with his wife and daughters.

ABOUT THE ILLUSTRATOR

PIERCE HARGAN was born in Los Angeles and is a graduate of the School of Visual Arts in New York City. His work is featured in the acclaimed anthology *Schmuck*. This is his first graphic novel. He lives in Brooklyn.

Thank you to Kim and
the girls; family, friends, teachers
(especially Glenn Davis); all the librarians
ever; comic shops who give a rip; Pierce Hargan,
Joan Hilty, Wyeth Yates, Samantha Ulban, Bob Mecoy;
all at Abrams; and you for reading.
—N. B.

This book would not have been possible without the help
and support of Samantha Ulban and Wyeth Yates. Thanks
to Nick Bertozzi, Joan Hilty, Bob Mecoy, Pamela
Notarantonio and Charlie Kochman for believing
in the vision of a young cartoonist.
—P. H.

TO MY
THREE SISTERS
—N.B.

FOR
MY FAMILY
AND LOVED
ONES
—P.H.

Editor: Joan Hilty
Project Manager: Charles Kochman
Designer: Pamela Notarantonio
Managing Editor: James Armstrong
Production Manager: Kathy Lovisolo

Library of Congress Control Number 2016931814

Hardcover ISBN 978-1-4197-1875-5
Paperback ISBN 978-1-4197-1876-2

Text copyright © 2016 Nick Bertozzi
Illustrations copyright © 2016 Pierce Hargan

Originally published in hardcover in 2016 by Abrams ComicArts®, an imprint of ABRAMS.
Published in paperback in 2018. All rights reserved.

Printed and bound in China
10 9 8 7 6 5 4 3 2 1

Abrams ComicArts books are available at special discounts when purchased in quantity for premiums
and promotions as well as fundraising or educational use. Special editions can also be created to
specification. For details, contact specialsales@abramsbooks.com or the address below.

Abrams ComicArts® is a registered trademark of Harry N. Abrams, Inc.

ABRAMS The Art of Books
195 Broadway, New York, NY 10007
abramsbooks.com